THE SCOTTISH FAMILY TREE DETECTIVE

MANCHESTER
1824

Manchester University Press

Also available

*The family tree detective: tracing your ancestors
in England and Wales*   Colin D. Rogers
*The Irish family tree detective: tracing your ancestors
in Ireland*   Francis Dowling (forthcoming)

The Scottish family tree detective

Tracing your ancestors in Scotland

Rosemary Bigwood

MANCHESTER UNIVERSITY PRESS
Manchester and New York
distributed exclusively in the USA by Palgrave

Published by Manchester University Press
Oxford Road, Manchester M13 9NR, UK
and Room 400, 175 Fifth Avenue, New York, NY 10010, USA
www.manchesteruniversitypress.co.uk

Distributed exclusively in the USA by
Palgrave, 175 Fifth Avenue, New York,
NY 10010, USA

Distributed exclusively in Canada by
UBC Press, University of British Columbia, 2029 West Mall,
Vancouver, BC, Canada V6T 1Z2

British Library Cataloguing-in-Publication Data
A catalogue record for this book is available from the British Library

Library of Congress Cataloging-in-Publication Data applied for

ISBN   0 7190 7184 4 hardback
EAN   978 0 7190 71843

ISBN   0 7190 7185 2 paperback
EAN   978 0 7190 71850

First published 2006

15 14 13 12 11 10 09 08 07 06   10 9 8 7 6 5 4 3 2 1

Typeset in Sabon 10.25/12 pt
by Servis Filmsetting Ltd, Manchester
Printed in Great Britain
by Bell & Bain Ltd, Glasgow

To my husband, children and grandchildren and to my friends of our lunchtime genealogical gatherings in appreciation of so much shared enthusiasm, curiosity and knowledge

Contents

List of maps and figures

Maps

Figures

Abbreviations

DIGROS	Digital Imaging of the Genealogical Records of Scotland's people
GROS	General Register Office for Scotland
IGI	International Genealogical Index
JP	Justice of the Peace
LDS	Church of Jesus Christ of the Latter-Day Saints
NAS	National Archives of Scotland (previously the Scottish Record Office)
NLS	National Library of Scotland
NRA	National Register of Archives
NRAS	National Register of Archives of Scotland
OPR	Old Parish Registers
SCAN	Scottish Archive Network
SHS	Scottish History Society
SRO	Scottish Record Office
SRS	Scottish Record Society
TNA	The National Archives, Kew, London (previously the Public Record Office, PRO)

Acknowledgements

I owe a debt of gratitude to Colin Rogers, who in *The family tree detective: tracing your ancestors in England and Wales*, opened my eyes to a new way of looking at family history – not by source but by topic – a method which I have attempted to follow in this book. My thanks to all at the National Archives of Scotland and the General Register Office of Scotland amongst whose records I have spent so many profitable and fascinating years. The support of the editorial staff at Manchester University Press have kept me on the right lines, and finally, a thank you to my husband for his patience in dealing with my incompetence in understanding the intricacies of computers and for his views on many subjects.

I *Introduction*

'Explore. Discover. Understand.' This is how Nasa summarises its objectives in exploring outer space, but the statement of their mission should also be adopted by all family historians in their earth-bound research.

In setting out to trace family history we embark on a journey into the past which may take us along many varied research roads and through much unfamiliar territory. Over the last few years there have been dramatic developments in opportunities for exploration of sources which can be used. Access to the internet is changing both methods of research and attitudes to it – expectations of what can be discovered and ideas as to what can be achieved. The ease of being able to consult catalogues, to discover interesting material in odd places, to find general information about almost anything and facilities to exchange news and views with others working in a related field often result in a vast expansion in knowledge about a particular family.

Despite this 'freedom to roam' and sometimes because of it, one hears two common cries when speaking to family historians. The first is: 'I have come up against a brick wall' and the second is: 'Where do I go next?'

The aim of *The Scottish family tree detective* is to provide guidance in dealing with these matters. In the past, having exhausted the possibilities of statutory registers, census returns and parish registers, many family historians reluctantly assumed that they had reached the end of the road, but there is now a growing awareness that the choice of source material is enormous. Faced with new challenges – and new problems – it is important to adopt a strategy – to locate, link, select and evaluate the sources available – to understand what they contain and how they can be used. Route planning and the ability to follow clues become priorities.

No guide book can cover everything and in travelling down the winding roads of family history, as on any journey, some of the greatest satisfaction will lie in making your own discoveries. It is hoped that this book will, at least, provide signposts to the main highways of research and also point to some lesser known tracks along which it will be rewarding to travel in tracing your ancestors.

Using the book

The first section of the book, 'Starting research', offers advice in establishing what you can find out about your family at home, deciding how you are going to record it and where you can go to find out more.

The second section, 'From birth to death', covers the three main 'facts' of life – birth, marriage and death. This is a guide to using the 'foundation' sources for genealogy – statutory registers, census returns and old parish registers, suggesting ways of solving problems in these fields. Other material is also examined which may fill gaps, compensate for deficiencies in these records and expand knowledge of the family.

In the third part of the book, 'Profiling the ancestors', a wide range of sources are explored and evaluated from the point of view of finding out more about people in the past, both in tracing ancestry beyond the parish registers and also in putting flesh on the bones of forebears through the reconstruction of their lives and of the communities in which they lived.

'Profiling the ancestors' views the subject from three angles:

'Where did they live?' This is an important question as the answer will determine what individuals, groups of people or authorities may have come in contact with your ancestors, resulting in the making of records at local or national level.

'When did they live?' What was going on in the world around them? War, politics, religious or economic change may have made an impact on their lives.

'What did they do?' The selection of source material relevant to various occupations or to persons in particular classes of society is the means of broadening research on individuals and their background.

The final section, 'Understanding legal documents', provides guidance in dealing with the often challenging matter of dealing with more complex records such as sasines, deeds and court records, looking at what these documents contain, their terminology and form.

II *Starting Research*

Discovering the past

'Why doesn't the past decently bury itself, instead of sitting and waiting to be admitted by the present?' This was a remark made by D. H. Lawrence but I hope that few would now agree with him. It is not easy to find any one reason for this ever growing fascination with bygone generations and the desire to be connected to them. Population movement, the loss of bonds with communities where families had lived for centuries, and, above all, the need to 'belong' in an often uncertain world, are perhaps all contributory factors. Conditions of life are changing rapidly and there is a growing realisation that the past cannot be buried or forgotten – nor do most people wish it. A more representative view is that given by Robert Louis Stevenson: 'the past is myself, my own history, the seed of my present thoughts, the mould of my present disposition.'

The concept of what is involved in family history varies. The dictionary defines genealogy as the history of the descent of families or the pedigree of a particular person or family. This often results in the recording of names and dates of vital events in each generation and nothing more – the construction of what one might term 'the skeleton' of the family tree. More and more people, however, are interested in family history in a wider sense, in putting flesh on the bones of their forebears, in examining and trying to understand what life was like in the past, what members of a family did, where they lived, and their place in society. Appreciation of what it was like to live in a Glasgow tenement in the early twentieth century or a black house in the Outer Isles in the nineteenth century, for example, cannot be achieved by indulging in pitying comparison with our lives today, but we need to see what our ancestors made of their lives and how they coped with everyday problems. This is 'real' history – a first-hand glimpse into the past. The study of family history expands into social history and involves research in associated areas which becomes an integral but often underexploited part of problem-solving in genealogy. These are some of the areas which this book sets out to explore.

Facilities for researchers have changed a great deal over the past years. Access to original source material such as statutory registers, census returns and old parish registers (OPRs) used to be confined to those able to visit New Register House in Edinburgh. Availability of microfilmed copies of these records in family history centres of the Church of Jesus Christ of the Latter-Day Saints (LDS), in archives and libraries worldwide, then enabled people to carry out research in any country. Technology in the form of the internet now makes it possible for people to communicate quickly, cheaply and easily round the world. There is access to information on an amazing range of topics – people, places, events and organisations. In the field of family and local history, an ever growing number of indexes and transcripts of documents can be viewed on websites, mostly without charge, and archives and libraries are putting catalogues of their holdings online. In Scotland, digital images are already accessible for statutory registers, census returns, old parish registers, testamentary material and kirk session records, showing the way ahead.

This revolution in technology and the amount of information now available result in choices for family historians which are stimulating but often bewildering. Some information provided on internet sites is wonderful, some misleading – some is downright wrong. Many families have without doubt a number of cuckoos in the nest due to the adoption of forebears of doubtful origin, often merely on the basis of a shared name on an ancestral tree. The advice and assertions of helpful contributors to message boards online can lead many astray, as enthusiasm is not always matched by knowledge or accuracy.

The other problem is that of being faced with too much choice. Online access to catalogues of source material held publicly or privately round the world reveals many possible new avenues for research but there are often difficulties in understanding what a particular document may contain, in assessing its value to you and knowing how to select from what is on offer. Is it worth spending time (and perhaps money) on consulting it? What will it reveal? Is it likely to be relevant? Will it be comprehensible? In the solving of all problems and in making selections, we have to develop strategies.

Planning a genealogical journey

Recording research

Interest in your family's past is something which may have crept up on you inadvertently – the result of finding a few documents or pieces of information at home and it may only be later that you make a conscious decision to develop this research and take it further. At some point, and sooner rather than later, it is wise to consider how you are going to record your research. The guiding principle should be to keep your findings in a form which is comprehensible to others – whether in narrative or note form. Scattered notes kept in shoe boxes may seem logical to the writer but are likely to be thrown away by anyone inheriting these treasures, and the remark 'I know I have it somewhere' is often the prelude to a long search. It is also important to adopt a system which can be extended backwards, forwards and sideways and which will take in any amount of information about an individual which is found later. There are a great many computer programs on the market and many have room for notes but some people still prefer to keep records on paper. For them the solution is usually loose-leaf files.

Charts of some kind are important as they provide a quick visual reference to what you know and avoid the possible pitfalls of mixing up generations, particularly those where father, grandfather and perhaps great-grandfather had the same Christian name. Our forebears tended to be conservative in the choice of names for their children.

There are various forms of charts. The drop-line chart (some computer programs will print out these charts) is the most complicated to draw up but also the most informative, headed by the furthest back known ancestor, with all the children ranged along the line below, and then the descendants of each below that. The successful family historian may end up with a room-wide roll of paper – wallpaper can be useful.

Pedigree charts (which can also be printed out from most genealogy computer programs or obtained from family history centres) show the main-line ancestors only – the most recent person being researched, the parents, four grandparents, eight great-grandparents and so on, with dates of birth, marriage and death. This 'skeleton' form is useful for quick reference but provides no information on siblings.

Family group sheets are also popular – recording names of parents and of all their children. Some sheets provide room for notes, and show a connecting link to the next generation either up or down. The choice of type of chart will depend on what you want from your research – something you may not know at the outset – but you should always bear in mind that the project is likely to expand.

Not everyone intends to publish their family history but at the least it is worth thinking of sharing your discoveries with relatives and descendants. Margaret Stuart (1978) provides a useful guide to writing the history of a family, dealing with the small family history, the anecdotal work or one which is a historical project.

There are certain important principles to bear in mind when recording your findings:

Always note the full reference for a source of information – name of book, author, date of publication or document reference, class mark, page and the archive or library where it is kept.
In searching a primary source, note years covered in your research or, in the case of a book, pages read.
Make it clear whether you have noted down an exact transcript of the text, made a paraphrase or notes on the original.
Record negative findings as well as positive ones so that you do not have to duplicate your search later. Negative findings can often reveal as much as positive ones.
Note the characteristic of a manuscript – whether it appears well-kept, has gaps or seems to have been written carelessly.
Note any known bias of the writer – affiliations to a particular cause, special reasons for writing, for example – as this can affect the value of the text and how you assess it.
Note when a document was written – at the time of a particular event or later.
Take down as much information as possible. Some details mean little when you read them first but may contain vital clues which are useful later on.

Working from home

In all detective work, it is important to start research from a firm base. Assess what you know – with certainty – and what you would like to know and only then set out to explore what else can be found and where relevant source material may be held. Even if you think you know all about your family history back to the time of a grandfather or great-grandfather, it is always worth spending some time confirming this. A number of unexpected facts may emerge in the course of this preliminary research – names of children who died young, second marriages, occupations and relationships – as well as corrections in what you have been told. Memory is very fallible.

Oral history

Most families hand down stories about the past and this information can be both interesting and valuable but needs to be backed up by proven fact. There are many tales of titled ancestors, usually concerning a daughter from a well-born family who ran away with the coachman or estate worker and whose name was then erased from all the records by her irate father. Rob Roy McGregor, Robert the Bruce and Robert Burns (among others) are attributed with a great many descendants whose authenticity has never been proved. Such stories should never be discarded out of hand. In most cases it is impossible to substantiate the claim but occasionally it turns out to be true.

In the Western Isles oral tradition is of particular importance. Bill and Chris Lawson over a number of years have compiled a research resource, *Co Leis Thu?*, made up of over 30,000 family tree sheets for most of the families who lived in the Outer Hebrides over the past 200 years, many of whom emigrated to Canada, America, Australia, New Zealand and elsewhere. This resource is now housed at the Seallam! Visitor Centre at Taobh Tuath (Northton), Isle of Harris (www.seallam.com/coleisthu.htm). Much of the information comes from recorded oral traditions both in Scotland and in places to which the islanders migrated, and this has been expanded and complemented by written sources such as statutory registers, parish registers, census returns, estate records, emigration lists and government papers.

If you are collecting oral information on your own family, consider the choice of questions to ask. This needs planning and tact as you need to think in advance what you would like to find out and what questions are most likely to produce the answers. Oral evidence will always have to be challenged and its accuracy proved by reference to other documentation as you will often get conflicting information from different members of the family, but it can be a valuable part of research into family history. It also gives a personal dimension to the past and is an individual contribution to social history.

Family letters and Bibles

In time to come our descendants may find that there is far less surviving memorabilia which can provide clues about our ancestors. Letter writing is being relegated to e-mail and photographs are now often stored on discs, all of which may result in their ultimate loss. Old letters can provide an insight into family life and often contain important clues in identifying relatives. Many letters have survived which were written by those who emigrated, either corresponding with relatives who remained in Scotland or setting down what is known of the family's origins in Scotland for the benefit of others. The facts given will range from the vague and irrelevant to the exact but can afford a base for research.

Many people still have old family Bibles in which births, marriages and deaths are entered on a flyleaf. Entries usually consist of a list of names and dates but some include fascinating and sometimes intimate details about the person concerned. One family Bible noted that a daughter died of a broken heart at the age of about thirty, one of her brothers enlisted in the army and died in India, while another became a carpenter and went to London. A story is told of one family that one entry in their Bible for Martha – with dates of birth and death – remained unidentified till later they found that she was the family cow.

Many people are worried when they find that dates given in a Bible do not always agree with those on statutory certificates or entries in a parish register. These apparent errors can sometimes be accounted for by the fact that the Bible records dates of baptism or burial rather than those of birth or death, but mistakes may have occurred if entries were made from memory some time after the event.

Medals and memorabilia

Medals were usually awarded to celebrate an event or achievement – in school, at work, for sport, for national or military service – often providing links with the past. The National Archives in London (TNA) hold records of many medals awarded for service in various campaigns or for gallantry which can now be searched online at www.nationalarchives.gov.uk/documentsonline/. At present (2006) there are details of over five million World War I campaign medals, as well as seamen's medals for World War II. These show name, rank, regiment or service and can be linked to other service records. School awards can also provide useful clues – and problems. The only evidence of one woman's links with Scotland was a medal given for excellence at St John's Episcopal School in 1841, which initiated a search to identify all such schools of this name in Scotland at that time, in the hope of then finding the family in census returns.

Engraved cups or other tokens of success in fields of sport or work may also provide clues which can be followed up in newspaper reports or other documents.

Family photographs

Old photographs offer the most tantalising glimpses into the past. Too often they are neither dated nor named, and clues to identification have to be found from a study of fashions or of styles of photographic backgrounds. Pols (1992), Oliver (1989) and Ginsburg (1982) include useful guidance in dating photographs.

In the nineteenth century, many people – some in quite modest circumstances – had their photographs taken professionally. The name of the studio is usually clearly marked and with the aid of a local directory it may be possible to date the photograph within a period of years by checking when the studio was in existence. Torrance (1998) provides a guide to nineteenth- and twentieth-century directories which have been published for Scottish towns and cities and some are now being reproduced on CD. Group photographs for a school, team or local organisation (which often appeared in local papers) may lead to the discovery of other records which provide clues.

One-name studies

The Scottish Genealogy Society and some other family history societies keep lists of those who are researching particular surnames. The *Genealogical research directory*, published annually by Johnson and Sainty, contains a list of surnames with details of people all over the world who are interested in particular names, showing the geographical area and period of time on which they are focusing. Each person listed is given a number and there are details of their address, so that contact can be made. A number of individual families and clans now have their own websites where information can be exchanged and queries placed. The Guild of One-name Studies can be contacted on www.mlfhs.org.uk.

Emigrant links

In the case of families who left Scotland a long time ago, is not always easy to establish a link back to their land of origin. A name on a chart – 'J. Cleland born in Scotland', for example – lacking a date, names of parents or residence – does not present a very good prognosis for identification. The minimum information needed to provide a starting point for research (but without a guarantee for success) is an approximate date of birth, marriage or death in Scotland and, unless the name is a very uncommon one, some additional details such as the name of a spouse or of parents or details of residence in Scotland to make identification of a relevant entry possible.

There are, however, a number of clues which can be followed up which may provide help in dealing with this problem. (See also 'Emigrants', p. 198.)

Collect as much oral history about the family's past as possible, but remember that different members of the family may have variant versions. Comparing what is remembered about the family is important.

Try to identify the approximate period of time when the emigrant left Scotland. This may provide a clue as to why he or she left – as a fugitive from persecution or from the law, as a prisoner, because of eviction or to seek a better life at a time of famine or economic and agrarian change. The circumstances that were the reason for emigration may indicate particular sources such as government papers, official records or estate papers which may include names or identify the area from which the family originated.

Passenger lists were usually kept at the port of debarkation and many have not survived. It was common for Scottish emigrants to travel to a port at a distance – either in Scotland or England – to find a ship and it is therefore important to consider that a person from Caithness, for example, might board a ship at Glasgow or Liverpool. Some of the most difficult people to trace are those who left Scotland for Ireland and then moved on to America. A considerable number of people who originated in Scotland emigrated more than once – moving from America or Canada to Australia and New Zealand. There are, however, many websites which provide information on surviving passenger lists and names of emigrants. Raymond (2002) and Stewart (2004) refer to a number of such sites and a search of the internet will reveal more. A great deal of work is being done in Australia and America and elsewhere in indexing passenger lists and other lists of arrivals. Passenger lists often give age, occupation and parish of origin but details are not always correct.

Immigration records, naturalisation papers, birth, marriage or death certificates in the country of settlement may include details of the country of origin. Some of these are now indexed online. Some certificates, such as those in New Zealand, contain a great deal of information, giving parish of birth as well as names of parents.

Census returns (in any country) for those born abroad too often only note the country of birth without giving details of the parish but they can be useful in indicating when the family left and in providing information where children were born – before or after the move.

Those who settled in another country often named new homes or properties after the places where they had lived before emigration.

If it appears that a couple arrived in their new country married and with children born in Scotland, then it is possible to search the indexes to the OPRs or statutory registers for both the marriage and births or baptisms to try to identify the family.

Newspaper obituaries in the country of settlement may provide details about the emigrant's origins.

Tombstones sometimes record where the person came from and some Scottish tombstones include details of members of the family who died abroad.

If the family was well-to-do, there may be legal documents – such as testaments – both in Scotland and in the country of settlement which provide a link and mention relatives who remained in Scotland.

Bear in mind the possibility that the surname may have changed at the time of emigration. Officials may have had difficulties in taking down Scottish names which were unfamiliar and changed the spelling. People sometimes made changes themselves and simplified the form of their names (see 'Scottish names', p. 23.)

The internet

The internet is the first port of call for many people looking for their ancestors. In any guide to using the internet in family history, you will find a range of phrases such as 'an explosion of data', 'a revolution in the work of family historians', 'a new adventure into Scottish genealogy', 'frustration', 'a bewildering range of information'. These expressions reflect both the good and the bad aspects of the internet which is now the preferred means of sharing information on genealogy and making contact with other branches of the family or with those interested in discovering more.

There are innumerable web pages for exchange of news and views on research on particular families and in many cases people in distant parts of the world are finding relatives of whom they previously knew nothing. On the other hand, the wish to establish blood connections is sometimes stronger than the honest resolve to prove the link. The sharing of a surname is no proof of relationship – it would be hard to establish a connection between all McGregors, for example – and a shared DNA does little to fill in the particulars of descent. A great deal of erroneous information and advice is, unfortunately, proffered on websites. You should always try to do your own research and check every fact and link obtained through internet sites.

Information on the internet and through websites can be divided broadly into six categories:

catalogues of holdings of libraries and archives and other bodies
digitised documents
indexes
transcripts
information on people, organisations, places, events
forums, chat sites and mailing lists.

Catalogues

Internet access to archive catalogues is one of the most important and exciting developments for the family historian at the present time as it opens the way to finding and exploring source material which was formerly unknown or very difficult to locate. Catalogues of an ever growing number of archive holdings and records of academic or professional bodies are in the process of being put online and their repertories can now be searched through the relevant website. (See also 'Profiling the ancestors – Using catalogues', p. 121.)

Published listings of internet addresses are apt to go out of date very quickly and it is often easiest to use a search engine to key in the name of a place, repository, person or subject in which you are interested. Appendix 2 includes some key internet addresses which provide links to the holdings of Scottish archives, museums and libraries.

Digitised documents

Digitisation of documents such as statutory certificates, census returns, old parish registers, testaments and inventories, kirk session records and an ever expanding range of other material makes it possible for researchers worldwide to access original sources at home, though not all access to the services is free. This is of enormous value to those living out of reach of archives such as the NAS. The ease of searching their website www.ScotlandsPeople.gov.uk for testaments and inventories and the facility to download reasonably priced copies is already appreciated by many but it is important to remember that digitised documents represent only a small proportion of what is available and that there is, for example, a wealth of other source material which relates to testamentary matters. (See 'From birth to death – Testamentary sources', p. 100.) Ease of access online to some material should not lead searchers to stop there or encourage them to close their eyes to the possibility of uncovering other associated documentation.

Transcripts and indexes

It is important to remember that transcripts and indexes which can be found on websites are not primary sources (see 'Profiling the ancestors – Finding sources', p. 119.) Transcripts and indexes can be very useful – especially when you are not able to get to see the originals – but you are dependant on the skills of the contributor and the way is open to personal interpretation, omission and error. Entries may be left out, the indexer may find it difficult to read Old Scots handwriting and get names wrong and documents may not be presented in their right context. There are a great many useful transcripts which can now be consulted online – of census returns or monumental inscriptions, for example – but this material needs to be used with care and the same is true of indexes.

Information sites

Included under this heading are information sites, forums, chat sites and mailing lists. When looking for general information and exchanging news and views through message boards or discussion groups or joining mailing lists, such sites can be of great interest but again it is essential to evaluate what you find. Who is providing the information? Does it come from a printed book or a personal contributor? Neither, in fact, may be trustworthy. Not infrequently, enthusiasm outruns expertise when answering questions or supplying information. Details are often provided which are not correct and the danger is that once something appears on a website it is often afforded uncritical acclaim and belief and assumed to be true. Publication on a website is no guarantee of accuracy.

Another problem in using the internet is to find what you want. When you key in a search word or phrase, a note will often appear at the top of the page stating that thousands of so-called matching entries have been found. The majority will be totally irrelevant but picking out the relevant ones may be a mammoth task and this is a complication which is only likely to get worse. Books have been published which provide guides to useful sites, such as Stewart (2004) and Raymond (2002), and the inclusion of references at the end of articles in *Family Tree Magazine* or other genealogical journals such as *Ancestors* listing websites which relate to a particular subject are extremely useful. Sites change and frequently become out-of-date and it is too easy to fail to note down the addresses of particular websites in serial publications which are of interest. Time, patience and skill are needed to make the most of the opportunities afforded by the internet.

Scottish resources overseas

Although the internet has opened up wide-ranging search facilities for those living at a distance from the homelands of ancestors, research at one remove can still be very frustrating – often made worse by website references to new and previously unexplored sources in archives far from you. If you live in England, America, Canada, Australia, New Zealand or elsewhere, it is important to discover first what sources are available locally, often in the form of copies on microfilm or fiche. You can next decide what may be found on the internet which may be helpful and also discover from looking at online catalogues what other sources look interesting. You then have to decide whether it is worth employing a researcher to look at certain records elsewhere. The final solution may be to save up and make a visit to Scotland to do it yourself.

Many family history societies throughout the world have Scottish interest groups and some have built up very large resources for research in Scotland as well as information about the lives of these Scottish immigrant families in their new homelands.

Archives, universities and libraries in America, Canada, Australia and New Zealand and elsewhere hold a great deal of Scottish material – copies of Scottish documents and originals, as well as books of Scottish interest and family papers. A considerable number of Scots settled in North Carolina and there are records relating to them in the state archives of North Carolina, as well as in several university collections in the state. Nova Scotia and Prince Edward Island were also settled by Scots and their archives hold material of value. The University of Guelph in Ontario runs a degree course in Scottish studies and The Waipu House of Memories in New Zealand (www.waipumuseum.com) is dedicated to the emigration from Scotland and Cape Breton of the Reverend Norman MacLeod and his followers. A great many Scots, particularly from Orkney, joined the Hudson's Bay Company, founded in 1670. In 1994 the Company gifted their records to the Archives of Manitoba, Winnipeg, Canada (www.gov.mb.ca/chc/archives/hbca/). The early records have all been microfilmed (work is still in progress) and they can now be consulted not only at the Manitoba Archives but also at the Canadian archives in Ottawa and at the National Archives at Kew, London. These are just a few of the many holdings of records of Scottish interest held outwith Scotland.

It should, of course, never be forgotten that many Scots crossed the border to settle in England. The Anglo-Scottish Family History Society (www.mlfhs.org.uk) may help in providing some links.

Clans and clan societies

The concept of the Scottish clan has become a cornerstone (often romanticised) of Scotland's highland heritage. Interest in clans, their chiefs and members has spread worldwide and while there are a great many clan societies in Scotland, branches are also to be found in most countries where Scots settled in any numbers. They hold meetings and organise gatherings and games and there is often a clan genealogist to answer questions. A number of clan societies hold a considerable amount of genealogical material. The archives of 135 Scottish clan societies in America are held in the Odom Library, Moultrie, GA. In Scotland the Clan Donnachaidh Museum at Bruar, Pitlochry holds extensive information about the clan and its members, the Clan MacMillan centre has a large genealogical collection of material, and at the Clan Donald centre library at Armadale on the Isle of Skye you can consult a vast range of material relating to Macdonalds and their estates. There are many other clan centres. The latest edition of *Burke's Peerage* (2003) includes sections on all the clan chiefs. Most clan societies have their own websites, both in Scotland and overseas.

There are, however, many misconceptions about the clans. The clan system is of Gaelic origin and does not apply to Lowlanders, nor does the fact that you have a 'clan' surname mean that you are necessarily related, even at some remove, to the chief. People in the past often adopted the name of a clan chief because they wanted his protection, worked for him or lived on his lands. Sometimes they would bear two names – their own surname and that of a clan as an alias. The septs were usually families who became associated with a main clan – perhaps through a distant blood relationship or as a diplomatic move – but they might also retain their own surnames. The concept of septs is used to bring many families within the umbrella of the main clan. A great many published histories of the clan families are listed by Stuart (1978).

LDS family history centres

In most countries throughout the world it is possible to find a family history centre of the Church of Jesus Christ of the Latter-Day Saints (LDS) which is accessible. At these centres, microfilm copies of a very wide range of Scottish records can be consulted or, if the LDS hold a copy in the Salt Lake City library, they will order it for you for a small fee. They have an extensive Scottish family history library and their catalogue is also online. Irvine (2003) provides a useful guide to what source material has been filmed by the LDS and can be consulted though their local libraries.

The International Genealogical Index

The most frequently used searching aid created by the LDS is the International Genealogical Index (commonly referred to as the IGI), which provides access to a vast collection of baptisms and marriages and temple ordinance details from over a hundred countries. Some entries are the result of systematic extraction of certain records (such as the OPRs) but others are taken from material submitted by members of the Church. There have been a number of different editions of the IGI, later ones having more entries. It is, however, important to bear in mind that alterations have been made in each edition and a number of entries found in the 1988 edition, for example, do not appear in the 1992 edition, though the latter does include many new entries. The early editions of the IGI are available on microfiche and can be found in family history centres, libraries and archives round the world. The most recent editions are on CD or online at www.familysearch.org, as well as being available in fiche format.

There are a number of options which enable you to search for a particular event, collect children of the same parents or access information submitted to the Church by the family (see Irvine, 2003). The indexes cover most births or baptisms (referred to as christenings, this date being given in preference to birth if both are known) and marriages (or proclamations) recorded in the parish registers, as well as a few additions referring to those of other denominations and births and marriages from the statutory registers from 1855–75. You can also search a section called 'ancestral file', which is a collection of material submitted by members of the LDS Church which provides information on a number of generations of a family. Deaths and burials are not included.

Used wisely, the IGI is a very useful searching aid but it needs to be utilised with great care. There are many omissions and it is not reliable. There are a considerable number of mistakes (you may find two slightly differing entries relating to the same event), not every birth, christening or marriage is listed (even among those extracted from the OPRs or statutory registers 1855–75), and some references originate from individual submissions for which you can find no entry in the original records. It is only an index and to get reliable results, it is always necessary to look at the full entry. This may provide valuable clues and additional information.

Research in Scotland – where to go

A question which is often asked by those planning to trace their ancestors in Scotland is: 'Should I start in Edinburgh or go to the district where my ancestors lived?' Because so many of our Scottish records are centralised in Edinburgh, it is usually advisable to start there. The National Archives of Scotland hold all the national records of Scotland and many local ones as well, while the Registrar General of Scotland has copies of statutory, census and parish records. In addition, you have opportunities to consult local collections of books and manuscript material in the National Library of Scotland (including in their map library), in the Central Library in Edinburgh, Edinburgh Castle and in other museums and libraries in the city. A study of online catalogues will give you some idea of what you may find and where and this should help you to assess the situation and Cox (1999) provides a useful guide to what is available and where.

Scottish Family History Service

By the beginning of 2007 a new Scottish Family History Service is planned to be in operation – a one-stop shop and family history campus situated at the east end of Princes Street, Edinburgh. This will link the present New Register House which is officially known as General Register Office for Scotland (GROS) with the adjoining National Archives of Scotland, providing access to the records of both and including the records of the Court of the Lord Lyon. This centre, to be known as the ScotlandsPeople Centre, will provide one place where there is access to some of the key genealogical records – statutory registers, parish registers, census returns, kirk session records and testaments. The intention is to allow free (but time-limited) access to the combined electronic genealogical resources of the General Register Office for Scotland and the National Archives of Scotland but there will be charges for longer periods of research and for certain services. Access to the other NAS records in the historical search rooms will remain free as at present.

When giving guidance in this book as to where documents are held, reference will be made to GROS (New Register House), the NAS (National Archives of Scotland) and the Lyon Office, although in the future many records will be included under the Scottish Family History Service.

General Register Office for Scotland

The GROS (New Register House) will become part of the Scottish Family History Service. Their website is www.gro-scotland.gov.uk and this provides details of opening hours, national and local holidays and fees payable for access to the records.

Records in the keeping of the Registrar General of Scotland which are open to the public are Scottish statutory registers of births, deaths and marriages from 1855 onwards, census returns 1841–1901, parish registers for the whole of Scotland and various minor records. Work will soon be complete (2006) on digitising all these records which will be indexed and linked to the images.

National Archives of Scotland

The National Archives of Scotland (also known as General Register House, GRH, and formerly known as the Scottish Record Office,

SRO) is the repository of records relating to the government and legal system of Scotland but it also holds a great many other records of both national and local significance – church records, deposits of private papers and local records, among others. Their website at www.nas.gov.uk gives general information about hours of opening and general regulation of access. The electronic catalogue of the holdings of the archive is also on this website. Access to the NAS is free.

The NAS at present has two search rooms – one at the east end of Princes Street, Edinburgh (next to New Register House) and the other at West Register House in Charlotte Square (about a mile away). Most court records and a very large collection of maps and plans are kept at West Register House. Many documents are out-housed and need to be ordered up twenty four hours in advance so that they can be brought in to one or other of the search rooms. If you know the class of record you wish to consult, ring up the NAS historical search room (telephone: 0131 535 1334) to check where the records can be consulted and if they need to be ordered up the day before. This information is not provided on the website catalogues.

A first visit to a large national archive is a daunting experience and therefore home-work done earlier in checking catalogues on the internet and selecting documents which are likely to be of value may save you a great deal of confusion, frustration and anxiety. The chapter in this book on 'Profiling the ancestors' (pp. 119–201) is designed to help you in sorting out which are likely to be the most useful records to consult in particular cases, according to where they lived, when they lived and what they did. The NAS website gives access to a number of fact sheets on various topics such as military records, emigration, deeds, sasines and taxation. *Tracing your Scottish ancestors* (NAS, 2003) is a valuable book to have at hand. Staff of the NAS will advise you in finding and ordering up records but will not do the research for you.

National Register of Archives of Scotland

In addition to deposits of private papers of families and businesses held by the NAS and other archives, many collections are still in private hands. A large number of these have been catalogued through the National Register of Archives of Scotland (NRAS) and an index to these catalogues can now be searched on the internet through www.nas.gov.uk/nras/reqister.asp. There are separate catalogues for business archives, organisations, personal papers, records of families and estates, and diaries and papers and a search can be made of one category or across all of them. Access to the documents can often be arranged – sometimes in the NRA, otherwise at the place where they are held – but permission to view the records must be requested through the National Register of Archives and this will take time.

Court of the Lord Lyon

The Court of the Lord Lyon is situated in New Register House, Edinburgh. The Lord Lyon King of Arms is responsible for administering all matters concerning armorial matters and matriculation of arms, as well as being judge of the Court of the Lord Lyon. Many cases concerning heraldic business and disputed clanship matters are heard in this court. A Public Register of All Arms and Bearings in Scotland was established in 1672 and is still kept. These grants of arms in most cases provide a considerable amount of information about the family concerned, tracing back from the petitioner for a number of generations. Enquiries about the material held in the Lyon Office should be made in writing to The Lyon Clerk, Court of the Lord Lyon, HM New Register House, Edinburgh EH1 3YT. A fee may be payable for searches carried out there. The Lyon Office also holds a public register of genealogies and birth brieves (certification of birth) in Scotland which was begun in 1727 but was discontinued over the years 1796–1827. An index has been published by the Scottish Record Society (Grant, 1908). Other records held by the Lyon Office are described in *Guide to the public records of Scotland* (Livingstone, 1905). The Lyon Office website is www.lyon-court.com.

National Library of Scotland

The National Library of Scotland is situated on George IV Bridge, Edinburgh and is a copyright library, holding a vast number of books and periodicals, and a large collection of manuscripts relating to Scottish history and literature. Catalogues of both the printed books and manuscripts are now online – www.nls.uk. Access to the library is free but it is necessary to obtain a reader's ticket valid for either four weeks or three years. Proofs of identity are needed for both and in applying for a general ticket, you will need to produce two passport-quality photographs. There are many reference books on the open shelves but most material will need to be brought to you. You can consult the catalogues online and order in advance.

National Library of Scotland map library

This is a department of the National Library but situated in a different building, at the Map Library, Causewayside Building, Salisbury Place, Edinburgh. The library holds a huge collection of maps, charts and atlases connected with Scotland (though it also has material for other parts of the world). Many of the maps can now be consulted online (use the NLS website www.nls.uk , click 'digital library' and then on 'maps'). These cover most parts of Scotland between 1560 and 1928 and the collection includes eighteenth-century military maps, Ordnance Survey maps and town plans for the period 1847–95 in a growing online collection.

Edinburgh Central Library

This is also known as the City Library, and is situated at George IV Bridge, Edinburgh. It has two specialised collections – the Edinburgh Room contains material relating to the city, including old newspapers, photographs, cuttings and directories, and in the Scottish Room there is a large collection of books relating to culture, social life and history for all parts of Scotland as well as pamphlets, photographs and some manuscript material. Access is free.

Local archives, libraries and collections

In 1996 Scotland's local government was reorganised and the country was divided into districts administered by thirty-two unitary author-ities. Each of these districts should have an archivist and the addresses of the archives are given in Appendix 2. The catalogues of many of their holdings are being put online. Consult the SCAN online cata-logue (www.scan.org.uk) and click on the archive in which you are interested. The presentation on individual sites is not standardised but you will find at least a brief summary of each holding, a note of the level at which the collection is described and finding aids available. For some archives there are very detailed catalogues.

In recent years it has been the policy of the NAS to return some local records held by them (burgh and kirk session records, for example) to the relevant local archive and you may find collections split, with some records in the NAS and others in the local archives. It is always wise to search the catalogues of both the NAS and local archives as the local authority archive will not necessarily hold all the manuscript material relevant to that area. Fife, for example, presents a particularly confusing picture, with some records in the NAS, many relating to the Fife burghs held by the University of St Andrews, and other local records scattered through various local history collections in archives, libraries and museums. (See Cox, 1999.)

The website www.archiveshub.ac.uk provides details of the holdings of archives held in universities and other higher education centres throughout the United Kingdom, and www.familia.org.uk is a guide to genealogical resources in public libraries which may include both

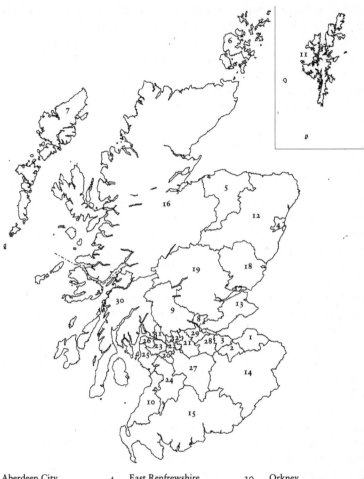

Aberdeen City	4	East Renfrewshire	20	Orkney	6
Aberdeenshire	12	Eilean Siar (Comhairle nan)	7	Perth and Kinross	19
Angus	18	Falkirk	13	Renfrewshire	23
Argyll and Bute	30	Fife	20	Scottish Borders	14
City of Edinburgh	3	Glasgow City	22	Shetland	11
Clackmannan	8	Highland	16	South Ayrshire	10
Dumfries and Galloway	15	Inverclyde	26	South Lanarkshire	27
Dundee City	17	Midlothian	2	Stirling	9
East Ayrshire	24	Moray	5	West Dunbartonshire	31
East Dunbartonshire	32	North Ayrshire	25	West Lothian	28
East Lothian	1	North Lanarkshire	21		

Based on maps issued by the Government Statistical Service ©
Crown Copyright 1995: with thanks to the School of Town and Regional Planning
University of Dundee.

Map 1   Scotland's local authorities

printed and manuscript material. The website www.archon.national archives.gov.uk also provides links to many archive collections.

Cox (1999) is a useful guide, not only to local archives but to many other specialised collections in Edinburgh and elsewhere in Scotland, such as army records, family history society holdings, university archives, museums, and those concerning medical or religious bodies.

When planning to visit local archives, it is wise to check on hours of opening and whether it is necessary to book a seat. Some archives are not open every day and search room facilities may be limited.

Getting professional help

We all like to do our own detective work but there may be occasions when the assistance of a specialist or local searcher is needed. Many people in the past put the whole task of finding out about their ancestors in the hands of a researcher. Now, with an increasing volume of material online, catalogues available for consultation worldwide and LDS and other family history libraries holding an ever growing amount of genealogical material, there are more opportunities to do it yourself or, at least, to be more selective in choosing what you want to have done for you.

Genealogical magazines contain many advertisements inserted by those who offer 'fast, friendly service', 'expert advice' and other good offices in undertaking genealogical research. Their names are often followed by a long list of membership of societies, most of which may be evidence of interest in family history but are not a proof of training, capability or experience. FSA is written after their names by many 'professional' researchers but in fact membership of the Society of Antiquaries has nothing to do with qualifications in undertaking genealogical research. The GROS publishes an annual list of those who undertake research but takes no responsibility for the quality of the work done. From all such advertisements it impossible to know how professional the work will be – unfortunately not every researcher is either reliable or knowledgeable and there are cowboys in this field as in most others.

The Association of Scottish Genealogists and Researchers in Archives (www.asgra.co.uk/index), publishes an annual list of its members, all of whom are accredited professional researchers and accept a code of practice. A minimum rate of charges for research is fixed by the Association each year, currently (2006) £20 an hour.

When choosing a researcher, study their advertisement. This should indicate the records with which that person deals – over the whole of

Scotland, in Edinburgh, for a particular locality or in a specialist field. If you want research done in the period before about 1710, make sure that the researcher can read Old Scots handwriting and if records such as pre-1781 sasines require consultation, these will require a knowledge of Latin.

Get an estimate as to what is involved in fulfilling your request and have a written agreement on the time to be spent on the work, the hourly rate and when you may expect a report. Some researchers work on a daily basis but most quote an hourly fee. Fees may vary considerably but the cheapest will not necessarily be the best. It is often wise to agree on a limited budget for the first instalment so that you can see what you are getting but it is rarely worth asking for just one or two hours' work unless you are requesting a particular piece of information.

Consider your options. Sometimes you may only need one specific source consulted or, on the other hand, you may want a full search carried out. If you have an old document which you cannot read, weigh up whether you want a full transcription or whether an extraction of all the relevant genealogical details will be sufficient. This will be much cheaper but you will lose the 'flavour' of the original.

You, too, have responsibilities in setting out clearly what you want to know and what you know already. You cannot expect to have satisfactory service if you hold back vital clues. On the other hand, take time to sort out the details you send your researcher – there is nothing more depressing than to receive a client's letter saying 'I just put together everything I had', resulting in a huge bundle of assorted notes and odd pieces of paper. You may be charged time for assessing all this!

Remember that even the best researcher cannot always produce positive results and research still has to be carried out to produce negative ones. And when you think that your researcher is charging an excessive fee, consider how much you pay to your plumber to fix a leaking pipe or to the mechanic to sort your car! A good researcher is a professional.

Scottish names

Spelling

'My family always wrote their name MacDonald, not McDonald' is an opinion one often hears but in fact there were few or no rules about spelling in the past. What was recorded was what was heard by the session clerk or registrar or other official or written down by the person concerned and this could result in many variants. If, for example, a Gaelic-speaking Highlander or an incomer from Ireland – perhaps unable to read and with a strong accent – came to register the birth of a child, the registrar had to take down the name as he heard it and this might differ from the interpretation of another registrar who had recorded the marriage.

It is not uncommon to find a statutory certificate with several different spellings of the same surname on it. A marriage certificate registered in Kilmorack, Inverness-shire in 1864 referred to the bridegroom as Donald Mackerlich but the same document named his father as Roderick McKearlich and one of the witnesses signed his name as Alexander McErlich.

Computerisation of indexes has brought many benefits but there are also some serious downsides. A computer only responds to the instructions given to it. If you key in a search for a John Rodger, no entry will come up for a John Roger, which is how your ancestor may have recorded the name. Unfortunately, even the prefixes Mc and Mac are not equated on most programs and you will have to search under both forms. Some indexes include a facility for using soundex for searching. This was a system patented in 1918 which takes the first letter of the word and divides the rest of the vowels into codes, offering alternative spellings of a name. It does solve many problems such as the Mc/Mac name variants, as well as Miller and Millar or Johnstone/Johnston alternatives but it also produces many names which are not valid alternatives. You also have to watch for names which escape the system, including those which change the initial letter or letters – the interchange of 'qu' for 'wh' or 'f' for 'ph', for example, is common in parts of Scotland. Various studies have been made of the success rate of using soundex and it is not encouraging.

Black's guide to the surnames of Scotland (1946) is a valuable reference book for all researchers as he quotes examples of spellings of surnames found in various documents over the centuries. It is not comprehensive but it is useful in highlighting variants and Gaelic and English forms of names.

Married women in Scotland were generally referred to by their maiden names – the inclusion of maiden names is one of the great advantages of researching Scottish genealogy.

Surname changes

It is very disconcerting when hunting for a family to find that the scent goes cold. If the family had Highland connections, the answer may be that the surname had changed. Towards the end of the eighteenth century, many families in Bute and Argyllshire (and elsewhere) anglicised their names. Sometimes the prefix 'O' or 'Mc' is dropped – O'Loynachan becomes Lang, O'Brolachan changes to Brolachan or Brodie and McFergish becomes Ferguson. The prefix 'McGille' is sometimes shortened to 'McIl'. The change could be more radical. McEachran appears as Cochrane, McSporran as Pursell, while if you lose a Henderson, look earlier under Hendry, McHendry or McKendrick. Black (1946) provides many of the answers and the name can be checked under either the Gaelic or English form and the entry will provide the link.

Patronymics – by which the son or daughter took the surname from the forename of the father – were widely used in Shetland until the nineteenth century or later but were in most cases given up much earlier in the Highlands though it persists, even today, among Gaelic-speakers who may have both an English name and a Gaelic one. Older Highland patronymics may provide the clues to a genealogy covering several generations, such as Finlay MacDhomhnuill mhic Aonghais – Finlay, son of Donald son of Angus.

In some districts, such as the fishing villages of the north-east, one surname might predominate and to distinguish between the various families people were given nicknames, also known as tee-names. Someone might be known by the name of their boat or distinguished by such additions as 'Lord', 'Beauty' or 'Carrot'. These nicknames sometimes occur even on statutory certificates and often are noted in census returns. In some Highland areas – Perthshire in particular – a surname common in the area in the eighteenth century or earlier has an added 'alias' – possibly a family name or one showing affiliation to a clan.

Christian names

There are also problems with spelling, shortened or variant forms of Christian names. It is not always easy, for example to be certain whether a person listed as Elisabeth (or Elizabeth) is the same as Isabella. This is not a common equivalent but it does occur. In other cases the variants represent the Gaelic and English form of the name. The list below gives some common Scottish names with their variants:

Agnes, Nancy
Angus, Aeneas, Aonghas
Christian, Christina, Christine, Kirsty
Donald, Daniel
Elisabeth, Elizabeth, Betty, Beatrice, Beatrix and sometimes Isabella
Helen, Ellen, Nellie

Hugh, Hew, Ewan, Aodh
Isabella, Isabel, Isobella, Bella
Jean, Jane, Jeanie, Jeannie, Janet, Jessie, Jenny
John, Ian, Iain, Eun, Eoin
Margaret, Maggie, Peggy
Morah, Morag, Sara, Sarah
Patrick, Peter
Samuel, Sorley

It was very common for boys' names such as Andrew, William or Donald to have 'ina' added at the end to make a girl's name. These children often appear as Ina. In records, Christian names are often shortened (and indexed under the shortened form) – Robt for Robert, Wm for William, Jn for John, Jas for James, Sandy for Alexander, Margt for Margaret.

The registrars sometimes had ideas about what names were suitable and substituted English equivalents for Gaelic Christian names when registering a birth. One registrar in 1858 entered a child's name as Harold, thinking that this was an English version of Torquil.

Place names

Spelling of place names can also be very variable and it is often helpful to vocalise what you think is written and see if there is a place known in the present time which might have been represented in that way. There have been various fashions in how names should be spelled on maps – according to the Gaelic form or anglicised. The most recent Ordnance Survey maps have adopted the Gaelic forms.

More radical alternatives have to be considered in cases where the old name has vanished or a different one been substituted. In the statistical accounts for Argyllshire parishes written in the 1790s, the minister often starts by stating that the parish formerly had another name. Glenorchy was known as Clachan Dysart, Ardchattan was Ballebhodan, while Campbeltown before 1700 was known as Ceann-loch, Lochhead or Kilkerran. Volume 20 of the *First Statistical Account* contains a 'List of Parishes suppressed, annexed to other parishes, or which have changed their names, with a corresponding List of the Parishes under which they are now included'. This list can be accessed online through www.stat-acc-scot.edina.ac.uk. It can be very useful in identifying parishes which are referred to in testaments and other older documents though it does not cover all of the older parish names.

There is the added complication that the same place name often occurs in various parts of Scotland. There are innumerable Kirktowns, several Kirkmichaels, and Pathhead is found in New Cumnock, Crichton and Kirkcaldy. It is never wise to assume that a place is where you think it is. Reference to maps, old and new, sometimes provide the answer and a gazetteer may indicate a likely solution to the problem. Groome's *Ordnance gazetteer of Scotland*, published in various editions in the 1880s, is widely available in libraries and is very useful.

A great many places – farms, villages, settlements or houses – have completely disappeared through depopulation, evictions and changes in farming methods and the names may appear on old maps and estate plans but are not on modern maps. The School of Scottish Studies, a department of Edinburgh University, holds a vast collection of records on Scottish place names, including field names. For some parts of the country covered by the 1:2,500 Ordnance Survey maps (published in the 1880's and known as the 'Parish Edition') there are accompanying books of reference which show acreage, land use and sometimes include information about names. These exist for much of central Scotland and the Borders, some lowland areas of Perthshire and the Highlands but unfortunately do not cover Fife, Midlothian, East Lothian, Wigtownshire and Kirkcudbright. They can be consulted in the NAS.

If you are trying to find a place within the period 1306–1659, it is always worth looking at the place name indexes to the *Register of the Great Seal of Scotland*. Reference is made to an enormous number of lands, all over Scotland, which belonged to the Crown as the feudal superior and it is usually possible to see from the charters who owned the lands and where they were situated. From 1781 to 1830 and from 1872 onwards there are indexes of places named in the sasine abridgements, arranged by county. Find the place (farm, estate or village) in the index (variant spellings are also given) and then look up the sasine in which it is mentioned. The information in the abridgement will usually make it possible to determine its location. These manuscript indexes can be consulted in the NAS and are being put online. (See also 'Understanding legal documents – The abridgements to the sasines: 1781 onwards', p. 216.)

Scottish language

Many Scots words are unfamiliar to those who are carrying out research. The *Dictionary of the Scots language* can be consulted online, without charge, at www.dsl.ac.uk/dsl. This is a combination of two previously published major works on Scots language – *Dictionary of the Older Scottish Tongue* covering language between the twelfth and seventeenth centuries, and *Scottish National Dictionary* dealing with the eighteenth century to the present day. Both these dictionaries can be consulted in various Scottish libraries. The online work can be searched by phrase or by word. There are also simpler printed options in *The concise Scots dictionary* (ed. Robinson, 1985) and *Chambers's Scots dictionary* compiled by A. Warrack and W. Grant (various editions, 1911–65).

Scottish handwriting

It can be very disconcerting and most frustrating when you find that you cannot read a document which may be of vital importance. From the first half of the sixteenth century onwards a style of handwriting developed which was designed to be written quickly and read easily by ordinary people. This became known as the 'secretary hand'. North and south of the border it developed in slightly different ways and there were a number of variant forms in Scotland. About 1700, however, the style of writing changed again and 'modern' handwriting appeared.

To decipher any Scottish document written in the seventeenth century or earlier may be challenging to the uninitiated. Letters were written in a different way, many abbreviations were used and words and terms may not be familiar. Reading Old Scots handwriting is a skill which has to be learnt. Palaeography classes are run in various places and the SCAN website includes tutorials in reading the older texts. Simpson (1973) has written a useful introduction to the subject and includes copies of a range of documents with transcripts and notes. The Scottish Records Association has published a self-help pack – *Scottish handwriting 1500–1700* (Rosie, 1994) – which provides a number of documents illustrating various styles of handwriting and gives a transcript and notes for each. For anyone who is intending to undertake extended study of pre-1700 documents, an ability to read secretary hand is very important. For others, who only need a transcription or abstract of one or two documents, there are researchers who will do this for a fee. Lists of professional researchers will include some who offer this service.

III *From Birth to Death*

'I am accustomed to have mystery at one end of my cases, but to have it at both ends is too confusing.' This comment by Sherlock Holmes underlines the importance of establishing facts step by step and following out the trail of evidence and clues. Genealogical research demands the same methods. There are three 'foundation' sources for genealogical research – statutory registers, census returns and the old parish registers, but these do not stand alone. In addition, church and legal records, family muniments and local records, among others, can complement and extend the information found in the 'foundation' records, and it is the 'big picture' of sources for birth, marriage and death which will be taken into account.

Methods of research

A printed history of a family will usually start with the first known ancestor and work forwards but in carrying out your own research you should always trace back, researching from the base of what you know and have confirmed already. A statutory certificate of birth, death or marriage may be the starting point. A birth certificate will tell you the name of the child, the names of the parents and usually the place and date of marriage of the parents. That marriage certificate will give the ages of bride and bridegroom and the names of their parents, thus taking the family tree back another generation. The information on a death certificate provides the basis for looking for a birth certificate and as you know the names of the parents, you can be sure when you have found the right entry. Census enumerations fill in information about each generation, provide leads back to an earlier census and give details of ages and places of birth which may be a bridge to the pre-1855 parish registers. There are times, however, when you need to look forwards to gain additional information – a tactic which is sometimes forgotten. Details on a marriage certificate, for example, can be confirmed by what is stated on the death certificate or the limited details given in a pre-1855 birth or marriage entry extended by finding a statutory certificate of death or census entry.

Searching for living relatives

Many of those who have traced their roots back to Scotland now want to make contact with living relatives. The internet is often the means of establishing links between families with common ancestors, and searches for descendants are also important in legal cases involving a need to find heirs.

Different research techniques are required in searching forwards. Starting from a post-1854 birth certificate (which names the child's parents) you can look through the death indexes for someone of approximately the right age and check whether the names of the parents given there match those on the birth certificate. If that death certificate states that the person was married, the name of the spouse will be given and you can look back for the marriage certificate and search for children born to the couple. Census returns (1841–1901) are often helpful, particularly in finding the names of children born in a family. From 1929 onwards the birth indexes include the maiden name of the child's mother, which makes it easier to pick out entries likely to be relevant, and from 1974 onwards an index entry for a death includes the maiden name of the mother of the deceased. There is, however, a nasty 'black hole' in the process of discovering the names of children born to a couple between 1902 and 1928, as there is a 100-year closure on access to census returns. The birth indexes only give the name of the child, the year of registration and the district in which the birth was registered. If a family moved around, you may have to check every birth under that surname which, in the case of a common surname, can take a very long time. The informant on the death of a parent is often a son or daughter and that name may provide a clue.

Local directories sometimes provide addresses but they do not include everyone. If the family you are researching owned property and you know where this was, then sasines may help in establishing who inherited and when. For professionals – doctors or lawyers for example – there are many publications which give details of careers. Voters' rolls can be of great assistance, particularly in modern times, in locating people and their addresses.

1. Birth

Statutory registration

Statutory registration was introduced in Scotland under the Registration of Births, Deaths and Marriages (Scotland) Act 1854 on

1 January 1855. The demand for statutory control over a compulsory system had been growing for a number of years and this had already been introduced in England in 1837 though it was not compulsory till 1875. During the eighteenth century a growing number of people in Scotland broke away from the Established Church and they did not always record baptisms or marriages in the Church of Scotland registers. The old parish system also came under increasing pressure, with large-scale migration of the population to the towns where the minister no longer knew all his parishioners. In many sectors of life – insurance, the law, local administration and medicine – statisticians were demanding accurate dates of birth, marriage and death. This information was no longer available from a study of the parish registers. Seton (1854) claimed that by 1850 'considerably less than a third of the probable births in the whole of Scotland were inserted in the registers' and in the cities the proportion was even smaller.

For the purposes of statutory registration, the country was divided into registration districts, which were usually based on the existing parishes, but large towns and cities were divided into a number of districts. The districts in large towns and cities have sometimes changed as populations grew.

From 1 January 1855 onwards, a birth, death or marriage had to be registered within a short time of the event at the local registrar's office – within twenty one days for births, eight days for deaths and three days for marriages. A copy of the certificate was kept in a book there while another copy of the book was later transmitted by the local registrar to the Registrar General in the General Register Office in Edinburgh.

Indexes have been compiled annually covering the whole of Scotland, made up from the indexes in the back of each of the local registrar's books. All the records of GROS are now digitised under their DIGROS project (Digital Imaging of the Genealogical Records of Scotland's people) and on payment of a moderate fee you can search indexes and view digital images of statutory registers, as well as some census returns and old parish registers on their website www.ScotlandsPeople.gov.uk. Online access to births is limited to birth records over one hundred years old, to marriages over seventy five years and deaths over fifty years. If, however, you are searching in person in the GROS, and have paid any requisite search fee, you have freedom to search indexes to within a year or so of the present and view digitised images of all certificates, from which you can take notes or make transcripts. There is no limit to the number of records you can consult. Cheap photocopies of certificates within the 'open' dates can be obtained by clicking on the 'copy' icon on your screen and these are available immediately. These copies cannot be used for legal or official purposes such as applications for passports.

If you want to visit a local registrar's office, it is wise to check in advance as search facilities may be limited. Local registrars' offices may now be linked to the online search facilities of the GROS. In most cases, a fee will be payable for a search there.

'Official' copies of certificates can be obtained from the local registrar's office or from the Registrar General in Edinburgh by personal application, by post or over the internet. If you are ordering and paying for an official certificate over the internet site, the certificate will be sent to you by post. In the case of a birth certificate, you can ask for an abbreviated certificate which only names the child and gives the date and place of birth without any information about the parents. This will cost less than a full certificate. The website of the GROS is www.gro-scotland.gov.uk.

Birth certificates

Information given

There were, without doubt, some births which were not registered in Scotland particularly in the early years of statutory registration, due to the inefficiencies of registrars and hostility of certain people to submit to the system, but the percentage does not seem to have been high. In England it is thought that up to a third of all births, marriages and deaths were not registered between 1837 and 1875.

The real bonus with regard to Scottish certificates is the amount of information which is recorded. In 1855, the scheme was ambitious in recording a great deal of information, but unfortunately the pressure on the registrars in taking down so much detail was too onerous and the following year the form was curtailed. Over the years there have been a number of variations in what was included on a birth certificate and it is important to bear these changes in mind as lack of certain details on the certificate of one member of the family may be supplemented by those given for another child born either later or earlier. If, for example, a child was born in 1856, you will find no details of when and where the parents were married but if another younger child can be found, born after 1860, that birth certificate will supply this information. It is always worth checking to see if a member of the family was born, married or died in 1855 as the extra details given on such certificates can be invaluable.

The following details are given on birth certificates:

1855: child's name(s), sex, date and time of birth, address where born, father's place of birth (if registered or not) and occupation, mother's maiden name, age and place of birth (if registered or not), usual address of parents if different from place of birth of child, date and place of parents' marriage, number (but not names) of children already born to parents, sex and whether alive or dead in 1855, signature of the informant and relationship to the child.

1856–60: child's name(s), date and time of birth, sex, address, name of father, and occupation, name of mother (with maiden name), name and signature of informant and relationship to child.

1861 onwards: as above but with the addition of the date and place of the parents' marriage.

If an informant is illiterate, that person will sign with a cross. It is sometimes interesting to note the spread of literacy as a father may sign the birth certificate of a first child with his mark but on those of later children there may be a rather hesitant signature. The informant is usually one of the parents but occasionally a grandparent, aunt or older sibling.

Stillbirths are not recorded till 1939 and all the registers are closed to the public. If however, a child breathed for only a very short time, the birth and death of the infant had to be registered.

Sometimes a birth is registered twice – in the district where the child was born (often a maternity home or hospital) and in the district which is the usual residence of the family. The details given on both certificates are identical. In the case of twins, it is very easy to miss one of the birth certificates, especially when using DIGROS. You may find an index entry to one of the children and look up the digitised entry but omit to look for a possible twin. As there is no 'browsing' facility to turn the page of the register on your screen and as the birth certificate of the other twin may be on the previous or next page, it can be overlooked. There is nothing on an index entry to indicate that a child had a twin brother or sister.

If the name of the child was changed, which did happen on a number of occasions, this was recorded in the Register of Corrected Entries (RCE). This is marked with a lozenge-shaped stamp on the left-hand side of the certificate with a volume and page number. There are microfiche copies of the Registers of Corrected Entries for each district and these can be consulted in New Register House but this information is being put online.

If your ancestor has more than one Christian name, this is a bonus, but before the twentieth century it was the exception rather than the rule. After this time it became a common occurrence. Middle names are often the maiden surname of the mother, grandmother or of another relative, providing a valuable clue in later research – but they might be chosen as a compliment to a local dignitary, landlord or minister.

Illegitimate births

A number of studies have been made of illegitimacy in Scotland (Mitchison and Leneman, 1989 and Flinn, 1977). Their conclusions are the same – that the rate of illegitimacy as a ratio of live births was high – though it varied from area to area. Both assume an illegitimacy percentage of births *circa* 1861 as 9.37 for the whole of Scotland, falling to 6.34 by about 1901. Within the different regions of Scotland there were variations, with the highest rates shown in the south-west of Scotland, followed by the north-east. Illegitimacy is found in a great many families.

When trying to locate all the children born to a couple, it is important to start looking from the time of the marriage onwards but bearing in mind the possibility that one may have been born before the marriage. Under Scots law, all illegitimate children were automatically legitimated by the subsequent marriage of their parents. Such a child might have been registered under the mother's maiden surname but if the parents did marry, then the child might later assume the father's name. There would be no official record of this change.

An illegitimate child may be registered under the maiden name of the mother or under the natural father's name and the certificate may be signed by the mother alone or sometimes by both parents. Often the paternity of the father is not acknowledged but in some cases there is a note on the side of the birth certificate showing that there is an entry in the Register of Corrected Entries relating to a decree of paternity issued by a sheriff court. The RCE entry will usually give the name of the father, his occupation and address, providing clues which can be followed up to identify him. Although the enthusiasm of the kirk session and minister to trace errant fathers had waned in most areas by the middle of the nineteenth century, in some parishes this practice continued longer. If you want to find the name of the father of an illegitimate child after 1855, it is always worth checking the kirk session records of the parish around the time of birth. If the mother applied for payment of maintenance by the father, the case may have been heard in the sheriff court.

Adopted children

A register of adopted children commenced in 1930. This can now only be searched by adoptees aged at least sixteen who are searching for their natural parents. Prior to 1930, you do sometimes come across a census entry describing a child in the family as adopted but this would have been the result of a private agreement. The original birth certificate of an adopted child will have a stamp against it indicating that adoption had taken place. The new birth certificate which is issued at the time of adoption for that child does not refer back to the original certificate but this information is retained by the Registrar General. The certificate showing the name of the birth parent or parents can only be accessed by the adoptee on application to the GROS in Edinburgh.

The adoptive parents may have a copy of the full adoption certificate (or this can be obtained from GROS), which includes the date of the adoption order and the name of the court which made the order. This is the information needed to gain access to the court process which will be held either by the sheriff court where the adoption order was granted or is kept in the National Archives of Scotland. The procedure for viewing the court process is clearly described in a booklet titled *Search guide for adopted people in Scotland* published by Family Care (1997). Information in the process is sometimes disappointing and sometimes valuable. It may provide the name of the birth father, consent to adoption by the natural parent or parents, possibly naming witnesses who may be members of the birth family, a report by the curator *ad litem*, including the name of the adoption agency, home or social work department involved, and perhaps some additional papers. Adoption agency records, particularly since 1950, may include quite a lot of detail about the birth parents and some agencies keep in touch with them. The Family Care booklet gives a useful summary of all the steps to be taken in locating a birth parent, starting from the information given on a birth certificate.

Minor records including births

The Registrar General holds a number of registers, listed as minor records. These are the marine register of births from 1855 (children born to Scottish parents on British registered merchant vessels at sea anywhere in the world), service records from 1881 (births of Scottish children at military stations abroad from 1881 to 1951), High Commissioners' returns of births from 1964 of children of Scottish descent, consular returns of births from 1914, and register of births in foreign countries 1860–1965, based on the evidence submitted by parents. All these entries will appear on the computerised indexes and are being made available through DIGROS.

Indexes to registers of births

Access to the vast source of information provided by statutory registers is through the annual indexes. The original annual 'paper' indexes covering the whole of Scotland for births, deaths and marriages, separating males and females, have now been put online but the 'paper' indexes are still retained by GROS and you can request to have a check made in them if you think that there is an error in the online index.

A birth index entry provides little information in itself. It gives the child's surname and Christian name or names, the name of the district in which the entry is registered, the number given to that registration district and the entry number of the certificate. From 1929 onwards the maiden name of the child's mother is given on the index entry which is an important aid in searching as it makes it possible to identify entries of likely relevance.

When you have keyed in the name of the child with surname and Christian name, and indicated male or female, all possible entries in that year will appear on the screen and if the surname is a common one, such as McLean or Miller for example, there may be a daunting number. Up till the beginning of the nineteenth century, the choice of Christian names was also often very limited.

If you are basing the date of birth on an age stated at death or marriage or in a census, then you will need to search at least one year either side of the expected year of birth and if the right entry is not found, a wider search may be required as ages are often stated inaccurately. There is no short-cut to the labour of checking the actual certificates to find the right one. If you have paid the required fee for access to the records, then you can look at a huge number of certificates in a day but when working through the pay-per-view website, the costs will mount up and any strategies which can limit the search and help to identify the correct certificate are useful.

Index problem-solving
Spelling of names

If you have problems in finding a relevant index entry, check possible alternative forms and spelling of the surname (see p. 23). Spelling in the past was infinitely variable and the registrar often had to do the best he could to represent what he heard as the correct name. It is sometimes helpful to say the name aloud and consider what alternatives there might be, particularly in the case of names of Gaelic-speakers or those from Ireland.

The soundex system of bringing up like-sounding names (based on the substitution of groups of consonants), which is an option you are given can be very useful and has to be used to cover the alternative forms of Mac/Mc which are indexed separately. The system is not foolproof: it will bring up a lot of names which are not alternatives but some quite common options are not covered.

Could the Christian name be wrong? If the Christian name changed soon after the birth was registered, this should be recorded in the Register of Corrected Entries and the fact that an alteration was made noted on the margin of the birth certificate. The amended name is the one which should appear on the index. A middle name which is found later in life may not be given on the birth certificate and so if you have found that an ancestor was named James Joseph, it is quite likely that at birth he was registered as James.

One of the difficulties in searching on computer is that it will only obey the instructions you give it and thus it is wise to check carefully what you have asked for. In a search for the birth certificate of a Peter Valentine, it is wise to key in only the initial letter of the Christian name as he may have been registered as Patrick. On the other hand, if you are looking for the birth of a John Campbell, keying in a search of births for J. Campbell will result in an overwhelming number of possible entries, including those for James. The alternative forms of Christian names – such as Jane/Jean/Janet or Jessie – can cause problems but if you key in the minimum information, such as the initial J, all possibilities will come up. It is more difficult to cover the cases when shortened forms are used – Dick for Richard or Mina for Williamina, Peggy for Margaret – which involve a different initial letter. Occasionally a child is registered without any Christian name at all, but this is usually only found when the infant dies at or soon after birth.

The IGI can be useful if you are looking for a birth between 1855 and 1875, as on their indexes against the name of the child and parish of birth, the names of the parents are given, making it possible to weed out irrelevant entries. The downside of this searching aid is that not every birth (or marriage) is on this index, there are a considerable number of omissions and wrong entries and all the later editions are arranged by county – and you may not know where your ancestor was born. The IGI is also valuable in drawing attention to the variant spellings of a surname. Surnames in these indexes are arranged under a standardised form – in some cases names are wrongly assumed to be variants of others but there is usually a cross-reference – but the original form of the name is retained. You can therefore look at the IGI entries listed under the name which you are researching and you will see possible alternative spellings which can be keyed in to the computer to try to find the relevant entry.

Clues in other records

If the surname and Christian names were common ones and you do not know in what district the child was born, look for clues which may help.

Have you found the family in census returns? This will state where children in the family were born.

Are there any later family events (such as a marriage) where a witness or informant appears who has an unusual Christian name and is possibly a brother or sister to bride or bridegroom? Looking for the birth certificate of a Prudence Miller, who appears as a witness on the marriage of Mary Miller, is likely to be quicker and easier (even if you do not know the approximate year of birth) than trying to find the birth of Mary Miller. The birth certificate of Prudence will show where the family were then living, possibly give you a lead into a census return and also (if after 1860) provide information when and where the parents were married – all details which may be of great assistance in identifying Mary.

If you have problems in finding a particular birth, look first for the marriage of the parents (cross-referencing the names of bride and bridegroom if this took place after 1854). The date and whereabouts of the marriage will show you where the family were living at the time. If you are looking for the birth of a child born about the time of this marriage, he or she might have been born before the marriage and be registered under the mother's maiden surname.

Where did the family live?

Knowledge of the part of Scotland in which a child may have been born is important, as you can often pick out the entries on the index which are likely to be relevant. Up till 1974 Scotland was divided into counties (see Map 2). The parishes of Scotland (on which most registration districts were based) were numbered county by county, from north to south, Bressay in Shetland being number 1 and Wigtown in Wigtownshire in the far south-west of the country being given the number 901. Thus by looking at the number of the registration district you have some idea as to which part of the country it refers.

If you are not familiar with the geography of Scotland, it is useful to look up a gazetteer such as Groome's *Ordnance gazetteer of*

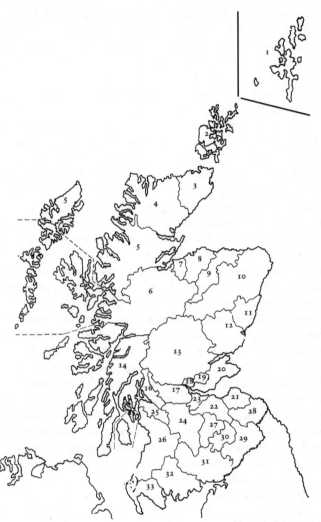

Aberdeenshire	10	Dunbartonshire	16	Nairnshire	7	Sutherland	4
Angus	12	East Lothian	21	Orkney	2	West Lothian	23
Argyllshire	14	Fife	20	Peebleshire	27	Wigtownshire	33
Ayrshire	26	Inverness-shire	6	Perthshire	13		
Banffshire	9	Kincardineshire	11	Renfrewshire	25		
Berwickshire	28	Kinross-shire	19	Ross and Cromarty	5		
Buteshire	15	Kirkcudbrightshire	32	Roxburghshire	29		
Caithness	3	Lanarkshire	24	Selkirkshire	30		
Clackmannanshire	18	Midlothian	22	Shetland	1		
Dumfriesshire	31	Morayshire	8	Stirlingshire	17		

Map 2 Scotland's former counties

Scotland (1882). Some quite sizeable towns did not have the same name as the parish or registration district till the twentieth century. Stonehaven was the county town of Kincardineshire but it was within the parishes of Fetteresso and Dunnottar and only became a registration district in 1935. There is a list of the names of many towns and large villages which did not coincide with that of the parish or registration district in Appendix 1.

The large cities are divided into a number of registration districts (which vary from time to time). Each district has a name and also a number which is common to all districts within the city (685 for Edinburgh, 282 for Dundee, 168 for Aberdeen, for example) with a superscript number for the particular district within that city. There are a few exceptions, such as Glasgow, where 644 is the number given to the greater part of the districts there but some come under 622 (the Gorbals area) and 646 covers the Govan area. If you are not sure of your geography, looking at the numbers can be helpful. For example, Castle and Portsburgh is a district of Edinburgh between 1855 and 1858 and it is easy to overlook this in searching for an entry in an Edinburgh district – but it has the district number 685^3 which indicates where it is.

The GROS has published a useful publication (available for reference or sale in New Register House) titled *The registration districts of Scotland from 1855*. This lists all the districts by number and also by name, showing any changes that took place in their numbering. There is a separate section dealing with the four big cities and their districts. A diagrammatic map of the Scottish parishes can also be of assistance. The GROS has also produced a *Civil parish map index* which shows the parishes of Scotland, dividing the country up into sections and there are similar publications published by various history societies and other organisations. Some have a page for each county but these have the disadvantage that they do not show the names of neighbouring parishes in the next county.

Elusive index entries

It is always worrying when you cannot find an entry which should be recorded within the period of statutory registration. Another concern may be that you find a certificate which does not agree in all details with other information you have uncovered. What steps should be taken to find missing entries? What are the possible reasons for the discrepancies?

The birth of a child born late in December may not be registered till the following year and will therefore be included in the indexes of that year.

Some births were not registered – particularly in the first few years of statutory registration – but there are other instances which sometimes, though not very often, were due to the incompetence of the registrar. This is a matter which is discussed by Sinclair (2000), who quotes cases where drink, age or lack of interest in the job impaired the registrar's efficiency.

A number of computerised index entries have been omitted and others entered wrongly, and a name entered with the wrong spelling is usually an entry lost. If you know the district of birth and the approximate date, you can check the individual index entered at the end of each annual district registration book. They are available on fiche (but not online) in New Register House. These indexes are also very useful if you are looking for an illegitimate birth and know the parish in which the child was born and the Christian name but not the surname. As long as the district is not too large, you can look down the lists of names and pick out possible entries and then check the certificates to see if the mother's name is correct. If you have good reason to think that an entry has been left out of the DIGROS index or wrongly entered, the staff of New Register House will search the original annual 'paper' indexes for you.

Check that you have filled in the search boxes on your computer screen correctly. It is very easy to forget to click on the male/female option, without which you may find no relevant entries. You may also have made a mistake in typing in the name.

Another hazard of searching indexes through a computerised system is that sometimes the computer may jump and miss an entry. When a search has proved negative despite the fact that you have positive knowledge of the place and date of a person's birth (or death or marriage), it is always worth going through the indexes again. In many cases – almost miraculously – the right entry appears.

Are you looking for the birth in the right place? It may help to do some lateral thinking as to where the event might have taken place. It was quite common for the first child to be born at the home of the maternal grandparents. In the twentieth century, an increasing number of children were born in hospital and this may be reflected in the district where the birth certificate was registered.

Some occupations make it likely that the family may have moved around. A railwayman, for example, can be difficult to trace as his employment may have involved moves to other places, some at a distance. Many agricultural labourers in the nineteenth century sought work on a new farm almost every year, looking for a better employer – it was also said that some wives liked the excitement of an annual 'hurl in a cart' – but the family is unlikely to have moved very far as it was difficult to transport belongings. On the other hand, if your ancestor was living in a big city – Glasgow, Edinburgh, Dundee or Aberdeen – there is a good chance that the family remained there because that is where the work was, but within that city or town the family is likely to have moved often.

Could the surname be wrong? If the child was illegitimate, the registration might be made under either the mother's maiden surname or the father's name. The fact of illegitimacy is often later concealed, on a marriage certificate, for example, and the surname given there may not be the same as that on the birth certificate. Sometimes the bride or bridegroom gave the names of grandparents (either maternal or paternal) in place of those of parents to conceal the fact of illegitimacy but the birth certificate will provide the correct information.

The second marriage of a parent can also cause confusion as the child of the first marriage sometimes assumed the surname of a step-father or later named a step-parent as parent. If a death certificate was used as the evidence for starting to look for the birth of the deceased, the informant may have been mistaken in naming the parents. An evaluation of the likely truth of the information on the death certificate may rest on the relationship of the informant to the deceased.

Ages stated in census returns and on certificates of marriage or death (of men as well as women) are frequently erroneous – sometimes years out. If you cannot find a birth certificate around the estimated date, search before and after the expected year.

Always make certain that you have the right entry! This may entail checking evidence of census returns and looking at the history of other members of the family.

Next steps in tracing the family

Researchers often get so excited in finding a relevant certificate for a member of their family that they forget to take down all the details and overlook the signposts which show where to go next. Figure 1 shows how the details given on a birth certificate can be used to take further steps.

Not everyone takes the time to collect details of siblings of the main line ancestor but time is never wasted in doing this. In the period from 1855 up to about 1914 families in most classes of society were large and you can expect to find a child born, on average, every two years. If there is a larger gap in the family, the birth of a child may have been

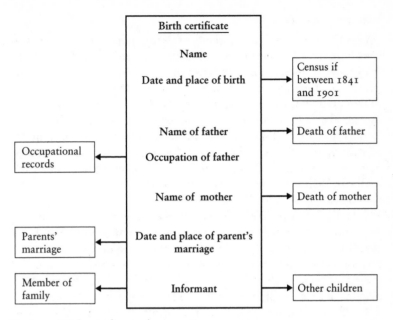

Figure 1   Birth certificate: where next?

missed or the mother may have had a miscarriage or stillbirth. The youngest child is sometimes a tail-ender – born some years after the previous sibling. From the 1920s onward there is a noticeable decrease in the size of families. The information gained from this exercise can be used in various ways. Some people, particularly those who are descended from emigrant ancestors, want to trace living descendants who remained in their country of origin. Birth certificates of other children provide addresses for the family (with possible links to census returns) and information about the occupation of the father. Christian names given to siblings may also contain clues.

Census returns

Census returns are an integral part of family history research. Information found there provides links to other censuses, leads in locating various members of the family and can act as a bridge between statutory registers and the pre-1855 parish registers. Censuses are also a fascinating source of social history, often revealing a silent tableau of the family once every ten years throughout the second half of the nineteenth century.

Censuses 1801–31

The earliest evidence in Scotland of interest in instituting official census returns for the whole population is found in the work of Alexander Webster, an Edinburgh minister, who in 1755 produced his account of the number of people in Scotland (Kyd, 1952). This was drawn up on information supplied by the parish ministers and listed the number of inhabitants in each parish, separating them into 'protestants' or 'papists'. He also included an estimate of the number of fighting men between the ages of eighteen and fifty six, estimated down to the fractions. Balingry in Fife with 464 inhabitants was credited with having 92⅗ fighting men. Unfortunately the census does not include names of individuals.

John Rickman, a clerk in the House of Commons, was the initiator of decennial censuses taken between 1801 and 1831 in England and Wales as well as in Scotland. In England those responsible for the enumerations were the overseers of the poor in each parish, but Scotland lacked a similar authority and schoolmasters 'or other fit person or persons in each parish' were appointed to undertake the task.

Little guidance was given as to the form that the early nineteenth-century censuses should take, but the returns were generally designed to answer a series of questions showing the number of inhabited houses and of persons of each sex in the parish, occupations of heads of houses in four main categories – agriculture, trade, manufactures or handicrafts, and others. It was generally agreed that the returns of 1801 reflected under-enumeration. In the 1821 and 1831 enumerations, some information was requested about ages of persons. Men serving in the army or navy were omitted but there was some confusion on the part of local enumerators as to whether local militiamen should be included in the returns or not.

Most of the 1801–31 returns were, unfortunately, only numerical but some enumerators in Scotland did make a fuller record of those in the parish, including names and other details. There was no official request for the submission of these census returns. Many were not kept or have been lost, others appear as part of the kirk session minutes or parish registers, are in the muniments of a local landowner or can be found in a local archive. Flinn (1977) gives a list of several parishes for which returns have been found, some of which are in the NAS (Annan, Dunnottar, Gordon, Jedburgh, Ladykirk and other Berwickshire parishes, Lochrutton, Lochwinnoch, Melrose, Moulin, Ormiston, Stow and Stromness) but there are others which have survived. Orkney archives hold a series of transcripts of enumerators' notes for the 1821 return for a number of Orkney parishes

(Irvine, 2004) while Baptie (2001) lists some more, usually titled 'lists of population' or 'census', found with kirk session records. It is, however, always worth checking with a local family history society as to whether work has been done locally in transcribing such records. The schoolmaster's returns for Annan 1801–21 have been published by the Scottish Record Society (1975) and state residence and names of all those living at each address, with an indication of occupation. Where they have survived, these early census returns can be very useful but it is not always easy to determine the identity of the person listed with certainty, as the information given is not detailed.

Census returns 1841–1901

In 1837 civil registration was introduced in England and from that time onwards there was a network of registrars who could administer a more detailed enumeration of the population. Despite the fact that a similar system was not in place in Scotland till 1855, national nominal census-taking was adopted there, too, from 1841 onwards.

The enumeration districts of Scotland were arranged by county and then by parish and if these were large (as in the case of big towns) they were divided again into smaller districts. The papers filled in for each household were collected and then copied into books. Those for 1841 and 1851 were removed to London and only returned in 1910 but the later enumerations went directly to the Registrar General of Scotland in Edinburgh.

The census was taken of everyone in a household on the following dates:

> 1841 census – the night of 6/7 June
> 1851 census – the night of 30/31 March
> 1861 census – the night of 7/8 April
> 1871 census – the night of 2/3 April
> 1881 census – the night of 3/4 April
> 1891 census – the night of 5/6 April
> 1901 census – the night of 31 March/1 April.

Censuses have continued to be taken decennially and only the 1941 census was missed, due to wartime conditions. No census can now be viewed by the public till after one hundred years have elapsed.

Microfilm copies of all the census returns open to the public, 1841–1901, are kept in New Register House, Edinburgh but are being replaced by digitised copies. Microfilm copies are also held by archives and family history centres in many places throughout the world, including in LDS family history centre libraries.

Work is nearly complete (2006) under the DIGROS project to digitise all the census returns 1841–1901 and then to link the images to indexes. This has already been done for the 1861, 1871, 1891 and 1901 returns, which can be searched on the pay-per-view website www.ScotlandsPeople.gov.uk and the facility will be extended as the project continues. Those searching the DIGROS images in GROS can use a browsing facility whereby you can turn the pages of the returns on your screen. This is important if you are trying to find other related families in the area. The 1881 census is available on CD and on computers in New Register House and a digitised version will be added.

There are microfiche or typescript copies of many indexes to individual census returns and a growing number are being put online by individuals or societies. The website www.freecen.org.uk provides online access, free of charge, to a growing number of Scottish census returns 1841–71 and these can be searched by name. The work done by individuals and societies in indexing the censuses is very valuable but some are more proficient than others and in some places there are many omissions or wrong transcriptions.

Be prepared for the fact that copies of some census returns are very poor. A number of the books were copied in ink which has faded and you may find that a few entries, pages or whole books cannot be read. There is no solution to this problem except to try to locate the family in another census but you should take a note of the imperfect condition of that census as it may be the reason why a family has not been traced in your searches. If you are working in New Register House and have difficulty in reading a particular entry, the staff may be willing to check the original enumeration book for you. Another problem is that in the process of checking the enumerators' books, a stroke was made on each entry by the examiner which often obscured part of what is written. It is often particularly difficult to read the stated age if there is a heavy mark across it.

Content of the 1841 census

Details given in the 1841 census – the first to include a nominal record of everyone in the country – are rather limited. They include the address, names of all those within the household but without a statement of their relationships to the head of the household, sex, occupations within broad categories (H. L. W. – handloom weaver, F. S – female servant, for example) and information as to whether an individual was born in the county where they were living or not, noted as Y(es) or N(o), E(ngland) or I(reland). Ages of adults are usually (but not always) given to within five years, rounded down. An age given as forty-five would cover those within the group aged forty-five to forty-nine) but the ages of those under sixteen are supposedly given accurately. Several families living in one building are divided by the mark / and separate buildings by //.

A few of the Scottish 1841 census returns were lost at sea when they were being returned from England in 1910. Most of these concerned Fife parishes – Auchtermuchty, Balmerino, Ceres, Collessie, Creich, Cults, Cupar, Dairsie, Dunbog, Kinghorn, Kinglassie, Kirkcaldy, Leslie – and Auchinleck in Ayrshire.

Content of the 1851–1901 censuses

From 1851 onwards the census returns provide a great deal more information – address, names of occupants, relationships to the head of the household, ages, status (widow, married, unmarried), occupations and parish of birth. There are, however, minor differences between the censuses.

In 1851 the schedule notes whether the occupant is blind, deaf or dumb. This information was omitted in 1861 but put in again thereafter.

From 1861 onwards, the census include a note of the number of children in each household at school and the number of rooms with one or more windows in which each family lived. This is an interesting detail as it provides an insight into the housing conditions of the times.

In 1891 and 1901 it is noted whether individuals speak Gaelic or English and Gaelic.

Occupants of institutions – poor-houses, prisons, hospitals or schools – are listed separately and the pages are usually placed at the end of the sections covering the relevant town. In the censuses from 1861 onwards there are lists of those on board merchant vessels in Scottish ports on the night of taking the enumeration and in 1871 and 1881 these include Scottish ships in English waters as well.

The 1881 census for Dunscore has been lost and the second half of the 1881 census for Dumfries.

Enumerators' comments

In the 1841 and 1851 censuses there is space in each book allotted to the minister, schoolmaster or enumerator, on which he might make any comments which he thought suitable, though many made no remarks. This is material which is often overlooked. The information contributed sometimes provides an interesting contemporary view on housing conditions, changes in farming methods, emigration and other matters. In 1841 the schoolmaster made the following comments on St Martins parish, Perthshire:

> There is a decrease of 64 from the census of 1831. This can be accounted for by the great no. of houses which have been thrown down when several pendicles have been joined in one large farm; and the greater part of these improvements have taken place during the last eight years. No. of parishioners absent on 7th June – 3: visitors in parish – 3: only one has removed to Buenos Ayres during the last six months.

Ten years later the minister recorded his remarks on the census of the same parish: 'Population decreasing. The pendicle or small farm system gradually giving way to the larger farming option and not a few of the natives of the parish leaving for America.' On the first page of a later book he added a list (including names and residences) of all those who had left the parish recently for America – a total of forty four persons.

Searching the censuses

Census returns contain an enormous amount of material which is of great value both to the genealogist and to the social historian. The fact that the first two nominal censuses – 1841 and 1851 – pre-date the introduction of civil registration is of particular value in Scotland as it is a means of obtaining some documentation on many people whose births or marriages may not have been recorded in the parish registers. Even the limited details given in the 1841 census can be useful.

Ease of access to a census through an index can limit the scope of your research and many clues may be missed. Whether you are searching through microfilm copies of the censuses (unindexed or indexed) or consulting the indexed censuses online, if the enumeration district is not too large it is often worth taking time to go through the whole return. You may discover grandparents, aunts, uncles, children staying with relatives or who are out at work – both girls and boys often left home at the age of about thirteen to take up employment elsewhere. A study of the area and the people who lived there may be both interesting and instructive. In large cities such as Glasgow, Dundee or Paisley it was not uncommon for migrants from a particular part of Scotland or Ireland to settle in the same district and information

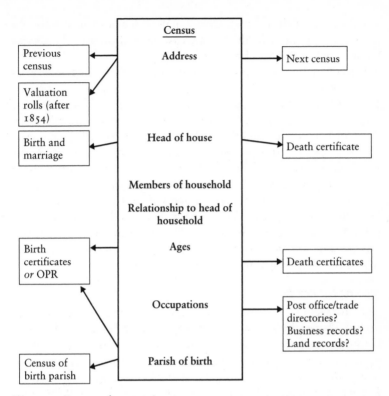

Figure 2   Census: where next?

about the origins of one family group may throw light on another. If you are searching online through a pay-per-view site where you do not have a facility to browse from page to page, it may be worth finding out where you can look at a microfilm copy of the census – at a local family history centre or library.

The information given about parish of birth of an individual is particularly important in the period before 1855 as it narrows your search and helps in proving the relevance of any entry found in the OPRs. In most cases the census will give the name of the parish of birth of each person but occasionally only the farm or village name is stated. In such a case you will then need to identify where the place is, using maps or gazetteers. The likelihood is that it is within the same census district and known to the enumerator who otherwise might have queried it. The county of birth should also be stated but is sometimes omitted – again a source of possible future problems as there are a considerable number of place names in Scotland which occur in various parts of the country. Occasionally it is not clear whether the reference to place of birth is to a parish or to a county of the same name – such as Perth or Inverness.

It is always worth trying to identify an individual or family in as many census returns as possible. You can then study the variations in the details recorded – age, parish of birth, occupation – and take these into consideration when following out the clues. The details taken down by enumerators in different returns may differ. Most enumerators just stated if someone was born in Ireland without giving the parish or county of birth but occasionally this additional information is given. Sometimes you may find details of the agricultural holding of a crofter or farmer – the number of acres of cultivated and how many labourers were employed. There is always a possible element of surprise in discovering the enumerator's description of your ancestor. One person was described as 'an unwanted guest' and in another household, the occupants were labelled as 'wild couple – very'.

Finding the family

The prospect of having access to indexes to all the census returns of Scotland is an alluring one and the progress already made in this work has made it possible to find many previously lost or lurking ancestors, particularly in large towns and cities where it was not practicable to search through the large number of books making up the census. Dependence on indexes, however, brings its own hazards; if the index is wrong, then the entry, to all intents and purposes, is lost. Inevitably there are mistakes in the indexing of the censuses and this has been particularly evident in the case of the 1881 census – though some of the most glaring errors have been corrected.

Once all the census returns are digitised, most people will have the option to search them with the aid of indexes on the ScotlandsPeople website but some may continue to use microfilm copies – a cheaper option. Even without the aid of indexes, much can be accomplished by basing searches on information found in statutory registers or OPRs. An address given at the time of a birth, marriage or death will pinpoint the location of a family or person at that time. Local directories (see Torrance, 1998) can also be useful as they give addresses of many people – professionals, gentlemen or in trade – but it is important to remember that the listings are not inclusive of everyone.

You may also sometimes want to see who lived at a particular address, without any knowledge as to who was there. This is done more easily by looking at a microfilm copy of the census. Returns for most of the larger towns are covered by street indexes which make it possible to identify a relevant district if you can find an address for the family. Even then a search may not be straightforward. Numbers of houses were altered from time to time or omitted by the enumerator and names of vennels or wynds leading off the main streets may change as these often depended on who owned the property on the corner. Local directories are useful in showing where the vennels and wynds led off the main streets. Returns for parts of the same street may also be scattered through many enumerators' books, depending on how his work was planned. At the beginning of each enumerator's book, there will be a description of the streets or particular area covered. Sometimes this is very detailed and will name all the farms or streets within his allocated district, but some enumerators only give a broad description of the area they visited or indicate that every household between one point and another have been listed. One street might be split into a number of sections which are listed in various books.

Locating the right family – and being sure that you have the right one – is not always straightforward. Your detective senses need to remain alert as a wrong turn can lead to serious consequences or great confusion. Identification of the right household must depend on such clues as matching information which you already have about children and parents, the Christian name of the wife (maiden names are rarely given in census returns though widows may sometimes revert to their maiden name), on knowledge of an address gained from another source (such as an earlier census or statutory certificate), occupation, or age. This is particularly difficult in areas where one or two surnames predominate. Black (1946) stated that in the middle of the nineteenth century there were twenty five persons named George Cowie in Buckie and a voter's roll of the 1920s showed that there were 128 families of that surname.

There may be other problems. Ages are not always given correctly on census returns – it is not uncommon for individuals (men as well as women) to age less than ten years in a decade. One enumerator commented: 'I may also observe that in a vast number of cases the ladies have understated their ages by from 5–10 or in some cases 20 years.'

You may find that not all the children known to have been born to a couple are at home when the census was taken. Do not assume that a young child who is not listed with the rest of the family had died as, particularly in large families, it was common for one to be boarded out with a grandparent. Many children did, however, die in infancy and it was common practice for a younger child to be given the Christian name of the deceased sibling. On the other hand, watch for a gap in the family or for what appears to be a mistake in the Christian name of the wife, as this may point to the death of the first wife and the addition of a second family to the father after a second marriage. Illegitimate children living with grandparents are sometimes described as sons or daughters rather than as grandchildren – or occasionally just as 'lodgers'.

The stated parish of birth of an individual may vary from one enumeration to another and descriptions of occupations may change. It is, for example, often difficult to determine whether someone described as a shoemaker in one census is the same person employed as an innkeeper in the next. Many people had more than one job. The designation 'farmer' changed ten years later to 'agricultural labourer' may reflect a downturn in fortunes, but it is much less likely that you will find the same person labelled as a mason in one census and a wright in another as these were occupations demanding a skill. Such a discrepancy should alert you to the possibility that you have got the wrong entry.

Much of Scotland's population was very mobile and even if a person remained in the same area, it is very likely that they frequently moved house. Indexing means that you can usually trace the family despite these movements but beware of jumping to conclusions that you have found a relevant entry when you find a person of the right name and age in a totally unexpected part of Scotland. Careful matching is required and it is wise to consider the likelihood of an individual moving not just from one urban district to another but from one part of the country to another. A shepherd in the nineteenth century might well have moved from the border counties to an estate in Sutherland, and an employee on the railways could be found anywhere on the rail network; masons went where the work was and there was a great deal of movement from Highland areas to the industrial centres of Scotland to seek employment. On the other hand, workers in the jute industry or other manual labourers tended to remain within a narrow area. Widowers and widows are sometimes elusive and may have moved to live with married children.

Interaction with statutory certificates is two-way. Addresses given on birth or marriage certificates may provide clues as to where the parents were living at the time of taking a census. On the other hand a census listing of a family will guide you when identifying all the children born in a family. If you find a family listed in a census and are not sure whether it is the right one, check the birth certificates of one or more children and this should provide proof as to the identity of the parents.

It is not always easy to determine the exact bounds of a parish or district and if a family lived on the borders of a parish or county, it will be worth looking at a map and checking the census returns for an adjacent district. If you have traced a family in the 1891 census and fail to find them in the 1901 census, the reason could be that as a result of the report of the Boundary Commissioners for Scotland in 1889 the place where they were living earlier was now officially in a different parish or even county. The Commission reported that sixty four parishes had parts which lay in more than one county. In Perthshire alone twelve parishes were partly in Perthshire and partly in adjoining counties and it was then enacted that each burgh and parish should lie within a single county. This resulted in a considerable number of adjustments. *The boundaries of the counties and parishes in Scotland* (Shennan, 1892) gives a detailed analysis of the changes.

Spelling of names presents the same problems in searching census returns as it does in other records and if you fail to find the entry you want in an index it is important to try all possible alternative forms of the name – using the soundex option will help. Christian names can also trip one up. The enumerator did not always put in the whole name and there are occurrences where only an initial is entered or a shortened form of the Christian name such as Wm. for William or Robt. for Robert.

Valuation rolls

From 1855 up to 1974, annual valuation rolls were compiled for all property in Scotland, county by county, with the burghs being listed separately. These name the proprietor, the tenant and the occupier, though those paying a yearly rent of less than £4 were not included. The rolls are not indexed by person and only a few are accompanied by street indexes. If you have an address for a family, valuation rolls can sometimes be used to find out more in the ten years between the censuses. You may, for example, discover when a family moved (but there will be no details of where they went) and if you find a relevant entry, it will tell you whether the family owned property. There is a complete set of valuation rolls in the NAS and many libraries and archives hold those for the local district.

The old parish registers

The date 1 January 1855 can be regarded as a line of demarcation when carrying out genealogical research. After the introduction of statutory registration, you can expect to find a certificate registered for most births and deaths in Scotland and a high proportion of marriages, and these certificates will provide a great deal of core information. Before this time, however, the main sources for 'growing' your family tree are the registers of birth or baptism and of proclamation or marriage kept in each parish. The death or burial records are the least well kept. To the Church, baptism and proclamation were the more important events to be recorded, though sometimes an entry will note both the birth and the baptism, and enter not only the proclamation but also give the date of marriage. It is not always clear to which event an entry refers and in that case you should assume that an entry is a baptism rather than a birth and a proclamation rather than a record of the marriage.

These records are known as the old parish registers (also sometimes referred to as the old parochial registers) or OPRs. In 1538 Thomas Cromwell, Vicar-General of Henry VIII in England, instructed every parish to keep a register in 'a sure coffer, with two locks and keys' in which were to be recorded weddings, christenings and burials. Thirteen years later, in 1551, the first similar move was made in Scotland. James Hamilton, Archbishop of St Andrews, ordained that every curate should keep a register of baptisms and of marriages, these records being preserved among the 'most precious treasures of the Church'. Registers of burials remained very deficient over the whole period up to 1854.

Despite repeated directions from Church and government in this matter that registers should be kept, records of only twenty one parishes have survived which commence between 1550 and 1600. Over the next fifty years, there are a further 127, with 266 dating to the period 1650–1700, 226 to 1700–50, 84 to 1750–1800 and 28 to 1800–54. Registers of some parishes in the Outer Isles and Skye did not start before the 1830s. The earliest Scottish register is for the parish of Errol in Perthshire in which the first entry is dated 1553. A few Scottish parish registers are still coming to light. A few years ago a register of baptisms for Inverkeithing covering the years 1711–44 was found among the processes of the Court of Session, where it had been retained as proof in a legal case which took place in 1745.

Characteristics of the OPRs

The parish registers differ from statutory registers in a number of ways and these characteristics influence how one should evaluate and use the information they contain, the strategies to be adopted in solving problems and the selection of other source material which may supply additional information or fill gaps.

Registration of all births and baptisms, proclamations and marriages and of burials (whatever the religious persuasion) was, in theory, compulsory before 1855 but it was never possible to enforce this and a high percentage of these events were not recorded.

There is no standard form of entry and you will find many variations in the content of entries, depending on the whim of the session clerk or minister.

Many of the parish registers are very deficient or lacking.

The dates of commencement of the registers vary widely.

The OPRs are mainly concerned with members of the Established Church of Scotland, though entries concerning some members of other denominations are found there.

Access to the registers

In 1854 a decision was taken to call in all the pre-1820 parish registers then kept by session clerks or ministers and to put them in the care of the Registrar General in Edinburgh. In 1872 the registers for the period 1820–54 were also transferred there. In a few parishes the records of births and baptisms, proclamations and marriage and of burial form part of the kirk session minutes or accounts and are not kept in a separate volume. These still remain as part of the kirk session records – many in the NAS, others in a local archive or kept locally. All of the kirk session records are being digitised. There is a list of these records in the GROS search rooms and the information is also available on the GROS website (www.gro-scotland.gov.uk). In some cases, the additional material has been filmed and added to the OPR microfilms but most of the entries are not included in the OPR indexes. Baptie (2001) has listed all kirk session records containing short or long runs of such entries but there are parishes in which occasional entries have been made as part of the accounts or minutes which are not included.

Under the GROS programme of digitising their records, work is in hand in digitising all the parish registers, linking them to the DIGROS indexes which can be searched on the pay-per-view website, www.Scot landsPeople.gov.uk. In the GROS (and in the new Scottish Family History Service centre in Edinburgh) there is access to all these records and to the indexes. The kirk session records will also be available through Scotlands People.

Microfilm copies of the registers

In the past the public had access to the original volumes of the parish registers in New Register House but there was growing concern about the wear and tear on the registers. The LDS church in consultation with the Registrar General performed a valuable service in microfilming the complete series of OPRs and the original volumes are no longer available for public consultation. These microfilms have made research in the parish registers possible worldwide, as copies are held in LDS family history libraries everywhere and are also in many local archives, libraries and society centres. The Scottish Genealogy Society Library in Edinburgh has a complete set of the OPR registers on microfilm. Some libraries also have facilities for printing out copies from the film.

In many cases one reel of microfilm includes the registers of several parishes and care is needed to make sure that you are looking at the registers for the right parish. For most parishes there are several volumes and in some large cities, such as Edinburgh, Glasgow, Dundee and Aberdeen, there are a considerable number of registers. Sometimes births/baptisms are recorded in a different volume from marriages and burials; more often (particularly in smaller parishes) you will find the birth/baptismal records at the beginning of the book, followed by proclamations and marriages and then by burials if they exist. Occasionally all the entries are intermixed. In nearly every parish there is a break in 1819, with a new volume commencing in 1820. This was due to the necessity to split the records at this point when it was decided to send the pre-1820 registers to Edinburgh.

The quality of the microfilms is very variable, due mainly to the problems of filming pages where different inks may have been used. In addition, many of the original pages are very faint or have been stained by water, attacked by insects or torn. This constitutes one of the hazards – and frustrations – of research. If you cannot read an entry, the members of staff in New Register House are always helpful and if they think that the original may be clearer, they may be willing to study it for you. This assistance is only available in the case of an individual entry and cannot involve searching a whole page or series of pages. The problems of legibility also affect the reading of the digitised records, though modern technology has been used to try to overcome some of the difficulties.

Indexes to the OPRs
DIGROS index

This is available in New Register House, Edinburgh and at a growing number of locations having a direct link to GROS such as the Family Records Centre in London and online on the pay-per-view website at www.ScotlandsPeople.gov.uk. It can be searched in various ways – either for an entry of birth/baptism (or proclamation/marriage) anywhere in Scotland, year by year, or by county over a decade (1750–59, 1760–69 for example). Searches can be made for all children born to particular parents by entering the surname of the child and the names of the parents. New refinements in the ways that the indexes can be searched are being introduced but care does need to be taken in determining your fields of search and considering possible exclusions. If you enter the names of both parents when looking for their children, a negative search may result if the session clerk of a particular parish only gave the father's name.

There is the usual problem of variant spellings of names, and Mc and Mac prefixes are not regarded as the same. You either have to search such names separately under both forms or use soundex. The soundex facility is helpful, though you should never rely on it, as a number of valid variants do not appear. This is an acknowledged difficulty and one hopes that in future the matter of dealing with spelling variants will be made easier.

Index entries give the name of the child, name of parent or parents, date of event (birth or baptism, marked B for birth, C for christening or baptism) and parish in which it is registered, with the number of parish and volume and in many cases a frame number.

If you are using these indexes in conjunction with microfilm copies of the OPRs, it is wise to check the reference number given for the volume in which the entry is said to be recorded. A number of mistakes have been made, particularly in the case of Edinburgh and Glasgow parish registers. There is a typescript list of the parish registers in New Register House giving the number of each volume and details of dates and events (birth, marriage or burial) included in that book. This information is also on the GROS website, www.gro-scotland.gov.uk. These lists only give the beginning and end dates of entries in each volume and do not indicate any gaps within them.

Microfiche index

This index was compiled after the microfilming of the OPRs. It is arranged by county with a separate series of fiches for births/baptisms and for proclamations/marriages. Deaths and burials are not covered though work is in progress to compile a national burial index. Unfortunately a great many entries were overlooked and there are three fiches of addenda which cover the whole of Scotland, not divided by county. The index is available in archives, libraries and family history centres throughout the world.

Male and female entries are not separated. Each entry is indexed alphabetically in the form in which it is found in the register but names with the prefix Mc and Mac are all indexed together under Mc. One of the advantages of this index is that by scanning the fiche entries you can see at a glance the alternative forms of a name. The name of the child is given, the date of birth or baptism, the name of the father or of both parents if given in the entry, and the parish in which the entry is recorded. If the entry gives both the date of birth and that of baptism, then the date indexed is that of the baptism.

The index may note a frame number referring to the microfilm copy (indicated as FR) which can help in finding the entry in cases where it has been recorded out of chronological order. Unfortunately, many of the frame numbers on the film are unreadable, which is very frustrating. (For the IGI indexes, see p. 15.)

Content of an OPR birth/baptismal entry

Some triumphant ancestor hunters after a day of searching through the parish registers claim to have been able to establish their ancestral line through several hundred years, but it then sometimes appears that this was achieved on the basis of looking only at the indexes. Always take the time to look up the full entries in the parish registers – index entries are not a substitute for the 'real thing', the actual record. Some official leaflets state that most entries contain relatively little information but this is very misleading. The OPRs may be very deficient in many respects but they do constitute the largest primary source of genealogical information for the period before the introduction of statutory registration and a great many entries contain valuable clues and interesting details which cannot be found from the index alone. Time saved in checking the full entries will result in ancestors lost.

Much of the frustration and also interest of searching for ancestors in the pre-1855 period is that you never know what details you will find in the parish registers. In most parishes it was the session clerk – often the schoolmaster but sometimes the minister – who was responsible for making the entries in the parish register and it was entirely up to this individual to decide what details should be recorded. The information which you *may* find is:

the name of the child
the name of the father and usually – but not always – the name of
   the mother under her maiden name
the occupation of the father
the residence of the family
the date of birth and/or baptism
witnesses to the baptism.

Not all birth or baptismal entries name both parents. Registers where only the name of the father is given can cause problems as it may appear that one man was fathering children with undue frequency. The solution is likely to be that there were two or more fathers with the same Christian name and surname. Details of residence may help to sort out this confusion and further help may be found by looking at local maps to study places of residence at the time of the baptisms of the children – whether near each other or far away. If you are lucky, the session clerk will change and the new one will include the name of the child's mother.

There was no ordinance that a child had to be baptised within a given period after birth. In some instances this took place on the day of birth, in others a number of weeks later or even after several years, though this was rare.

You may find that several children are recorded together in a multiple entry. In 1854, just before statutory registration was introduced, many parents realised that it might be important to record the baptisms of their children which had been neglected and the parish registers often have pages of late entries, recording together all the children born to a family, sometimes dating back many years. In other parishes, a new session clerk might try to compensate for the deficiencies of a previous incumbent by collecting together information about earlier baptisms. Computerised indexes have eliminated the problems of locating these entries which are out of chronological order.

An entry may indicate exactly where the family lived – on what farm or in what township – but it may only state the name of the parish. It is, unfortunately, unusual to find an entry as informative as the following one recorded in Edinburgh parish register:

23 March 1789
John Campbell sixth lawful son of William Campbell of Glenfalloch Esq. and Mrs. Janet Butter his spouse (High Kirk Parish) Daughter of Mr. William Butter, Architect in Edinb^h Twin children Born 14th March last, a Son named Charles William, a Daughter named Jean Bap^d 23rd March by Rev^d Mr. Robt Bell. W^{ts} the s^d Mr. William Butter, Mrs Jean M^{c}farlane his spouse Miss Anne & Jean Butter.

On the other hand, details which have been recorded may be rather unusual and throw light on more than the date of baptism of a child. In Birsay, Orkney, the entry for a child born to George Anderson reads:

Sept. 29 1751
To George Anderson in Swanayside (a scoundrall a knave a scrub a rascall a villain a cheat) a son called Andrew.

N.B. He had been in the Northwest and has been years in Sascra.

Underneath was added:

The above George Anderson is as honest, just, obliging man as any other man in this parish.

The names of witnesses to the baptism often provide clues which can be invaluable in later research. Not every entry includes these and sometimes a child was baptised 'before the whole congregation'. It may be stated that the congregation was a dissenting one, leading to a search for registers of that church. Witnesses were often relatives – grandparents of the child or uncles and aunts, occasionally a much older brother or sister. The relationship of the witness to the child is rarely stated. The baptism of John Campbell quoted above was witnessed by his maternal grandparents and probably by two unmarried aunts. In some of the Dundee registers there is a column which gives the name of the relation after whom the child is named. On 4 May 1849 James Cunningham and Catherine Ogilvie had a son born, baptised in Dundee two days later by the name of William Ogilvie and a note is given in the register that he is named after his maternal grandfather.

Naming the child

It was customary for a child to be given only one Christian name and the good fortune of having an easily identifiable ancestor such as one called Waterloo Wellington Kennedy (Dumfries, 1853) is rare. Sometimes a middle name was included, often the maiden name of the mother or grandmother or surname of another relative. A child might also be named after the local minister or landowner. This can be confusing if you expect to find these names in earlier generations of forebears. It was common practice in cases where a child died at birth or in infancy for another child to be given the same Christian name.

Many families (but by no means all) followed the Scottish traditional naming pattern.

The eldest son was named after the paternal grandfather.
The eldest daughter was named after the maternal grandmother.
The second son was named after the maternal grandfather.
The second daughter was named after the paternal grandmother.
The third son was named after his father.
The third daughter was named after her mother.

There could be variants on this, the eldest son being named after the maternal grandfather, for example, and if both sets of grandparents had the same Christian names, this would alter the naming patterns. In some areas, particularly the West Highlands, it was considered so important to follow this tradition that more than one surviving child in a family might be given the same Christian name, differentiated later by a nickname. You should not, therefore, always assume that an earlier child of the same name has died.

Spelling of Christian names can be as idiosyncratic as the representation of surnames, and the baptism of a child as William All-Mina (Morton parish, 1769) might open the way to wrong assumptions as to the sex. Nicholas is a name used for both boys and girls, which can cause confusion.

Imperfections in the registers

By the mid-nineteenth century the recognition of 'the lamentably defective condition of these local records' (Seton, 1854) was one of the main reasons for public pressure for the introduction of statutory registration. The starting dates of the registers of parishes vary widely but another problem is that many have been lost or destroyed, and most are deficient at some period. Fire, water, mice and human malice have played their part and the *First Statistical Accounts* written in the 1790s reveal a catalogue of disasters. At Halkirk in Caithness it was reported that 'the old registers of this parish were destroyed many years ago by some ill-disposed persons'; in Abertarff the volume was dropped by the person carrying it 'in the act of crossing a rapid stream'. 'Some unaccountable accident' was the cause of the loss of the older registers for Aberdour in Aberdeenshire and a number were taken from the parish as evidence in legal proceedings and never returned.

Defects were often attributable to the carelessness of the session clerks or ministers who were responsible for keeping the records. In 1779 Arnot, commenting on the registers kept in Edinburgh, reported that they were 'the infallible sources of error'. A committee was appointed by Dundonald kirk session in 1839 to examine the state of the registers and reported back that for the last three years they were 'a mass of confusion and in one case a child was represented to have been baptised about a week before birth'. The comment was added that this was not very likely to have happened. In Dumfries there is a despairing note in the register for the years 1792–1805: 'Here is a chasm or blank', and one session clerk of Petty in Inverness-shire refused to make any entries in the parish registers in the mid-eighteenth century because he had not been paid his fees.

A small fee for making an entry in a parish register was usually requested by the session clerk (it was waived in case of need) but in

1783, a Stamp Act was introduced putting a national tax of 3*d*. on every entry made. The Act was repealed in 1794 but it had acted as a direct disincentive to registration and a fall in the number of entries over these years is noticeable in many places.

During the eighteenth and nineteenth centuries, the growing number of dissenting congregations had a marked impact on registration in the parish registers of the Established Church. Migration to large towns and a loss of social cohesion also meant that the Church had less hold on the parishioners.

When searching for a relevant entry, it may save a lot of time if you first check on the state of the registers of a particular parish in which you are interested. *The detailed list of the old parochial registers of Scotland* was published in 1872 and this lists the parishes in each county, the dates covered by each register for that parish (under births, marriages and deaths or burials) and includes a note 'relative to blanks, defects, condition of registers etc.'. This does not cover every deficiency but it is a useful guide to the quality of the register and what is recorded there. Copies of the *Detailed list* can be found (not always placed very obviously) in the search rooms of New Register House and in some family history centres. The book has been reprinted and revised by Bloxham (1970).

Research strategies

The information given in statutory certificates, with additional clues and evidence from census returns, in most cases will lead you back to a birth or marriage that took place before 1855. For example, James Wright, a gardener in North Berwick, died in 1882 at the age of fifty seven. His parents were named as James Wright, a deceased coachman and Isabella Dingwall or Wright, also deceased. Census returns indicated that he was born in North Berwick. Armed with this information, the next move was to search the indexes to the parish registers to see if his birth or baptism was recorded there *circa* 1825. Knowing the names of James's parents, it was possible to be certain that the right entry had been found – or to assume that it had not been registered.

If a relevant OPR baptismal entry is found, the following steps can then be taken:

Search for all siblings of the direct ancestor. Their baptisms may provide clues through naming patterns, show where the parents were living at various times and possibly provide the names of witnesses who may be relatives. Knowing when the first child was born will help in finding the proclamation or marriage of the parents. Many women bore children over a twenty-year period (or longer) with the first child often appearing soon after (or before) the marriage.

Search for the marriage of the parents.

If there is any likelihood that the parents might have survived into the period of statutory registration, search for their deaths after 1854 as these death certificates, if found, will name *their* parents.

If there are pre-1855 death or burial records for the parish, search these in the hope of finding a relevant entry giving an age at death.

If there is any likelihood that the parents were alive when the 1851 census returns were made, search for a relevant entry to gain details of where and when they were born. Even the 1841 census will give you an approximate age (within five years), indicate whether the person was born in the county or not and possibly show other members of the family.

The next step back in time is the one which often proves a stumbling block. If you have found an ancestor who was married before about 1780 or born a little earlier, that person is unlikely to have survived into the period of statutory registration. You do not know when or where he or she was born or the names of the parents. What then?

You can assume that it is likely that age at marriage was at least seventeen and therefore you can start searching the indexes to births and baptisms in the parish registers (initially limiting the search to the county of residence at the time of marriage) for a birth seventeen years before the date of the marriage, going back for perhaps twenty years before that. (Second marriages can upset your calculations as the bride or groom may have been quite old at the time of that marriage.) You may be faced with several scenarios:

You find no baptismal entry of possible relevance over the years and parishes searched.

You find that there are several entries of possible relevance and need to prove which, if any, refers to the ancestral line.

You find just one entry of possible relevance but need to prove that it is the right one.

Missing entries

If the baptism for which you are looking is not recorded in the OPRs, you need to try to discover why this is so and to look for ways round the problem. First, study the condition of the registers of the parish in which you think your ancestor was born to see whether they are defective at the period in which you are interested. The *Detailed list* may provide the answer. For example, the entry for Nigg, Kincardineshire reads:

> Births: No entries Jan. 1693–1718, Nov. 1741–May 1743, and Dec. 1745–July 1747. The original record 1718–1790 has suffered exceedingly from dampness. There is, however, a copy of the portion 1732–91. Mothers' names are not recorded until Jan. 1684 and again omitted 1718–1727 inclusive.

Clearly there were several periods when no entries of baptism were made in this parish register, and the condition of part was dubious. The *Detailed list* only notes the most serious deficiencies. If you can look through a number of pages of a particular register (on microfilm, for example) around the time of the expected entry it may become clear that the register was not well kept, that the number of entries recorded for each year varied greatly, that it was carelessly written or that entries were inserted out of chronological order. This is a 'wake-up call' that the register is not reliable, but it does not provide information about either the extent of under-registration or even the quality of record keeping in the parish. It is hardly reassuring to come across an entry such as the following in Kirkmahoe on 11 April 1813:

> Janet lawful daughter of James Copland and . . . I forget the name . . . in Kirkton and baptised. Sunday evening. I think the name is Janet and almost certain.

In fact, an inkling of the level of record keeping in Kirkmahoe may have been gained from the *Detailed list*, which notes that there are eleven pages of irregular entries of whole families registered together covering the period 1771–1818.

If you are searching through an online system which does not allow for turning the pages of the volume, it may be worth finding a microfilm copy of the register so that you can make an assessment of its condition. Once the OPRs are digitised, it is anticipated that it will be possible to browse in these records, though this may only be allowed on payment of a fee.

The limitations of using an index linked to a particular entry are underlined when problem-solving. In searching the registers, it is important to note whether there were other families of the same name recording children at that time. If you find that the surname is very rare in the register, possibly the family did not belong to that parish – or perhaps they were dissenters. You should then plan to search not just the parishes of one county but over a wider area and consider going outside the OPRs.

Consideration of the period of time when a couple were having their children may be important. (See 'Timelines 1560–1900', pp. 149–54.) In the late eighteenth and early nineteenth century the agricultural revolution changed the lives of many of those in the country. Numerous families were cleared from their lands – at the time of the Sutherland clearances, for example – or moved elsewhere voluntarily, often to seek work in the towns. With the coming of the railways, people might move from one end of Scotland to the other in the course of their work.

Witnesses to baptisms of children born to other families of the same surname may also provide vital clues. Robert Motion married Mary Halkerston in 1775 and their children were born in Pittenweem, Fife, where he died on 24 February 1833 at the age of eighty three years and six months – giving an estimated birth year of 1749. There was no index entry in any parish register for Fife for his birth or baptism. The *Detailed list* noted that the baptismal register for Pittenweem was blank between November 1746 and July 1750 – the crucial period within which it was assumed that Robert was born. His parish of birth was not known but this blank in the register was a possible explanation for the failure to find his birth or baptism. Robert Motion and Mary Halkerston had six children, but at only one of the baptisms was a Motion witness named – John Motion was a witness when the eldest known son, James, was born in 1776 – possibly the child's grandfather or an uncle. There were several other Motions recording children in the area in the 1770s and 1780s. David Banes and Janet Motion had a son born in 1779 and the witnesses were Robert and John Motion, while a witness for the baptism of the child of Robert Duncan and Beatrix Motion was Robert Motion. From these entries one could guess that Robert, John, Janet and Beatrix were brothers and sisters. A search of the indexes to baptisms recorded in the parish registers of Fife then brought to light the following entries for children born to a Robert Motion and Helen Broun: Janet baptised 1741 in Dunino; James baptised 1744 in Dunino; Bathia (a form of the name Beatrix) baptised 1746 in Cameron; John baptised 1753 in Carnbee; Isabel baptised 1756 in Carnbee. There is a gap in the family between 1746 and 1753 when Robert's baptism in 1749 would fit and the circumstantial evidence is such that Robert, whose baptism was not recorded, was the son of Robert Motion and Helen Broun, probably born in Pittenweem at a time when the parish register was deficient. This was a search which could only be carried out by searching through the registers and looking at the entries; results would not have been achieved through an online search for particular entries or by reliance on indexes.

Failure to find a relevant entry may be the result of working from incorrect information. Ages given on death certificates are often inaccurate and many mistakes were made in census returns (both in stating age and parish of birth). Parentage stated on a death certificate may also be wrong. A grandson informing on the death of his grandfather is required to state the names of his great-grandparents and it is hardly surprising to find that many statutory certificates contain errors. An illegitimate birth may have been concealed by indicating that the parents were married and sometimes grandparents' names are given instead of a parent's name.

Finding the right entry

Access to indexes encourages a 'pick and mix' mentality and the temptation to select a likely entry without any proof as to its relevance. As with all detective work, clues to selecting the right entry among several or proving that the one entry you find does refer to the ancestral line can often be found in looking at what is known already.

The traditional Scottish naming patterns were followed in many families and if you can show that this is reflected in one side of the family (naming the eldest daughter and second son after the maternal grandparents, for example) then it is likely that this will also be true of the other side.

George Matthewson was a seaman living with his family in Dysart at the time of taking the 1851 census. He was described as aged forty one and born in Dysart. He appears to have died before 1855. There was no entry for a birth or baptism in Dysart parish *circa* 1810 but a George Matthewson was born in the adjoining (inland) parish of Markinch in 1810, son of James Matthewson. George had named his eldest son George and his second daughter Christian (possibly following the traditional naming patterns) and it was noted that a couple named George Matthewson and Christian Smith were proclaimed in Dysart in 1798, having two children there in 1813 and 1824. One can assume that there were others who were born between 1798 and 1824 but whose births or baptisms were not recorded. It seemed as likely – and possibly more likely – that George and Christian were the parents of George born (but not recorded) in 1810, rather than James who had a son George born (and registered) in a parish which was not the one indicated by the census return – but unfortunately it cannot be proved conclusively. This case is an illustration of the dangers of forgetting to consider the possibility that the relevant entry is not recorded, while giving undue weight to another entry just because it has been recorded. Sometimes a problem of this kind can be resolved by checking all deaths after 1854 – in this case of a George Matthewson – in the hope of being able to eliminate one of the candidates.

Some more unusual names may occur in a family from generation to generation which may provide a clue in weighting the likely relevance of two possible entries. The terms 'junior' and 'senior' have to be treated with care as they may be used to identify close relatives with the same Christian name rather than refer to father and son.

The incidence of twins in a family can be a clue as it is noticeable that families may continue to have twins from generation to generation.

If possible, check whether a child survived infancy. Infant mortality was high and if another child of the same Christian name is born (too late to be the sought-after ancestor) this may eliminate one ancestral contender when you have a choice of possible alternatives.

Look at the names of witnesses to the baptisms of the children of the person for whose birth you are researching. They may have included a grandfather of the child or aunts or uncles (as in the Motion case quoted above).

Farmers in some areas stayed on the same lands for many generations and therefore the place of residence may indicate that one entry is more likely to be relevant than another.

Information in kirk session records

The births or baptisms of illegitimate (or 'natural') children are sometimes recorded in the parish register but more often their names are omitted. If there is a possibility that the child was illegitimate, information can often be found in the kirk session minutes. In such cases, the minister and elders would go to great lengths to establish the paternity of the child. The evidence collected so that a claim could be made against the father for support of his child was often very detailed, involving both parties concerned, their families and neighbours. The minutes of the kirk sessions can also be useful in other ways. The following case illustrates the information which can be found on an illegitimate birth but also how the gap of a missing birth was filled.

Robert Condie, a labourer, married Mary Russell in Clackmannan in 1707. There was no information as to how old he was at this time and no entry was found for his birth in or near Clackmannan prior to 1690. Between 1680 and 1690, however, it was noted that there was one family of Condies in Clackmannan – Robert Condie and Christian Cowie, who had a daughter named Bessie baptised in 1684 and another entry referred to an unnamed child born to the same parents. A search of the kirk session records of the parish between 1700 and

1710 brought to light a case concerning Bessie Condie who had a long-standing affair with a married man, James Hunter. Bessie, sadly, died in childbirth but her mother, Christian Cowie, was given financial help by the session in bringing up her motherless grandchild. Various members of Bessie's family appeared to give evidence in the many hearings, including her mother, Christian Cowie, and her brother Robert and his wife Mary Russell. This case proved the parentage of Robert and indicated that the entry for the unnamed child in Clackmannan parish register almost certainly concerned his baptism, but it also provided a lot of information about Bessie and her child. (For further information on kirk session records, see p. 130 and p. 156.)

Was your ancestor a dissenter?

Although officially all baptisms were supposed to be entered in the parish registers, in fact this did not happen. The parish registers, in the main, were concerned with members of the Established Church of Scotland – whether this was during the episcopal or presbyterian regimes – and adherence to a dissenting or 'nonconformist' congregation may be the reason for failure to find a baptism in the OPRs.

In 1560 the Scottish Parliament adopted the reformed Confession of Faith and celebration of the Catholic mass was forbidden. Over the next 130 years the presbyterian church underwent many changes in direction. During the seventeenth century there was a continuing struggle for the ascendancy of episcopacy or presbyterianism: in 1610 the General Assembly voted to bring in episcopacy; in 1638 presbyterianism was reintroduced and in 1661 episcopacy was restored. The period from this date till the Revolution Settlement of 1689 was a time of religious persecution, marked by the struggles of the Covenanters, but in 1690 Parliament restored Scottish presbyterianism and episcopacy was declared as 'contrary to the generality of the people'. (See 'Timelines 1560–1900', pp. 149–54.) Over all this time, as the ecclesiastical climate changed, many ministers were ousted, but the pastoral care and discipline in the parish continued and people still recorded baptisms and marriages in the parish registers, whether episcopal or presbyterian government was 'the face of the kirk'.

During the eighteenth century there were a growing number of groups of 'nonconformists', among whom were the Episcopalians, now regarded as a separate denomination, and congregations who split from the Established Church of Scotland (and who themselves splintered into separate congregations) at varying times to form the Associate Session, Relief Church and others. In 1843 the Free Church was formed – this event being known as the Disruption.

Quite often entries for baptisms of dissenters do appear in the parish registers, stating that the baptism had been performed by a minister of the Associate Session or Relief or other church and sometimes duplicate entries can be found in the records of the particular dissenting congregation. A few Roman Catholic entries are also found in the parish registers. On the other hand, the growing level of religious dissent did have an enormous impact on the number of entries made in the OPRs and membership of one of these other congregations may be the reason for a failure to find baptismal entries of children in the OPRs.

Which church?

Discovering whether your forebears were dissenters and the church of which they were members may take some sleuthing. Starting with post-1854 records, you may have noted on a marriage certificate that the ceremony was conducted according to the rites of the United Presbyterian Church, Free Church, Roman Catholic or other church. This should alert you to the possibility that at least one side of the family may not have been members of the Established Church. Look up the entry for the parish concerned in a gazetteer. Groome's *Gazetteer*, for example, provides details on churches in the parish and when they were built, providing a starting point for a search for records of that congregation.

One of the questions which each minister was required to answer when compiling both the *First* and *Second Statistical Accounts* was on the church attendance of the parishioners in his parish. Not all ministers complied but the majority provided some details of the number of dissenters and the churches which they attended. A study of both accounts of Ayrshire parishes showed that in Fenwick by the 1790s two-thirds of the churchgoers had left the Established Church and by the early 1840s in thirteen Ayrshire parishes at least a quarter of their churchgoing members had become dissenters. On the other hand, some Ayrshire ministers reported very small numbers of dissenters in their parishes, fourteen of them claiming over 90 per cent attendance at the parish church (see Bigwood, 1987). The formation of the Free Church in 1843 further reduced the numbers of those belonging to the Church of Scotland and according to Steel (1970) by 1851 there were 889 Free Church places of worship.

A detailed account of the religious constituents of a number of Scottish parishes (unfortunately not all) can be found in a series of parliamentary reports published in the late 1830s by the commissioners of religious instruction in Scotland, 'inquiring into the opportunities of public religious worship and means of religious instruction, and the pastoral superintendence afforded to the people of Scotland'. The commissioners visited 552 parishes and their reports show the number of those who belonged to dissenting congregations, many of whom attended a church outside their parish of residence. In Duns in Berwickshire they reported that there were 1,700 members of the Established Church of Scotland, and 1,737 belonging to other congregations. The First United Secession Congregation had been established in Duns in 1738 and had 510 adherents, 388 of whom belonged to the parish but 84 of whom lived in the parish of Preston and Bunkle. A second United Secession congregation was established in 1768 with over 1,000 members, nearly half of whom lived outside the parish, 197 belonging to the parish of Edrom.

These figures highlight another important aspect of the problem of tracing dissenting families as they show that the church attended may not be in the parish of residence. In such a case, a child may be listed in a census as born in a certain parish but the baptism may be registered in a different parish where there was a dissenting congregation.

Records of dissenters

Unlike the parish registers of birth, death and marriage (OPRs) which were deposited in the General Register Office of Scotland in Edinburgh under the Registration Act of 1854, there was no such legal directive regarding records of other denominations. For many of these congregations there are no known records of pre-1855 baptisms, marriages or burials (though there may be minutes or other documents) and for those which have survived, you may have to look in a variety of places.

The NAS houses a large collection and also has microfilm copies of some (but by no means all) records which are held by local archives, while others still remain in private hands or with the church concerned. Many were either not kept or have been lost. As more and more catalogues of archives come online, it becomes easier to find out what records exist and where they can be found. Remember that the name of the congregation may not include the name of the parish in which it was situated.

The first place to search is the NAS electronic catalogue. CH3 is the class reference number given to records of the United Presbyterian Church, which includes those congregations which had come together by 1900 – the Associate Synod, Relief Church, Burghers and Anti-Burghers, the Free Church, United Original Secession and Reformed Presbyterian Church. Key in CH3 plus the name of the parish, and you will find details of the records of any of these congregations in that parish, the beginning and end dates of the records and the reference number given to the collection. You can bring up details of a particular holding on your screen. A search under 'CH3' and 'Kirkcaldy' produced details of twelve dissenting congregations with records dating from 1743 to 1982. Clicking on the entry for CH3/1144, Kirkcaldy Associate Session, then showed that there were records of baptisms for this congregation for the periods 1760–74, 1786–91, 1794–99, 1807–29, 1831–36 and 1839–76. Baptie (2000) lists most of the CH3 records in the NAS which contain registers of baptisms, marriages or deaths.

As well as searching online catalogues of other archives, some holdings are listed in the National Register of Archives. When searching the NRA catalogue online under 'Organisations', you can refine the search to look for records of a particular religious denomination. When you select the category 'Nonconformist and other churches' and then the sub-category 'Scottish secession churches', a list of twenty four holdings comes up. Clicking on a selected entry produces a more detailed description of the holding. An entry for St Andrew's Erskine kirk session, Dunfermline, shows that there are minutes, accounts, lists of baptisms, communicants' roll books, miscellaneous correspondence, and architectural plans and drawings covering the period 1745 to 1974 – and that this holding is in private hands. There is also a separate website for the National Register of Archives of Scotland (NRAS) – www.nas.gov.uk/nras/researchers.asp – which can be searched. The online register has only been available in the NAS search rooms but is being added to the internet, giving access to details of a growing number of surveys.

Quakers

The earliest meeting in Scotland of the Society of Friends, as the Quakers were known, was in 1653. There is a collection of material concerning the Quakers in the NAS (CH10), including a list of Scottish Quaker births, marriages and deaths compiled by A. Strath Maxwell, covering the period up to 1890. A copy of this can be found in the NAS.

Episcopalians

It was only after 1690 when presbyterianism was restored as the established religion in Scotland that the Episcopal Church became a separate entity and in many parts of the country it remained strong till the middle of the eighteenth century, particularly in the north-east of

Scotland and parts of the West Highlands. It is often difficult to find records of Episcopalians as many of their records are still in private hands. Steel (1970) reported on a survey made in 1965 regarding surviving registers. Twenty two congregations reported that they did not hold any pre-1855 registers and twenty one failed to reply to the questionnaire. The NAS has microfilm copies of some church registers, arranged by diocese, listed in their catalogue RH4/179-85. More may be found by searching the website of the National Register of Archives. The Episcopal Church's *Year Books* are also useful in showing where there are episcopal congregations and contact can then be made with the church concerned.

Roman Catholics

The best guide to the surviving registers of Roman Catholic missions and churches has been compiled by Michael Gandy (1993a) in *Catholic missions and registers 1700–1880*. He has also published an accompanying atlas of the Catholic parishes of England, Wales and Scotland (1993). The earliest known register of births is that for St Andrew, Braemar, which starts in 1703, but most of the registers commence in the nineteenth century. The NAS has photocopies of Catholic registers of birth, marriage and death, arranged by diocese, catalogued under RH21. Most registers of baptisms name the child and the parents (usually giving the mother's maiden name) and the names of the sponsors. The date of birth may also be given but no details of residence.

There are a number of named lists of Catholics (termed 'papists') in the General Assembly papers in the NAS (CH1) for the years 1708–28. In some areas everyone in a household was listed and a Protestant relative named who was held responsible for the Catholic members of the family. Some idea of the number of Catholics living in a parish in the middle of the eighteenth century is provided by Webster's *Analysis of population* of 1755. Under the heading 'number of inhabitants' he gives the number of Protestants and the number of papists – but no names.

2. Marriage

Regular marriage

Scotland has its own legal system, distinct from that of England, and this affects the laws relating to marriage. A regular marriage in Scotland was one performed after publication of banns in the parish churches of both parties by a minister of religion in the presence of at least two witnesses. The marriage could take place in any building – not just a church – and marriage certificates often show that it took place in a public building (hotel or hall), at the manse or in the home of the bride. Originally, the officiating clergyman had to be the parish minister but under the Toleration Act of 1712 an Episcopalian clergyman might solemnise marriages on various conditions, one of which was that prayers should be said for the Royal Family. The Marriage (Scotland) Act of 1834 allowed other dissenting ministers (including Roman Catholic priests) to celebrate marriage as long as banns were proclaimed in the parish church.

Until 1929, a woman could marry from the age of twelve, a man from the age of fourteen: after 1929, the age for both was raised to sixteen.

Irregular marriage

There were several kinds of irregular marriage. A clandestine marriage, known as an 'inorderly marriage', was one celebrated by a minister of religion of some congregation but without the preceding publication of banns. Clandestine marriages were always acknowledged to be as valid as a regular marriage in the eyes of the law but penalties might be incurred by the parties concerned, including the witnesses. The Act of 1834 ended the possible penalties for 'unauthorised' clergymen taking the service but continued the requirement that banns should be proclaimed. Some of the border marriages were regarded as clandestine marriages because they were performed by clergymen but others, when not celebrated by a qualified clergyman, were regarded as irregular.

There were also other kinds of irregular marriage:

By declaration – *de praesenti*: this was marriage by consent without witnesses (which included marriages by cohabitation and repute). The man and woman declared that they were man and wife without any need for formalities but the consent constituted a present condition, not future intention.

By promise with subsequent intercourse: betrothal followed by intercourse was regarded as a marriage contract and though the Church did not always approve, it was regarded as a union which had to be dissolved before either of the parties could enter into another marriage. This form of irregular marriage was abolished in the Marriage (Scotland) Act of 1939.

Cohabitation with habit and repute: marriage could be legally inferred from an acknowledgement that the parties had lived together as man and wife for some time but this would not be valid if there was some impediment to a legal marriage, such as a previous marriage which had not been nullified. This form of marriage was not mentioned in the 1939 Act.

Marriage by consent before witnesses: such marriages were the result of a declaration of the two parties concerned before witnesses, celebrated by someone other than the parish minister and without proclamation of banns. A great many such marriages are found in Scotland. No record might be made of the event, though there were a number of persons in the towns and other places who acted as 'marriage brokers' and who often handed out a written assertion that the marriage had taken place. The Church did not approve of such marriages and when the minister found that a couple had entered into such a union, they were usually summoned before the session, fined and then their marriage was acknowledged by the Church. Many of these irregular marriages were performed in the borders at places such as Lamberton Toll Bar, Coldstream and Gretna. Marriage by consent was only abolished in 1939, after which a valid marriage had to be contracted in the office of a registrar on production of a certificate of the publication of banns or notice of intended marriage.

After the introduction of statutory registration in 1855, some of those who entered into irregular marriages wanted legal evidence of their marriage and such persons were able to apply to the sheriff of the county within three months of their marriage for a warrant to register such a marriage, which was then entered in the statutory registers. Many 'irregular' marriages, however, were not recorded by the registrars, particularly during the rest of the nineteenth century.

Statutory registers of marriage

Statutory certificates of marriage can be consulted at the office of the registrar in which they are registered, in the GROS or online, with a seventy-five-year closure on viewing the image on the website www.ScotlandsPeople.gov.uk. Marriage certificates provide yet another stepping stone in the journey back into the past and post-1854 certificates contain a great deal of information. It is always important to take down all details as these may provide clues which can be of value in further searches.

Minor records of marriage

The Registrar General of Scotland also holds various records relating to marriages contracted outside Scotland but many of these registers are very incomplete. These are being added to the online images (DIGROS).

Service records, including army returns of marriages of Scottish persons at military stations abroad 1881–1959, service department registers from 1959 for marriages taking place outside the United Kingdom of persons usually resident in Scotland serving in the HM Forces, marriage certificates performed by army chaplains outside the United Kingdom since 1892 where one of the parties is Scottish and one of the parties is serving in the HM Forces.

Consular returns of marriage 1917 onwards.

Register of marriages of Scots in foreign countries 1860–1965 – made on the basis of information supplied by the parties concerned.

Foreign marriages after 1946 (of Scots in certain foreign countries without the presence of a British consular officer).

Information on a marriage certificate

As is the case with other statutory certificates, some changes were made at various times regarding what information was included.

1855: date and place of marriage.
Denomination of church (United Presbyterian, Church of Scotland, Roman Catholic etc.) in which the ceremony was performed or by warrant of sheriff.
For both bridegroom and bride – name, occupation, age, any previous marriage and number but not names of children by earlier marriages, present and usual address.
Names and occupation of parents of bride and groom – including mothers' maiden names and whether they are alive or deceased at the time of this marriage.
Birthplace of bride and bridegroom, date, and if registered.
Name of officiating minister or clergyman – or in cases of 'irregular marriage', by warrant of the relevant sheriff.
Names (and sometimes addresses) of witnesses.
1856 onwards: as above but omitting information on previous marriage(s) and children by these marriages, date and place of birth of bride and bridegroom. The marital status of bride and groom (widow, widower, divorced or single) is noted.

The actual signatures of bride and bridegroom are on the certificate held by the local registrar but those on the certificate sent to the Registrar General are only copies.

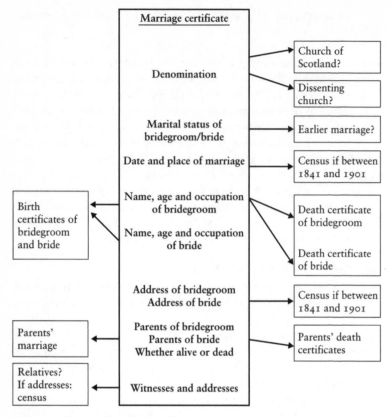

Figure 3   Marriage certificate: where next?

Many people had more than one marriage following the death of a spouse. Mortality of women in childbirth was high in the nineteenth century. Tuberculosis was rife, contributing to many deaths of both men and women in their twenties and thirties. In the event of the death of a wife, especially when there were young children in the family, it was usual for the husband to remarry, quite soon.

How reliable is the information?

In most cases details given on marriage certificates, being supplied by the couple themselves, are correct. Statement of age, however, is not always accurate, particularly if there is a disparity in age between the bride and bridegroom. In such cases, one or the other may alter their age to close the gap. Occasionally (as in cases of bigamy) there are deliberate attempts to hide a real identity.

If the bride or bridegroom was illegitimate, this fact is sometimes concealed and it is made to appear that the parents were married, the woman being referred to by her maiden name and her married name ('Isabella Clarke, m[aiden] s[urname] McLean') – not just by her maiden name, which would usually indicate that she had not married.

The marriage certificate states whether the parents of bride and groom were alive or deceased when the son or daughter married – details which are usually correct but occasionally are not.

Indexes to statutory registers of marriage

Indexes can be searched online through DIGROS. You can search either under the name of bride (under her maiden name) or bridegroom or cross-reference both surnames. This has the advantage of making it possible to pick out a relevant entry by looking at the index alone. The DIGROS indexes are linked to the images but there is a seventy-five-year closure of access to the images (not to the indexes), except in New Register House. If the certificate is within the closure period, those using the pay-per-view system will have to order a copy of the certificate.

The index entry will give you the surname and forename of either the bride or bridegroom (tick which is required), the district where the certificate is registered and entry number.

LDS libraries and the IGI

Microfilm copies of the indexes for marriages up to the middle of the twentieth century are available through family history libraries of the Church of the Latter-Day Saints and they also hold microfilms of marriage certificates for the years 1855–75. Males and females are listed separately in the indexes and there are no cross-referencing facilities except for the years 1855–63, when the indexes for the bride show her maiden name with her married name in brackets. Irvine (2003) has a detailed discussion of the uses of material in the LDS libraries.

Indexes to statutory registers of marriage from 1855 to 1875 are also included in the IGI, arranged under standardised forms of the surnames and intermixed with births. This should not be regarded as a complete list of all marriages which have been registered. It is, however, useful as the name of the spouse is given on the index entry. The fiche editions of the IGI (except the 1988 one) are arranged by county but editions of the IGI on computer or CD can be searched to cover the whole of Scotland.

Lost entries

The date and place of marriage of a child's parents is given on a birth certificate, except for the years 1856–60. In many cases, the information is erroneous – wrong place, wrong date or wrong year. A check on birth certificates of siblings of the ancestor may provide some alternative dates or details which can then be followed up. If the marriage certificate is not found in the expected year, extend the search both backwards and forwards.

There may be a mistake in the indexing. In some cases, when using the cross-referencing facility on the computer, having entered the names of both bride and bridegroom no relevant entry will come up but when the name of the bride or bridegroom alone is entered, the correct entry appears. If, therefore, you cannot find a marriage which you are sure should be registered in Scotland, choose the surname of either the bride or bridegroom and search the indexes again, checking any entry which is possibly relevant. It will save time if you search under the party which has the more unusual name or for which there are not a lot of spelling alternatives.

Christian names were sometimes shortened or entered on the marriage certificate under initials only. If you key in William Allison, for example, and the index entry is under W. Allison, no reference will come up on your screen. The full Christian name will be on the original certificate held by the local registrar but may not be on the copy sent to the Registrar General.

Consider all possible spelling alternatives of the surname, including names prefixed by Mc and Mac.

If the woman has been married before and is now a widow or divorcee, at the time of her second marriage she should be indexed under her maiden name, not her first married name but if difficulties occur, check under the surname of her first husband as well.

The marriage may never have been registered. Throughout the nineteenth century (and beyond) irregular marriages continued, including cohabitation with habit and repute. Two Royal Commissions examined the law of marriage during the nineteenth century – the first in 1848 and the second in 1865. In 1848 it was estimated that up to a third of marriages were irregular, though at the time of the second Royal Commission it was reported that this was no longer considered very respectable. By 1884 it was stated that only 2.4 per cent of all marriages were irregular but the figure rose by 1913 to 9.1 per cent (Walker, vol. 6, 2001). The increase may, however, reflect the instances when the parties concerned requested certificates leading to registration. Walker commented: 'How many irregular marriages went unregistered is unknown.'

Newspaper notices

Both before and after 1855, entries can be found in newspapers announcing a forthcoming marriage or reporting one which has taken place. In national newspapers or publications such as *The Scots Magazine* or *The Gentleman's Magazine* only those of some standing are likely to be mentioned unless the circumstances were very noteworthy. *The Scots Magazine* was first published in 1739 and a card index to births, marriages and deaths noted there is kept in the office of the Lord Lyon in Edinburgh.

Local newspapers are more socially inclusive and entries may include details of the guests and comments on the bride's wedding dress. Much work is being done in indexing local papers (contact a local library or family history society to find out what has been undertaken) and work is in hand to put online a number of nineteenth-century local, regional and national newspapers held by the British Library (www.bl.uk). *The Scotsman* has already launched a digital archive (http://archive.scotsman.com), where you can, for a small fee, read every article from every edition of the newspaper from its launch on 25 January 1817 to the end of 1900, and this will be extended up to the present day. There is an easy-to-use search facility.

Information given in newspaper notices varies but may contain valuable details. The following is an entry in the *Glasgow Herald* for 2 September 1893:

> Cowan–Neilson. At Warriston, Helensburgh on the 1st inst., by the Rev. John Lindsay, John Cowan, Earlybraes, Shettleston, to Agnes Stenhouse [Steel], daughter of the late John Steel, Sweethope, Bothwell and widow of Hugh Neilson, Clydebridge Steel-works, Cambuslang.

OPR proclamations and marriages

Under the presbyterian doctrine, marriage was not a sacrament and the minister could declare that a couple were married because of their mutual consent and the lack of any known impediment to this marriage. The consent of parents was not required. The age of marriage was fourteen for boys and twelve for girls, neither party could already be married to someone else and certain degrees of affinity were forbidden, but this did not include 'cousins german' – first cousins.

Regular marriage consisted of the proclamation of banns in the parish church or churches of the couple and the exchange of consents, followed by marriage by the minister. The minister might give the couple a certificate showing that the banns had been proclaimed and some families still have copies of these documents, which are not recorded in the parish register. A sum of money – referred to as a pand, pawn or consignation money – was sometimes requested by the session clerk as a pledge that the couple intended to marry within forty days and to behave chastely till their marriage. The pawn was then returned to them if they had fulfilled their promises. Originally the proclamation was made on three consecutive Sundays but by the eighteenth century it seems that this was not insisted upon. Many entries indicate that there was only one proclamation or that all three were made at the same time – for which the kirk might demand an extra payment for the church funds. The marriage usually took place in the parish of the bride.

Form of an OPR entry

Proclamations and/or marriages are recorded in most of the OPR registers after the section covering baptisms, though in some parishes births/baptisms and proclamations or marriages are in separate volumes or occasionally interleaved with baptisms. It is reported that in the registers for the Angus parishes of Kinnettles, Mains and Strathmartine, and Monikie the entries of baptisms and marriages are 'recorded promiscuously with other matters' (Seton, 1854). The arrangement of the volumes in each parish is commented on in the *Detailed list* – this becomes important when searching through micro-film copies of the registers.

There was no set form for an entry and what is recorded by the session clerk or minister varies from time to time and parish to parish. At its bleakest, the entry may only record the date of proclamation, the names of the two parties and their respective parishes of residence. If there is no specific indication (as in the following entry) that the date refers to the marriage, you should assume that it refers to the proclamation.

Paisley Low parish: 13 September 1771
John Orr and Margaret McIlhose

From the fact that no parish of residence is given for either person, one can deduce that both lived in the parish where the entry is recorded. If one of them had resided in a different parish, this would have been noted. There is no indication as to how many times the banns were proclaimed and when – or if – they were married. Sometimes the fact and date of subsequent marriage is given but not always. There was a complaint that in the parish of Dunipace the session clerk, appointed in 1843, endeavoured to keep a record of marriages but though he asked the parties concerned to let him know the date of their marriage, they very often neglected to do so.

If the bride and bridegroom lived in different parishes the proclamation for their marriage should be recorded in both parishes, the banns often being called on different days, but this was not always done. Some researchers are confused when they find that there are two entries with different dates for what is assumed to be a marriage and wonder whether there are two couples of the same names or whether a mistake has been made. The answer is that these proclamations are for the same intended marriage. It is always worth looking at both entries as one session clerk may have put in more information than the other. On 6 January 1828 the following entry is recorded in the parish of St Ninians:

Revd Archibald Hamilton Duthie, Stirling and Mary Murray St. N[inians].

On the same day, the proclamation was also recorded in the bridegroom's parish of Stirling:

The Reverend Archibald Hamilton Duthie of this Parish and Mary, eldest daughter of John Murray Esq. of Livelands, Parish of St. Ninians.

There is considerable value in finding this second entry which provides the name of the bride's father and his territorial designation. It is unfortunately rare to find the fathers of both parties given.

The names of witnesses or cautioners for the good behaviour of both parties, if they are named in the entry, can provide useful clues as they are often related to the bride or bridegroom, though the exact relationship is rarely described. Details of occupation and residence may also be included.

Sometimes an entry may hint at a family drama. In 1818 in Latheron, Caithness, the following entry for a marriage is recorded:

25 April 1818
Peter Sutherland, Achurah whose lovely wife eloped about 18 years ago with a sea captain and Margaret Cormack, Achnagar – married 18 June.

This entry was also interesting in showing that a number of weeks might elapse between the proclamation and the marriage – though it was usually not more than six weeks. The happy outcome of marriage does not seem so likely in the case of the couple from Campbeltown,

Argyll, and it is not clear whether the match was ever made:

> Hugh Thomson and Jean Greenlies both in this congregation 26th December 1723. She rewed.

Only on rare occasions is the breakdown of a contract recorded. In Midmar on 25 June 1720, the following entry was made in the parish register:

> Patrick Cheyne, schoolmaster in Echt and Miss Sophia Garioch daughter of Alexander Garioch farmer in Glach in the parish of Kinernie were contracted in order to marriage but by mutual consent of both parties the match was broke off.

Underneath, in a different hand was written the comment: 'Ha ha ha! He he he!'

When there were accusations of broken contracts of marriage, the kirk session would sometimes hear the arguments on both sides, the case being recorded in the kirk session minutes. Sometimes (before 1823) a settlement was reached in a hearing before the local commissary court. After 1823 the case would be heard in the sheriff court.

Missing marriages

Many proclamation and marriage records are missing from the registers. Check in the *Detailed list* for the main gaps in the registers and, if you know in which parish the couple were married, it is worth spending time in browsing through the register itself to make a visual assessment as to how well the register was kept. In addition to deficient registers, a great many people did not record their marriages.

Although most men married a woman from their own or a neighbouring parish, this was not always so. Lateral thinking may provide ideas as to where a man might meet his bride-to-be. Did his work take him away from home? Those who had to travel because of their occupation – such as fishermen or seamen – might find a bride far from home. Did political events or economic trends influence his life? At the time of the Napoleonic Wars many of those who served in the militia married a woman from the town where they were stationed and the Edinburgh parish registers at the end of the eighteenth and in the early nineteenth century list many proclamations of soldiers described as serving with a particular regiment, then at Edinburgh Castle, who were intending to marry local girls.

A considerable number of references to marriages can be found in the kirk session records rather than in the parish register. In Aberlady, for example, there are entries for marriages among the kirk session accounts for the years 1828–48. (See Baptie, 2001.)

Irregular marriages

A great many marriages took place in Scotland which were termed irregular or clandestine (see p. 73). Sometimes an irregular marriage is entered in the parish register with a note to this effect but more commonly it does not appear there. When the minister found that two of his parishioners had been married irregularly, the couple were usually summoned to appear before the kirk session and ordered to produce satisfactory evidence that they had been married elsewhere, albeit irregularly. They were then fined and admitted to be lawfully married. Records of these irregular marriages appear in the kirk session minutes. A reference to an irregular marriage may also be entered briefly in the kirk session accounts in the form of the fine paid.

All entries of irregular marriage found in the South Leith kirk session records for the years 1697–1818 have been extracted (SRS, 1968): there were 1,543 entries. People of all classes of society are represented. There are a considerable number of mariners and sailors, some local men, others described as members of the crew of certain vessels, soldiers – even a general. On 30 January 1755 General Humphrey Bland married Elizabeth Dalrymple, sister of the 5th Earl of Stair, irregularly.

Matters did not always go smoothly and in 1760 an irregular marriage was reported to the session whereby the marriage of John Cattanach, master of an Aberdeen sloop, to Mary Cecilia McLean, daughter of a Leith porter, was denied by the groom, who 'averred it to be a forgery'. The session sometimes required further proofs. Jean Lift married William Duncan in 1741 but when summoned by the session admitted that she had been irregularly married to Robert Gillies six years earlier but he had disappeared and she could not find proof of his death. This case was then referred to the Edinburgh presbytery.

Cases of irregular marriage might also be heard in the commissary, sheriff or burgh courts or before a Justice of the Peace. A number of couples were summoned to appear before Peebles burgh court in the mid-eighteenth century who admitted that they had been married irregularly in Edinburgh or elsewhere and were fined. The fines varied according to the assumed ability of the parties to pay. A watchmaker was fined £50 Scots in 1764, while a stocking weaver in 1772 was charged just 10 shillings. In some cases the name of the bride's father may be given. Searching court records is time-consuming and for it to be worthwhile, you would need to know the court in which a case was heard and the approximate date.

Border marriages

There were a number of places where irregular border and Scottish runaway marriages took place and a detailed list of known registers was compiled in 2000 by Ronald Nicholson. Most were on the border between England and Scotland – at Gretna, Coldstream and Lamberton. This booklet can be consulted in the GROS and is online on the GROS website, listed under GROS family records. The list gives the covering dates of entries for each place, the earliest of which is dated 1754, the place at which the marriages were celebrated and a reference to where copies of the records are held. The actual entries are not quoted. Some custodians require a fee for searching and copying entries.

Marriages of dissenters

Some persons who were not members of the Established Church of Scotland did register their marriages in the parish registers but many, having been married by someone other than the parish minister, only appear when fined by the kirk session for irregular marriages. These entries could refer to Catholics, Episcopalians or others but information as to their religious persuasion is very rarely given.

A number of registers of marriages for members of the secession congregations have survived but less than those for baptisms. The first problem is to identify the church to which the couple may have belonged and then to trace any registers. These may be in private hands, in a local archive or in the National Archives of Scotland (CH3). The CH3 catalogue can be consulted online – enter CH3 and the name of the parish to see the contents of the holding. Sometimes the church did not bear the name of the parish – for example, Lauriston was the name of the Cameronian congregation in Falkirk, for which there is a marriage register for the years 1822–61.

Gandy (1993a) provides a guide to registers known to have survived for the Roman Catholic Church. Dates of the registers vary and only a few go back as far as the middle of the eighteenth century.

Records of the Scottish Episcopal Church are often difficult to locate. Those held in the NAS are catalogued under CH12. Local archives may hold some registers but many are still with the churches concerned.

Marriage contracts

In the case of those who were well-off – burgesses, landowners or professional men but also sometimes shopkeepers – financial arrangements concerning the couple were often made around the time of marriage in the form of a pre-nuptial or post-nuptial contract. Three hundred and sixty marriage contracts are recorded in Perth sheriff court register of deeds between 1687 and 1809 (Hamilton-Edwards, 1978) and these refer to people of various social classes – fleshers, merchants, wrights, weavers, sailors, portioners, tenants and shipmasters. An agreement would be drawn up by the two parties, with the fathers on both sides named and usually present – important information for the family historian. Sometimes a brother might stand in for a father. The bride's tocher or dowry to be paid by her family was agreed (in early times this was repaid if the marriage was dissolved within a year and a day if there was no living child) and the husband made provision for his wife and any children to be born of the union.

A marriage settlement was not always registered but if it was, then it would be in a register of deeds – the Books of Council and Session, or register of deeds of a sheriff court, burgh court, commissary court or franchise court. Copies of these documents are also sometimes found in collections of family papers. Marriage contracts were usually registered not at the time of the marriage but at the time of death of the husband or wife or shortly afterwards, as this was when arguments might take place regarding the fulfilment of the terms of the contract. A testament or trust disposition will often refer to the existence of a marriage contract and if it has been registered, it may mention where.

Marriage and sasines

At the time of marriage, either as part of the marriage settlement or as a separate agreement, it was usual for a landowner to give his wife (or future wife) a liferent in certain of his lands. The lands were then held jointly by husband and wife, with the liferent going to the longest liver of the two and after the death of the survivor, the property was passed to the heir 'in fee' (in outright ownership). The transaction was completed by registering a sasine in the general or particular registers of sasines or in a burgh register. (See 'Understanding legal documents – Sasines', p. 24.) A sasine may therefore provide evidence of a marriage for which no contract or entry has been recorded elsewhere.

In the sixteenth century some such contracts were recorded in the protocol books of a notary. These may be difficult to locate as a notary might carry out his business over a wide area but protocol books of the burgh notaries can be very informative. On 29 March 1573 Christian Lauder, wife of Alexander Robeson junior, son and apparent heir of Alexander Robeson senior of Willisburn, was given legal possession of (infeft in) a third part of certain lands in the constabulary of Haddington for her life rent use. Only a few of the protocol books have been transcribed and indexed.

Dissolution of marriage

Before the Reformation, marriage could be annulled on grounds such as insanity, or being within the prohibited degrees, or on account of impotency or existence of a prior marriage, but it could not be dissolved. Protestantism did not regard marriage as a sacrament and from 1560 onwards, while grounds for nullity remained and the laws governing prohibited degrees were emended, adultery and desertion were now regarded as reasons for divorce. After 1566 (when the commissary courts were re-established) cases of divorce were heard in the Edinburgh commissary court. This was the head court and the only one competent to hear such cases, though from the seventeenth century onwards, there was a right of appeal to the Court of Session.

When the commissary courts were abolished, the responsibilities for hearing divorce cases passed to the Court of Session but from 1984 onwards most divorces have been heard in a sheriff court and registered in the GROS Register of Divorces.

Divorce after 1830

From 1855 onwards the fact that a marriage ended in divorce in Scotland is marked by an oval stamp on the left-hand margin of a marriage certificate, marked with the word 'Divorce', followed by a reference to a volume and page number in the Register of Corrected Entries (RCE). These entries are being added to the DIGROS images. The entry gives the date and place of divorce and states at whose instance this took place. Addresses of both parties are usually included.

After 1983 there is a Register of Divorces, covering the whole of Scotland. This is indexed. The Register gives the names of both parties, date and place of marriage, date and place of divorce and details of any court orders concerning care of the children.

There is no indication on a marriage or proclamation entry in the parish registers to indicate that it ended in divorce.

If it is known that a divorce took place after 1830, the relevant records can be found by searching the printed minute books of the Court of Session. The minute may name not only the parties concerned but also various other members of the family and their circumstances. The minute will lead you to the unextracted processes of the Court of Session, which are indexed and which will provide further details. Work is in progress to make the unextracted processes searchable on the electronic catalogue of the NAS (see 'Understanding legal documents – Civil jurisdiction: the Court of Session – Processes', p. 224).

Divorce 1560–1830

During this period, judicial divorce was granted by the Edinburgh commissary court after a hearing there. Leneman (2003) shows that over this period there was a dramatic rise in the number of divorce suits heard. Between 1684 and 1770 only 118 cases are recorded but between 1771 and 1830 the number rose to 786 cases. There is a catalogue in the NAS of divorce and consistorial cases heard by the Edinburgh commissaries between 1658 and 1835 which supersedes the printed calendar of consistorial processes and decreets published by the Scottish Record Society (1909). Cases were concerned with all aspects of marriage, divorce and separation. The value of this material as a source of social history has been highlighted by Leneman.

Desertion

Before the mid-nineteenth century, relatively few marriages ended in divorce but desertion was not uncommon. Such cases came within the remit of the kirk sessions as it was usually a woman with children who was deserted, who then had to call upon the poor's funds for financial help, though every effort was made to make the husband stand by his responsibilities. These circumstances might also cause problems when a deserted wife wished to marry someone else and the session required proof of the death of the first – absent – spouse.

The commissary courts were also concerned with cases concerning marriage disputes and alimony, and detailed evidence has sometimes survived in processes in this court. There are some manuscript indexes to the commissary courts processes but unless you have some detailed knowledge that the marriage was disputed and that there was a court case, it is rarely worth taking the time to look for possible documentation.

3. Death

In the cycle of human existence, it is ironic that death is the event which creates most records relating to a family, in looking forward to the next generation and back in settling the business of the life which has ended.

Statutory registers of death

A death certificate, like that of birth and marriage, can be viewed at the office of the local registrar where it is registered or in GROS. There is a fifty-year closure on viewing the certificates on the pay-per-view site but they can be consulted through DIGROS in New Register House up till about two years before the present time.

Information on a death certificate

Death certificates of 1855 contain many details which are omitted in subsequent years and for this reason it is always worth looking for a death certificate not only of your direct ancestor but of any other relative who might have died in that year. In subsequent years, some details are omitted.

The information recorded on death certificates is as follows:

1855: name, occupation, sex and age of the deceased.
　Address where death took place and usual residence if different.
　Name of spouse or spouses, if any.
　Where born and how long in the district where the death took place. (If the birth was in Ireland, the place may be named.)
　Name of father – occupation and then alive or deceased.
　Mother's maiden name, then alive or deceased.
　Names and ages of children in order of birth and if deceased, age at death.
　Date, time and place of death.
　Cause of death, how long suffering from complaint and name of medical attendant, if any.
　Burial place.
　Informant (with relationship) and sometimes address of informant.
1856–60: same as above but the name of the spouse of a married person is not given though marital status is noted. Information on place of birth of the deceased and details of children are omitted.
1861 onwards: as above but the name of spouse is included.
　Details of burial place omitted.

Lack of information concerning the name of a spouse on certificates of 1856–60 can sometimes by solved if the informant was the husband or wife of the deceased. The information on a certificate provides many leads which can be followed out in other sources.

As well as being a most important source of genealogical information, death certificates reflect many social issues – the number of

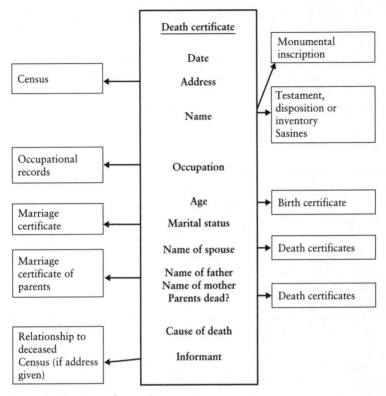

Figure 4   Death certificate: where next?

women dying in childbirth, the scourge of tuberculosis (phthisis), the mortality of infants from teething, croup, whooping cough and measles, as well as epidemics of cholera, diphtheria and smallpox. While a great many children died young and accidents often claimed the lives of young men, a surprising number of people lived to a great age. Patterns of health can sometimes be traced in certain families and there are now a number of medical programs which trace the families of persons who have died from certain diseases so that genealogical and genetic research can be based on what is found.

   In certain cases there may be an entry in the Register of Corrected Entries (marked on the left-hand side of the certificate). This usually refers to a sudden and unexplained death or sometimes to an accident. The entry will report (briefly) on the findings of the sheriff court in the matter. The Fatal Accidents Inquiry (Scotland) Act, 1895 provided for public inquiries into such accidents and the records are listed with the relevant sheriff court. Before 1895 if a record has been kept (which is not always the case), it will be with the ordinary business of the court.

Among the 'Minor Records' held in GROS are records of stillborn children after 1938 (the register is not open to the public), High Commissioners' returns of deaths 1964 onwards for those of Scottish descent or birth from some Commonwealth countries, and deaths of some Scots in foreign countries 1860–1965 based on information supplied by families concerned.

Indexes to death registers

Annual indexes to the death registers post-1854 can be searched in New Register House, through a centre having access to DIGROS or on the ScotlandsPeople pay-per-view website.

The index entry gives the name of the deceased person, the name and number of the district in which the death is registered and the entry number. Ages are given in the indexes from 1855 to 1858 and from 1861 onwards but work is in hand to add this information to the indexes for the missing years 1859–60.

From 1974 onwards, the index entry includes the maiden name of the mother of the deceased, which helps in identifying an entry of likely relevance.

Married women are indexed both under their maiden and married names and names can be cross-referenced. When there is a possibility that either name might have alternative spellings, this can be difficult as there are no facilities for searching like-sounding names. If a woman had been married more than once, she should be entered both under her maiden name and any married name but an earlier married surname is sometimes not given.

If you fail to find a relevant cross-matched entry, search the index either under the married name or the maiden name. Sometimes the maiden name of a deceased woman will not be known by the informant on the death and she will, therefore, only be entered under her married name.

Entries recorded in the High Commissioners' and Commonwealth returns are included in the DIGROS indexes.

Indexes to deaths 1855–75 are not included on the IGI.

Searching for a death certificate

The search for a death certificate will probably be based on age given in a census entry or marriage certificate – possibly on knowledge of a date of birth. Ages given in census returns are often incorrect. When looking for a death certificate, you can key in an exact age or – a wiser choice – search within a range of years. If the surname is an unusual one, it may be better to omit the age when searching but in cases of common surnames – Ross, McLean, Campbell for example – you will need to narrow the search by putting in an age range. There are a number of mistakes concerning ages on the indexes and an age of seventy four transposed to read forty seven means that the right entry may never be found.

It is wise to check your search parameters with care. Sometimes the age range on the screen sets itself to 0 and only entries for the deaths of those under one year will come up.

When looking for a relevant death certificate it is helpful to know where the death was likely to have taken place. In the nineteenth century and first decades of the twentieth century people usually died at home but it has now become common for death to take place in a hospital which can be quite some distance from home. The certificate may, therefore, be registered in an unexpected district. Elderly people often went to stay with a married son or daughter and again this may result in death in an unexpected area.

Death information: true or false?

All information given on certificates must be evaluated and this is par- ticularly true with regard to death certificates. Who was providing the information? Were they in a position to know the truth? As the details are not submitted by the person concerned (as is the case on a mar- riage certificate) there is a considerable chance of error.

The important fact to note is the relationship of the informant to the deceased. If this was a grandson, then he was being asked to name his grandfather's parents – the great-grandparents of the infor- mant – including the maiden name of his great-grandmother. It is hardly surprising that mistakes occurred. One would, however, expect sons or daughters acting as informants to be more reliable than grandchildren, distant relatives or mere neighbours, though they too seem to have suffered from occasional amnesia. The parent- age of those who died in the poor-house or an institution is also, sometimes, stated as 'unknown', even though the family may have known it.

Ages as stated are always suspect and in a case where a man married more than once, the earlier marriage is not always mentioned. The occupation of the deceased as stated on the certificate may also be unexpected as there was sometimes a tendency to raise social status. A hawker may appear as a merchant and a labourer as a farmer.

War deaths

The Registrar General holds a number of records relating to war deaths or deaths of members of service families in its collection of 'Minor Records'. These are being added to DIGROS.

Deaths from 1855 onwards on any British-registered merchant vessel at sea in any part of the world.

Air register from 1948 covering a death in any British-registered aircraft if the deceased was usually resident in Scotland.

Service records from 1881 including deaths of Scots at military stations abroad 1881–1959.

Service Departments registers from 1959 onwards for deaths of persons usually living in Scotland serving in HM Forces, including families of members of the Forces.

South African War registers 1899–1902 for deaths of Scottish soldiers.

World War I deaths (1914–18) for Scottish warrant officers, non-commissioned officers or men (not officers), and petty officers or men in the Royal Navy.

World War II (1939–45) – incomplete returns of deaths of Scottish members of the Armed Forces.

The entries for the World War I deaths are not very informative and in many cases it is not easy to determine whether the entry is relevant as the only details given are the name of the person, age, regiment, rank and where they died. Details of the regiment, however, can lead you to find out more by searching in the National Archives at Kew, London, where most army records are held. A number of records relating to British war deaths and service personnel can be found on www.1837online.co.uk.

There are, however, various other sources for war deaths. The Commonwealth War Graves Commission (www.cwgc.org) provides details of all the graves and memorials in its care, covering the war dead of the two World Wars. Casualty details include name, nationality, rank, regiment, unit, age, date of death, service number, grave reference and cemetery. In some cases additional information is available by clicking on the entry. Jonathan Beattie died in 1918 at the age of twenty five and was described as son of Jonathan and Isabella Beattie of Montrose. He was said to be a native of Fordhouse, Dun, Forfarshire.

Local war memorials have been erected in nearly every town and village in Scotland and a number of local societies have recorded the names on websites. There is, for example, a Roll of Honour 1914–19 for the county of Angus, another for army dead in Caithness for the First World War and a growing number of others. Work is in hand to make a register of all war memorials.

Work has recently been completed in the NAS in putting together sets of soldiers' wills for the First and Second World Wars and a detailed description of these records is given in the NAS guide *Tracing your Scottish ancestors* (2003).

Many records concerning war deaths will be found in the National Archives (TNA) in London. A search of internet sites under the name of a particular battle, campaign or war will almost certainly bring to light a great deal of information. Many Scotsmen served in the East India Company (HEICS) whose records are held by the British Library in London (www.bl.uk/) and include a number of registers of deaths, as well as of births and marriages. Genealogical magazines such as *Ancestors* and *Family Tree Magazine* publish many articles which have a bearing on war and its casualties and quote websites which contain relevant material.

Pre-1855 deaths and burials

In 1565 at a convention of the General Assembly a request was put forward by the commissaries of Edinburgh that every minister should keep a register of the names and residences of those who had died in the parish 'that pupils and creditors be not defrauded'. Various subsequent injunctions that deaths or burials should be recorded were largely ignored. In 1779 Arnot reported that the registers of births and burials were 'the infallible sources of error, the burial registers being kept by people whose faculties were impaired by drinking, who forget today what was done yesterday'. It was generally acknowledged by the middle of the nineteenth century that the burial registers were the least well kept of the parish records. In many parishes none have survived: in others the records cover only a few years and include only a fraction of all burials which took place. In 1804 an entry in Peterhead kirk session minutes reported that there was no grave-digger or sexton in the parish as the man performing these duties had been put in prison. A new grave-digger was appointed who was required to meet with parishioners, who would point out the places of interment of their relatives, and to keep a correct register of all burials. In such circumstances it is not surprising that the records of some parishes leave much to be desired.

Many of the OPR entries only concern the receipt of a payment for hire of the mortcloth – the pall owned by the parish to cover the coffin – but a number of people did not use the parish mortcloth and so their burials – and the burials of their children – went unrecorded. Deaths at sea are usually omitted and in remote areas people sometimes buried their own dead.

There are other problems in finding burial records. Many people were not buried in the parish where they had been living but in another parish with other members of their family. This often happened in farming communities. Sir John Sinclair in *Analysis of the Statistical Account of Scotland* commented on burials of those who died in Dunnottar: 'Not one half of the people who die are buried in it but are carried to the neighbouring parish of Fetteresso.' The 'home' parish might be far away and in some areas of the Highlands there are routes known as coffin roads. Mackenzie (1921) described how a laird of Dundonnell died in Edinburgh but his body was transported by sea and cart to Garve and from there it was intended to carry the coffin to Dundonnell for burial, but the necessary refreshment had been so generous that on the road it was remembered that the coffin had been left behind. Such stories are not uncommon.

Work is in progress to create a national Scottish burial index to all entries in the parish registers. Meanwhile it is necessary to check whether there is a register of burials or deaths (burial was the event usually recorded) for the parish in which you are interested. This may form part of the parish register, usually a section after marriages, but many burial records are recorded in kirk session records, either in the accounts (as payment for the hire of a mortcloth) or in a bill of mortality or burial register. Some dissenting congregations kept their own registers of burials and there are also some Roman Catholic records (see Gandy, 1993a). A few burial registers have been published (see Stevenson, 1987) and many are now being transcribed and printed by local family history societies. A search of the website of a local family history society may provide information as to what work has been done.

Content of a burial entry

Records of burial (or death) vary considerably in the amount of information they provide. Mortcloth payments give few details and it is often difficult to be certain whether an entry is relevant as it will usually only note the name (sometimes without a Christian name) and the fee paid for the hire of the mortcloth. In many parishes there were several grades of mortcloth – the 'best' or 'second best' – and from this one can sometimes gain an idea of the social standing of the deceased. Some entries of burials include age and cause of death.

Records of deaths of those of higher social status often include considerable detail and unusual or tragic accidents may also receive notice. The Banff register on 12 January 1739 has the following entry:

> William Haddo, George Syme in Melrose, Charles Shand in Gellyhill, Christian Wilson, daughter to Hary Wilson in Down, Elspet Lyell there, and Elspet Nicol, spouse to the above Hary Wilson were unluckily driven out to sea in the ferry boat and lost.

Entries relating to loss of life in the fishing communities of Fife provide many detailed descriptions of the events and occasionally one strikes gold in a death entry. In Rathen, Aberdeenshire, the death of an eight-month-old baby occasioned this entry:

> Thomas Ogilvie born 2nd January 1798, died 21st September. 5th son, 10th child of George Ogilvie by Rebecca Irvine his wife. This infant is the only descendant of his maternal grandparents that is yet deceased, all their six children, twenty four grandchildren being still living, whose joint ages amount to upwards of five hundred and twenty two years.

Graveyard records

Monumental inscriptions

Until the eighteenth century, most persons in Scotland were buried in the parish churchyard (the earlier custom of burial in the floor of the church was discouraged). In large towns and cities (Edinburgh, Aberdeen, Glasgow and Dundee among others) there were a number of burial grounds but some country parishes such as Killin and certain areas of the Highlands had numerous small places of burial. As more dissenting congregations were formed, particularly in towns such as Paisley, some churches bought their own land for the burial of their members. Stones in many of the early non-Church of Scotland burial grounds have not survived but Steel (1970) gives an interesting list of the few known to exist for Episcopalians, Quakers, Jews, Moravians, and a very few Roman Catholics.

An entry in the Clackmannan kirk session minutes of the late seventeenth century noted that a young man was accused of throwing down a gravestone and cursing. His defence was that he just laid his hand on the stone and it fell over. It is, therefore, hardly surprising that many tombstones have not survived to the present day and of those that have, the condition is deteriorating. Robert Monteith in 1704 and 1713 published collections of inscriptions in Scotland which are probably some of the oldest records of stones and include many which have now disappeared. In the nineteenth century interest in recording inscriptions grew and many transcriptions were included in works dealing with the history of particular places. The two-volume *Annals of Banff* (Cramond, 1893) contains a complete transcript of all monumental inscriptions within the churchyard of Banff totalling 568 stones, with additional sections covering the inscriptions within the parish church, in the Fife Mausoleum and in St Andrew's Episcopal Church.

A great deal of work is now in progress in recording inscriptions on the stones in burial grounds throughout Scotland. The Scottish Genealogy Society has published many of them and others are produced by various local history and genealogical societies. The SGS library also holds a collection of unprinted inscriptions. Some inscriptions are now on family and local history society websites – search under the name of the parish or church.

Various formats have been used in recording inscriptions. Many of those published by the SGS in the past only include details of pre-1855 stones and provide an abstract of the information on the stone – not a full transcription. Interesting information may thus be omitted, as well as details of more modern members of a family. Recordings of stones in other burial grounds cover everything inscribed on the stones. Work done recently by the Gullane and Dirleton Local History Society has built on this by collecting further details of the persons and families commemorated on the stones taken from oral information, primary and printed sources and newspapers.

There is often scope for a great deal of interesting detective work which can be carried out in reconstituting missing or unreadable details on badly weathered stones and extending the knowledge of the deceased by strategic use of the parish registers, census returns or statutory certificates. The value of the interplay between various classes of records is illustrated by the case of a weaver, Adam George, who was buried in Paisley Abbey burial ground. The published information taken from his tombstone reads:

> Adam George 5.12.1850 – 71: son George 28.4.1843 – 22; two chn.
> inf. By wife Ann Henderson.

The fact that Adam's wife was named meant that it was possible to make a positive identification of the family. There is also a well-kept burial register for the Abbey parish of Paisley and further details came to light there about the deaths in 1850 and 1843. It now appeared that 'son George' actually referred to a son whose name was James,

George being the surname. The burial register of Abbey proved to be unusually helpful in supplementing the inscription information on Adam George. The number of the lair was given, date of burial (five days after death), Adam's occupation (grocer), residence (Williamsburgh), cause of death (palsy), age (seventy one – as on the stone) and place of birth (Morayshire). This was a vital clue in tracing earlier generations of the family and making the leap from Renfrewshire to a completely different part of Scotland.

It is unfortunate that many mistakes have been made in transcribing inscriptions. These include omissions (in some cases only half the stone has been recorded), wrong readings and failure to read stones which can still be deciphered. It is often difficult to read figures and the numbers 8 and 3 may be confused. If you take a photograph of a tombstone in various lights, it is surprising how much can be read which cannot otherwise be seen. The mistakes, however, are not all the fault of the transcriber. Dates and ages clearly stated on a stone are often prone to error.

The information given on a tombstone varies greatly. In 1619, the kirk session in Brechin took steps to control the use of what were considered to be unsuitable epitaphs:

> The session considering that monie abuses are admittat in making epitaphs be young men in this citie affixing on burial stanes anie thing they ples, partlie ridiculous and partlie ontrew, ordain that no epitaph shall be put on any monuments without the approval of the session.

Despite this injunction, tombstones have recorded many strange characteristics of our ancestors.

A stone may commemorate one person or several generations. Full names are usually given but in some instances only initials are used. The decoration on an older tombstone is often revealing, providing details of the occupation of the deceased – the cooper's hammer, the ship of a ship-owner, the mason's level or a blacksmith's tools (Willsher, 1985). A mid-eighteenth-century stone for a well-to-do farmer in Liberton burial ground in Midlothian illustrates farming methods of the time with a beautiful engraving of horses and oxen yoked together for ploughing.

Although only a small number of families are remembered on gravestones, monumental inscriptions provide a valuable source of information about families and refer to a surprisingly wide section of the community, especially in country communities. Farmers, millers, craftsmen, crofters and labourers are all represented, as well as merchants and landowners. References are sometimes made to members of a family who emigrated or moved away and died elsewhere.

Whenever possible, visit a graveyard where your ancestors are buried. You can then check any transcription which has been made. Previously unknown relatives can sometimes be located, commemorated on stones near one in which you are interested, but some graveyards have been 'tidied up', which has involved the re-siting of stones, previously next to each other. Many churches have memorial plaques on the walls of the church – usually concerning landed families.

Lair registers and cemetery records

Many people thought it important to own a lair and bought land in the burial ground from the kirk session or burgh magistrates for this purpose. Later, when cemeteries became the property of private companies, plots could be bought there. Lairs might be inherited or sold and ownership was sometimes recorded by the kirk session. Disputes were not uncommon and records could reveal many family linkings. The ownership of plots also necessitated the keeping of plans of the lairs in a parish burial ground or cemetery. When looking for lair records for a parish burial ground, get in touch with the session clerk of the parish concerned. A copy is usually kept locally. There may also be information with the kirk session records and occasionally the local district registrar may have a copy.

Information concerning lairs sometimes amounts to a mini-genealogy. Testimony was taken in Clackmannan parish in 1668 as to who lay beneath an unmarked stone: 'John Wightman deponet that he knew that John Quhyt's ancestors lay under that stone belonging to the Quhyts lying towards the west end of the kirk, to witt his great grandmother Agnes Clerk with Margaret Blackwood his grandmother.' These details traced some of the family back to the sixteenth century.

Lair records concerned with the ownership of the plots are often rather confusing as the names may not match up with those on gravestones. A register of mortality for Auchterarder covers the years 1742–1878 and is, in effect, a lair book. It illustrates the problems of using such records. In June 1761 there is the following entry:

On the 8th current Archbald Smith from Gatherlys was interd in the north most grave save on in the Brynochs Lair James Brynochs stone at his head & but 5 graves in sd Antient Lair but John Maxton hath taken posesion of the southmost grave.

It would appear that this was an example of several people being buried in a lair owned by someone else. Another entry in that month reads:

12th current [June 1761] Christian Dun was intterd beneth the southmost stone & was most length in Deins Lair her husband being put in in the month of Agust 1743 all in old kirk yeard.

Without indexes to these records, there is no short-cut to searching through them and the fact that the reference to the burial of Christian Dun's husband only appeared eighteen years after his burial is an added complication.

Lair books can sometimes supplement other known information. In Dirleton graveyard a tombstone inscription reads: 'In loving memory of our dear father, George Dippie died 26th October 1924 aged 69 also our dear mother Elizabeth Laidlaw Dippie died 11th July 1932 aged 74'. The lair book has two entries: 'George Dippie, Chapel 1924' and 'Mrs. Dippie, Newcastle 1932' indicating connections with England. In the same graveyard, the tombstone of Euphemia Hutt gives her death as 17 July – the year is unreadable – but the lair book fills in 1859, making it possible to check her death certificate and find the names of her parents.

As urban populations grew, local authorities had to make arrangements for new burial grounds, provision being made under the 1855 Burial Grounds (Scotland) Act. Some cemeteries are privately owned, others are run by the local councils. The telephone book's classified directory will list cemeteries in the area, and on payment of a fee you can usually have a search made for the burial of a certain person or ownership of a particular lair. You will need to know the approximate date of burial. Information about older town cemeteries can be found in local directories (see Torrance, 1998). Some cemetery records are in local archives. The Edinburgh Cemetery Company, for example, administered seven city cemeteries and these records are now in the Edinburgh City Archives.

Obituaries

Notices of death in a newspaper can provide much valuable information and also relate to deaths outside Scotland. In the *Edinburgh Evening Courant* of 23 November 1833, the following notice appeared:

Died on the 5th June last, at Moorshedabad, Marie Daney, wife of George Gordon Macpherson Esq. surgeon, honourable East India Company's Service, after having given birth to a still-born son.

This may be the only known record of the death of Marie Daney or Gordon and would open the way to further research in the records of the East India Company in the British Library. Unfortunately, without an index to newspapers for this year, it would almost certainly be impossible to locate the relevant obituary, published nearly six months after the event. Musgrave (1899–1901) has made an index to deaths prior to 1800 extracted from *The Gentleman's Magazine*, *The Scots Magazine* and other periodicals.

National newspapers are mainly concerned with those in the higher ranks of society but the deaths of local worthies often appear in a local newspaper, with details of life and work. An obituary appeared in the *Jedburgh Gazette* in 1925 for John Keir Young, who had been a schoolmaster in the town. It noted that he was in his 84th year, had married twice, had one daughter who was married and living in Argentina and that he was born in Methven, Perthshire. If the newspaper is not indexed, searching may be very time-consuming. (See 'Newspapers', p. 127.)

Testamentary sources

Finding that a forebear left a testament is always exciting as in many cases it can provide a lot of personal information about the deceased. In Scotland, a testament, often referred to mistakenly as a 'will', concerned the confirmation of an executor and the taking of an inventory. If the person died testate, the document will include what is commonly called in Scots a 'legacie' or 'latterwill' containing the personal wishes of the deceased as to the disposal of their moveable property. Moveables included such items as furniture, money or cattle, but not land, which was regarded as heritable property. Up till about 1823 (the date varied a little from court to court) the registering of testaments was the responsibility of the commissary courts (see 'Profiling the ancestors – Commissary courts', p. 141) and after that the sheriff courts took over this part of their business.

Commissary court registers of testaments (pre-1824)

Everyone had the option to register a testament in the local commissary court or the head court at Edinburgh and particularly in the case of merchants or gentlemen this was often done. Members of the Tran family were burgesses (and provosts) of Irvine in the seventeenth and eighteenth centuries and later merchants in Glasgow. Between 1602 and 1764 thirteen Tran testaments are registered in the 'local' commissary court of Glasgow but a further testament for one of the Tran provosts is registered in Edinburgh commissary court in 1604. Appeals from local commissary courts might be heard in the head court – later by the Court of Session.

Unfortunately only a small number of people left testaments as in many cases there was little to leave or no argument about the appointment of executors and division of the property. On the other hand, if dissension was likely or if debts were owed by or to the deceased (however small), a testament might be recorded. Do not assume because an ancestor was poor that you are unlikely to find a registered testament. A search of indexes reveals a wide social mix – merchants, schoolmasters, maltmen, tenants, indwellers, packmen, weavers, shoemakers, mariners, tailors and servants (among others) and numerous persons described as 'in' a place, indicating that they did not own property.

The dates of commencement of the registers vary widely and there are many deficiencies and lost volumes. The registers for Edinburgh, for example, go back to 1514 but a fire has resulted in the destruction of most records of Aberdeen commissary court before 1722.

Searching the indexes

The indexes to testaments recorded in each of the twenty two commissary courts up to 1800 have been published by the Scottish Record Society. Bound copies of these indexes (one volume will usually contain the indexes to several commissary courts) are widely available in libraries and family history centres throughout Scotland and elsewhere. From 1800 to *circa* 1823 there are typescript indexes, with separate ones for the courts of Edinburgh, Glasgow, Inverness, Orkney, Peebles, St Andrews and Wigtown and a general volume covering the rest.

Work has now been completed in digitising testaments recorded in the commissary courts (pre-1824) and in the sheriff courts up to 1901, linking the images to the index entries. Access to the indexes on the *ScotlandsPeople* website is free but there is a fee for downloading a document. If you are working in the NAS historical search room, you can search the indexes and view the image without charge – but you still pay if you want a copy.

The facility to search the online indexes for a testament has brought many advantages. You have options to search by forename, surname, place, occupation or designation, date, in a particular court or in all the courts, whether of commissary or sheriff, up to 1901. This provides easy access to a wonderful source of both family and social history. It makes it possible to locate not only main-line ancestors but to check on other relatives in the area and to study the way of life of persons of all classes of society through the inventories of the furnishings of their houses, crops grown, their clothes and cattle.

As with all online indexing, however, there are problems. If the name is a very common one and you know the parish in which the person is likely to have died, you can narrow your selection of entries by searching only the relevant commissary court or sheriff court (see Appendix 1). The index entry gives the forename and surname of the deceased, possibly occupation or place of residence (which may be the name of the parish or of a township or farm) and date of the registration of the testament. A testament was often registered within a short time of the death but sometimes an interval of several years might elapse – occasionally a considerable period of time.

A married woman is indexed under her maiden name and the index entry will state the name of her spouse but there is no cross-reference under the husband's name. This information, however, is supplied in the printed indexes and is useful, particularly if you know the name of the man but not that of his wife. For example, there is no registered testament for James Bruce in Achloche in the commissary court of Brechin but the printed index notes 'Bruce, James in Achloche. See Chrystie Bessie'. Under Chrystie, Bessie is entered: 'spouse to James Bruce in Achloche, par. of Lochlie 6 Aug. 1627'.

The online indexes to the commissary registers of testaments indicate whether the deceased died testate or intestate but this information is not provided in the printed indexes.

Problems with spelling

The online indexes represent the name as it appears on the testament. If you fail to find an entry, consult the website 'research tools' which will list most of the alternative spellings of the name found in testaments. If, for example, you are looking for a testament for a McAdam, the name may appear as McAdame, McCaddame, Makadame, Makcadam, Makcaddam, Makcaddum, Makkaddam, McAddam, McAddame, McCadam, McCaddam, McCaddum or McKadame, as well as in other forms. Another option is to search using soundex which may bring up a different lot of variants. If the person for whom you are searching had an unusual forename or lived in a place for which there are likely to be few spelling variants, using the online option to search under the place (or even Christian name) rather than under the surname may solve the problem.

In the pre-1800 printed indexes, spelling of names has been standardised and it can be very confusing to locate an entry there but find that it fails to appear online when you enter it in that form. In the printed index for Brechin commissary court there are sixteen entries under the surname Falconer. When you enter this name on the ScotlandsPeople website index, only eight will appear because the other entries are spelled in a different way. A study of the printed indexes therefore is often very useful as this will alert you to the existence of a testament which may be of interest.

Identifying the place

There are some further problems in identifying a place name. In some testaments the parish of residence is given (occasionally an old parish name – the list of suppressed parishes printed in Vol. 20 of the *Old Statistical Account* may help). In others you will find only the farm or township noted, which may be very difficult to identify. John Fenton who died in 1662 was living in Bellemenay, which is stated to be in the parish of Glenisla, but William Lyon (testament registered in 1724) is only described as 'of Easter Ogill' without any parish description. For the period up to 1668, the indexes to places given in the printed volumes of the *Registers of the Great Seal* are of great assistance in identifying places and their relevant parishes. For later references, *A Directory of landownership in Scotland c.1770* (Timperley, 1976) can sometimes be useful. It lists the names of the principal landowners in each parish at that time and includes an outline of the lands they owned – but not all. In the case of William Lyon who was described as 'of' Easter Ogill, he must have owned land there and research revealed that these lands were in the parish of Tannadice.

For the eighteenth century, the manuscript 'Index to places' (which is being put online) for the abridgements to the registers of sasines can be helpful, as the sasine in which the name occurs will usually indicate the location of the place. Maps, local lists of names or gazetteers may also solve the problem, though many small farms and settlements have disappeared over the years.

Content of a testament

In Scotland, the term 'testament' refers to the confirmation of executors. If the deceased had died intestate, then it was the duty of the commissary court to confirm an executor in what is known as a testament dative. If, however, the deceased person had drawn up a 'latterwill' or 'legacie' during their lifetime, naming executors, this would result in a testament testamentar. When someone drew up a settlement before death which was later recorded in a register of deeds but did not name executors then, though the person died legally testate, a testament dative would also have to be registered whereby the commissary officer confirmed the appointment of executors who came forward after the death. This only happened on rare occasions.

Some claim that testaments dative are of little value to the family historian but they should never be overlooked as they often contain details of genealogical value and are of interest in throwing light on the family background.

The form and wording of a testament varies very little and therefore, even if the handwriting presents difficulties, knowing what to expect in each section of the document and the phrases which are likely to be used is a great help in reading the document. The opening sentence states whether this is a testament dative or a testament testamentar, and goes on to give the name of the deceased (umquhile) person, with their place of residence and often occupation or social standing – merchant, for example. In the case of a married woman, referred to by her maiden name, she will be described as wife (spouse) or widow (relict) of so and so. If the wife died before the husband, the testament will probably include the husband as joint owner of the moveable property.

If the deceased died intestate, then the commissary confirmed as executor the person who was assumed to have a right to this position. Often the surviving spouse acted on behalf of the children who were still minors: sometimes a son or daughter was the executor and anyone who was owed money by the deceased might apply to be the executor *qua creditor*. In this case, the executor was able to claim for the repayment of the debt from the value of the moveable goods and no reference is likely to be made to the names of surviving members of the family. These testaments rarely contain genealogical information unless the creditor was related to the deceased but they can throw light on the circumstances of the deceased.

The opening section, therefore, usually mentions one or more close relatives of the deceased but it must never be assumed that everyone in the family is named. The eldest son, if he also inherited heritable property (a house or land) did not have a share in his parent's moveable property but might claim the 'heirship moveables', often the best of the farm stock, to make it possible to run his property. His name, therefore, may not appear in a testament. The date of death of the person concerned should be given but is often left blank.

If both husband and wife had testaments, you may find that they provide different information. The testament dative of Robert Walker in North Berwick was recorded in Edinburgh commissary court on 24 June 1670. One only learns that he was living in North Berwick and that his widow, Marion Oliver, was appointed as his executor. She, however, died testate, her testament being registered in the same court on 20 June 1672. This document supplied further information on her husband. He was a burgess of North Berwick – a fact which pointed the way to new avenues for research in burgh records. Marion Oliver's testament also proved to be a source of much genealogical information. She and her husband had no surviving children and she left all her goods and gear to be divided among her nephews and nieces on both her own and her husband's side of the family. This illustrates the value of testaments of unmarried or childless members of the family who often name relatives to whom bequests were made.

The inventory

The first duty of the executor was to make up an inventory of the moveable goods of the deceased person and this information takes up the second paragraph of a testament. This is a most interesting source of social history and sometimes reveals the background or trade of the person concerned. Robert Walker's inventory referred to bolls of barley (bear) and a few horses but his wife's inventory listed a considerable amount of malt, which led one to think that Robert was a maltster. The inventory often provides evidence of crops grown, usually valued on the basis of the expected yield of grain sown ('valued to the third corne' – a yield of three or, occasionally on good land, four times was common in the seventeenth century), insight into farming methods through itemised farming implements, as well as detailed descriptions of furnishings of houses, whether crofts or castles. John Buttar was a minor laird in Perthshire who died in 1694, the inventory of his moveable goods being valued at £51. 14s. Scots. The inventory provides a picture of his modestly furnished home – two old chests, a cupboard, a feather bed, some bedding, a few kitchen utensils (an oak cask, water stoups, pots, plates, cogs, wooden drinking cups and an iron hook), a fishing rod and a plough. There may be details of contents of a wardrobe – Lord Lauderdale's factor died in 1807 and had twenty eight waistcoats, twenty three pairs of pantaloons and nineteen pairs of silk stockings. To keep down the estimated value of the possessions and thereby to lower the amount of tax due, goods and gear are often described as in bad condition – the horse lame, the pot broken and the table lacking a leg. The online facility to search for testaments for all those who belonged to a certain trade – shoemakers in Dunkeld or tailors in Jedburgh, for example – over set periods of time offers opportunities for studying and comparing the social standing and possessions of persons of a certain trade or class of society.

Debts in and out

After the inventory, the next section deals with the 'debts in' (owed to the deceased) and 'debts out' (owed by the deceased). There is less likely to be any genealogical information in this part (though sometimes members of the family were owed or owing sums of money), but it should not be overlooked and some interesting information can be gleaned. Accounts (sometimes quoted) for the cost of the funeral are often included for money paid out in 'mournings', for making the coffin and for food and quantities of drink supplied at the funeral. Robert Walker was owed money by a number of local people, which indicates that he was probably in trade, and sometimes the list of debts indicate financial problems. If the debts were large ones, this could point to the possible value of searching diligence records for any legal action taken by the creditors. The deceased often died with rent unpaid to his landlord (who will be named) – a clue which may lead to discovering further information on the deceased in the estate accounts or rentals of the landowner concerned.

Sometimes the indexes to testaments indicate that there is more than one testament registered in the name of a deceased person. The additional document will be an 'eik' – usually referring to debts in or out which have come to light after giving in the original inventory. An 'eik' may supply extra information – the name of a spouse or child which has not been given in the original testament – and it is always worth checking.

Division of the moveable property

The net value of the moveable estate after debts in and out had been taken into account, known as 'free gear', was then calculated and the commissary levied his tax or 'quot'. Sometimes the sum owed was more than the total value of the estate and the commissary notes this as *debita bona excedunt*.

The division of the free gear was laid down by law and provides information about those legally entitled to share the moveable goods.

If a person was survived by spouse and children, one third went to the spouse (*jus relictae*), one third to a child or children (*legitim*) divided equally among them, and one third was regarded as the 'deid's part'. This could be bequeathed according to the wishes of the deceased person as expressed in a legacie or latterwill.

If the deceased was survived only by a spouse or by a child or children (but not both), then the division was in two, one part again being the 'deid's part'.

If there was no surviving spouse and no children, the testament will state 'na division' and everything might be left as the deceased wished or in cases of intestacy, this could be claimed by surviving brothers and sisters, who took equal shares.

If a married woman died childless within a year and a day of her marriage, her moveable goods returned to her father.

The latterwill

The most interesting section in a testament testamentar is the legacie or latterwill. The deceased usually commended his or her soul to God, expressed any particular wishes for burial and set out any bequests of the free moveables. This can provide a great deal of genealogical information. There may be references back to the obligations of a marriage settlement (sometimes registered in a register of deeds, sometimes not registered at all) and names of members of the family and other relations. Illegitimate children may be mentioned and sometimes there are veiled references to a black sheep in the family who is left money under supervisory terms rather than outright. In his testament registered in 1767, Edward Orr, a merchant in Campbeltown, left his best feather bed to a younger daughter, but his eldest daughter, on account that she had made a bad marriage, received a bequest only on condition that she no longer cohabited with her husband 'who left her destitute and a heavy burden upon me'. His grandson (son of this daughter) was only to receive his £5 bequest if he pursued his trade carefully and well 'and not otherwise' – apparently a precaution in case he took after his father.

The date when the latterwill was written is recorded which can provide a useful guide as to when the writer died and witnesses to the writing of the document are named.

The final two paragraphs in both a testament dative and a testament testamentar are concerned with the ratification and approval of the inventory, the official confirmation by the commissary and the date of registration (this date may occur in either the last paragraph or the last but one). A cautioner, often a relative, was appointed to be responsible for seeing that the inventory was properly taken and the terms of the testament carried out.

Warrants of testaments

A testament was first written out on a piece of paper. This is known as the warrant and it was then copied into the register. In a few cases where a register is deficient or has been lost, warrants have survived. Where the register of testaments has been shown to be deficient but warrants are extant, some have been digitised. Most warrants, however, have not been put online and there may be some for which there is no registered testament. The inventory of records for each commissary court will indicate whether there are warrants. Search the NAS electronic catalogue online – www.nas.gov.uk/ – checking under the class reference CC with the relevant number of the commissary court with which you are dealing. The numbers of the commissary courts are given in Appendix 1.

Other records of the commissary court

If you look at a repertory of records for each commissary court, you will see that there are a number of different classes of documents. *Guide to the National Archives of Scotland* (SRO, 1996) lists the records of each court and the repertory can also be viewed online on the NAS website. What has survived varies from court to court as many records have been lost. Although the commissary court was not only concerned with executry business, in every class of record – in warrants, edicts, petitions, inventories or processes – there may be evidence of a death for which there is no testament or in which you will find additional information on the circumstances of a person for whom there is a registered testament.

The documents in each class are preserved in bundles (rarely bound into volumes), each bundle usually covering a year, and stored in boxes. On the outside of each document there is a superscription with a note of the kind of document it is and the name of the party concerned. This makes searching relatively quick and easy. In many cases, there is a certain amount of confusion among the papers. Copies of testaments may be attached to edicts or processes, inventories kept in a separate box, bundled up with edicts or tied up with copies of old bills, while disputed executries may be with processes or again with the edict. Patience in wading through this mass of material is rarely wasted; though you may not find exactly what you were looking for, a great deal of information may be found relative to social behaviour at the time.

The records are outhoused in the NAS repository, Thomas Thomson House, and have to be ordered twenty four hours in advance. They can only be viewed in the NAS historical search room. There is a manuscript inventory of most of the records in each commissary court which list by year the names of the persons concerned. This provides a basic searching aid but if you know the approximate date of death, it may be easier to go through the bundles for the relevant period.

Edicts and inventories

The registration of a testament only took place after the publication of an edict, which was the first step in the business of confirming an executor, leading to the registration of a testament. Following a request made by an intending executor to the commissary officer, a notice was put up (and read aloud) in the parish of the deceased, asking that any who might have claims to be appointed executor should come forward and naming the person who had expressed a wish to be the executor.

The great value of edicts is that they are evidence of a great many deaths which are not documented by a registered testament. A calendar of the records of the Argyll commissary court (Bigwood, 2001a) illustrates how valuable all these records are. A study of testaments and edicts recorded in the Argyll commissary court showed that between 1730 and 1733 there are thirty two registered testaments but also nineteen edicts for which there are no registered testaments, while between 1770 and 1771 there are seven registered testaments and twenty six edicts for which there are no registered testaments. A similar proportion of surviving edicts to unregistered testaments has been found in other commissary courts.

An edict contains most of the genealogical information which you find in a testament dative – the name of the deceased, and often occupation and residence, and the name of the executor – whether this is *qua creditor* or as nearest of kin, in which case the relationship is stated. The following is an example of information given in an edict for which there is no surviving registered testament:

> Angus Campbell, only child of Catharine Campbell, spouse of John Campbell tacksman of Balligown, decerned executor dative qua nearest of kin with John Campbell, his father as his tutor in law and administrator, parish of Kilmore 17 May 1754.

Edicts of tutory and curatory appointed curators to look after the affairs of 'pupils' – fatherless boys under fourteen or girls under twelve – or tutors for children between pupillarity and full age at 'twenty one years complete'. These may be included with other edicts or kept in a separate series of boxes. As close relatives on both sides of the family were usually chosen as tutors, such edicts can produce a great deal of genealogical information. When John Kerr of Moriston, husband of Grissell Cochran, died, the children were still under age and the Lauder commissary in 1707 appointed as their tutors Mr Mark Kerr of Houndswood and Andrew Kerr of Littleden, representing the father's side, and Sir John Cochran of Ochiltree and

William Cochran younger of Ochiltree for the mother's side. This was a landed family but there are many examples of edicts of tutory and curatory concerning those of lower social standing.

With the edicts there are often various other attached documents such as accounts for funeral expenses of the deceased, for medical expenses (often including whisky), for hire of the mortcloth, for providing mourning clothes and, most commonly, for the food and drink (in quantity) taken at the 'funerals', the Scottish term used for all the preparations and ceremonies in burying the dead.

Inventories of moveable goods of persons of all classes of society are also sometimes found with the edicts. In a number of courts there are separate registers of inventories and also warrants (first drafts) of inventories, which again may relate to deaths which are not followed by registered testaments. Moir Lamont in Gortenloiske, parish of Inverchaolain in Argyll, died in January 1701 and the inventory of her moveable goods was given up by John Broun, her son, for himself and in name of Finlay and Mary Broun, her other children. There is no surviving testament.

Processes

Processes are the papers accompanying a case heard in the commissary court and if you do find one relating to your family, it may reveal a great deal. Many of the cases dealt with slander and debt but others were concerned with settling the affairs of a deceased person – again usually claims for payment of debt but sometimes revealing dubious cases of pressure on dying persons to change their wills or disputes over inheritance.

The appointment of executors was not always uncontested and the process may throw considerable light on the circumstances of the family and provide information on a number of relatives. Second marriages were frequently a source of dispute. On the death of James Boyd, a gardener in Falkirk in 1770, his widow claimed to be the executor. A counter-claim was put in by a married daughter as she stated that her mother was now 'cloathed with a second husband' and 'co-habits with a young fellow as such and if speed be not used, there is little reason to expect any good out of the defunct's subjects'. The court found in favour of the married daughter. Suggestions of forgery were also sometimes examined.

Petitions

There were often cases of hardship following a death. Widows unable to access money to pay for a funeral petitioned the commissary officer for permission to roup goods to pay for a funeral, sustain the family or settle pressing debts. The petition might be followed by the taking of an inventory of the goods to be sold. George Milligan was a druggist and chirurgeon in Moffat and died in 1736. A testament and three 'eiks' were registered in Dumfries commissary court but his partner had problems in carrying on the business while testamentary matters were being settled. He wished to sell some perishable drugs and sought permission to do this before George's executries had been completed. The result was a full inventory of the contents of the shop, listing all the medicaments stocked there. It was followed by a list of all those who owed money to the druggist – one hundred persons in Moffat – which included not only their names but also occupations and residences.

Sheriff court commissary business (post-1823)

Under the Commissary Courts (Scotland) Act 1823, the commissary courts ceased to exist and their jurisdiction concerning executries and other matters with which they previously dealt passed to the relevant sheriff courts. In some areas, there was an overlap in the transfer of responsibilities from the commissaries to the sheriff court officers over the years 1823–29 and you may have to check the records of both the sheriff court and commissary court.

In a catalogue of the records of a sheriff court, there is a section titled 'commissary business'. Although there were often several sheriff courts in a county, in most areas only one would deal with commissary business (see p. 136). There are variations in how the sections of the sheriff court are arranged and labelled. Wills and inventories may be listed together or separately. Moveable estates of those who died outwith Scotland were dealt with only in Edinburgh sheriff court.

From 1823 to 1875 there are manuscript indexes in the NAS of recorded inventories under each sheriff court but there are also printed indexes for Edinburghshire, Haddingtonshire and Linlithgowshire from 1827 to 1865 and for the rest of Scotland from 1846 to 1867, titled *Indexes to personal estates of defuncts*. An annual printed calendar of confirmations, covering the whole of Scotland, commences in 1876. The calendar names the deceased, their residence and occupation, whether they died testate (and where the will is registered) or intestate, name of executor and net value of the moveable property. Both these sets of printed indexes are in the NAS and in various libraries and can be accessed through the LDS family history centres.

One of the useful aspects of the indexing and digitisation of testaments and wills is that it is now possible to undertake 'seamless' searching both before and after 1823, up to 1901. In the sheriff court records, if the deceased died testate, the testamentary deed is often copied at the end of the inventory and in such cases, if you pay for the right to download the inventory, it will include the deed. The settlement, however, may be recorded in a separate register (in the Books of Council and Session, in a sheriff court or burgh register of deeds) and may not have been digitised. There will be a note in the inventory indicating in which court and when the document was registered and you will have to order a copy (on payment of a separate fee) through the NAS. It cannot be downloaded from the website on your own computer.

Inventories and wills registered in the sheriff courts are indexed under the woman's married name – 'Mrs. Jane Lawson, alias Cargill, widow of David Lawson, shipmaster in Arbroath' in 1867 in Forfar sheriff court, for example. There is no reference in the online indexes to testacy or intestacy but entries in the printed indexes to *Inventories of defuncts* are marked with the letters D, F or H to indicate intestacy, C, E or G to show testacy, while A and B do not indicate either testacy or intestacy. The date of death is also given there and the year in which the document was registered, written in abbreviated form – '48' for '1848', for example. There is sometimes confusion in thinking that this was the age at death.

From 1876 onwards (when the printed indexes to confirmations start) married women are still indexed online under their married names only but the entries do note whether the person died testate or intestate: 'Lawson, Elizabeth Black or Ferrier, wife of Thomas Lawson, sometime farmer of Sandyford, Kirriemuir, Forfarshire, now residing at Fort Worth, Texas, USA, d. 12.08.1881 at Sandyford aforesaid, intestate'. The online index does not include details of the executor appointed or the value of the estate.

Testamentary dispositions

One of the dangers of easy online access to certain records is to induce 'tunnel vision', leading researchers to overlook other valuable associated source material. The digitised registers of testaments in the commissary courts and inventories and wills recorded in the sheriff courts do not include testamentary dispositions recorded in registers of deeds.

The important difference between a testament and a disposition recorded in a register of deeds is that a testament is only concerned with moveables, while a deed (registered in any court) could also deal with heritable property. A disposition registered in Lanark burgh court register of deeds in 1766 by Thomas Hutton, maltman and burgess of Lanark, left to his wife in liferent and his children in fee (full ownership) his tenement of houses, barn and yards, as well as malt kilns and land. All the children are named in the document. His eldest son was already in a trade, while the other children were minors and left in the care of their mother.

If the estate is a large one, everything may be left in the hands of appointed executors who act as trustees under the terms of a trust disposition and they then administered matters according to the wishes of the deceased. Such administration did not always go uncontested and a number of cases were taken to the Court of Session. Deeds may reveal a great deal. Arrangements may be made for the care of previously unknown children, lawful or illegitimate. There may be bequests to immediate members of the family (money, pictures, land), as well as to distant relatives, providing clues for further research, while debts and obligations may reflect business interests. Reference may also be made to marriage settlements and other earlier legal contracts.

Deeds could be recorded in the books of any competent court – the Court of Session, sheriff court, burgh court, commissary court or franchise court – regality, bailiery or stewartry but not barony, which was regarded as a lower court. (See 'Understanding legal documents – Registers of deeds', p. 202.)

As there are so many courts in which a disposition or settlement could have been recorded, the problem is to know where to look first. The decision will depend on several considerations – where the deceased lived (what records are there for the area?), when they died, their station in life, whether there are indexes to the records, and an assessment of the size of the task which faces you. It is usually wisest to search indexed or more local registers before starting to work through unindexed and bulky records. Most of these records can only be consulted in the NAS (a few have been microfilmed by the LDS) and some burgh registers may be in local archives.

Family muniments

If you are researching a landed family, you should consult the NAS electronic catalogue or catalogue for a local archive (a growing number can now be searched online, see www.scan.org.uk) to see if there is a collection of relevant family papers which includes legal documents. Many well-to-do families preserved copies of testamentary material, correspondence or accounts dealing with a death in the family. In the Biel muniments there are funeral accounts dated 1685–1834, while Clerk of Penicuik papers include testaments dated between 1665 and 1827. Some muniments are still in private hands. Most of the latter have been surveyed and catalogued for the National Register of Archives and the list of NRA catalogues is online at www.nra.nationalarchives.gov.uk/nra. The catalogues can also be consulted in the NAS.

Inheritance

Sasines

(For more detailed information about sasines and retours (also known as 'services of heirs'), see 'Understanding legal documents' – Land ownership', pp. 208–21.)

When someone died who owned heritable property, the heir was legally bound to have himself or herself served heir through a retour or precept of *clare constat* and they could then be given legal possession of the property – the terms used being infeft in, seised in or given sasine of the lands concerned, the sasine constituting a right title to it. This process did not always take place immediately after a death and there was sometimes a considerable delay – possibly of years and even missing a generation– before the legal transfer of land took place.

The importance of this process in the context of family history research is that death resulted in records. Only some Scots owned property but, particularly by the nineteenth century, it is surprising how widely land ownership was spread though the social classes. Even in the eighteenth century, one finds references to innumerable persons described as shoemakers, maltsters, plasterers, wrights, weavers or carters, as well as merchants or portioners who were involved in land transactions.

The sasine was the act of giving legal possession of land and from 1781 onwards, there are good searching aids in finding out whether an ancestor did own land as there are printed abridgements of most sasines. The next step is to ascertain how the deceased person acquired that land and from whom. Was it bought? Was it only owned as security for a loan or was it inherited? If it had been inherited, you can find information on an earlier generation.

Understanding the abridgements can present problems but it is not too difficult to pick out those which are concerned with inheritance, though this is not indicated by the index entry. Reference to 'heir to' or 'special service' or 'general service' is one of the principal clues. A general retour established a right to be acknowledged as heir, a special retour specified the lands to which the heir was entitled to succeed.

The following abridgement is dated 11 January 1865, from Aberdeenshire:

John Manson of Oakhill, Minister of the Free Church of Scotland, Woodhead, as heir to Mary Blyth, relict of Alexander Manson of Oakhill, merchant, Old Meldrum, his mother, registers sp[ecial] and gen[eral] serv[ice] December 1864.

Then follows a description of the lands which he inherited. This is an example of how much information can be found in an abridged sasine – the occupation and residence of John Manson, the occupation of his father, the maiden name of his mother and the fact that both were now deceased. In the case of large landowners, you may find that it is not the heir who is infeft in the property but trustees who were appointed to administer the estate and there may be a reference in the sasine to the trust disposition made by the deceased which will be recorded in a register of deeds.

The abridgements do not cover property within the royal burghs. They kept their own registers.

Before 1781 when the abridgements start, it is not always so easy to find a sasine relating to inheritance. It may be registered in a particular register of sasines (relating to one county) or in the general register of sasines, covering the whole country and possibly dealing with pieces of land held in different parts of the country or in a burgh register of sasines if burgage property is involved. The general register of sasines is now indexed up to 1735 and there are separate indexes, printed or typed, for a number of the particular registers for part or all of the period 1617–1780 (see p. 217). Some burgh registers are indexed but most only from 1809 onwards.

The indexes themselves can often provide a guide to relationships and sometimes to more than one generation of owners. The index to the Lanarkshire particular register of sasines 1721–80 lists 'John Dykes, portioner of Kirkwood, son of William Dykes, merchant, Glasgow' and then under William Dykes is noted 'portioner of Kirkwood and merchant, Glasgow, formerly merchant Strathaven, his spouse – Jean Callander'. Under each index entry the sasine volume and page number is given and you can therefore cross-check which entries refer to both William and his son John. These entries provide the names of two generations of Dykes, the occupation and residence of John's father and his former residence, as well as the name of William's wife. If there is no index, then you will have to use minute books. These are quite informative but do take time to search. An entry names the main parties concerned in the sasine and includes a brief description of the lands transferred and the date of registration of the sasine.

Services of heirs

(See 'Understanding legal documents – Services of heirs (retours)', p. 211.)

The legal process of proving that an heir had the right to inherit has resulted in records known as retours or services of heirs, which are a godsend for many of those lucky enough to have ancestors who owned land, especially those who held their lands of the Crown as superior. Many books on tracing ancestry indicate, erroneously, that every heir should appear in the Chancery register of services of heirs but it is important to remember that someone inheriting lands held of a subject superior – not directly from the Crown – only had to be issued with a precept of *clare constat* by that superior who had been satisfied that the heir had a rightful claim to be seised in the lands concerned. In cases which were complicated or contentious in any way, a retour of this kind might still go through Chancery. Most retours concerned the better-off members of society but retours do also include a number of persons of less exalted social status.

If you are dealing with a landed family who held their lands of the Crown, the printed indexes to retours from 1700 onwards can sometimes make it possible to trace succeeding generations of a family over several centuries from this source alone. If the link is a direct father to son relationship, then the abstract will, in most cases, provide all the information you need, but if the lands were passing from grandfather to grandson or from great uncle to great nephew, for example, the missing family links will only be named in the full text of the retour, not in the abstract. On 13 August 1742 Hugh Mathie in Bent was retoured to his cousin, Helen Mathie, grand daughter of Alexander Mathie, a weaver in Glasgow. The full text of the retour provides a great deal of genealogical information. Helen Mathie was daughter of Alexander Mathie deceased. He was only son of another Alexander Mathie deceased, a weaver in Glasgow, and the latter was only son of the deceased John Mathie, also a weaver in Glasgow. Hugh Mathie was son of Thomas Mathie, farmer, who was brother of the deceased John Mathie.

The retour is the final document at the end of the process of proving a right to inherit certain lands. It starts with the issue of a brieve of Chancery, instructing the sheriff or burgh court to hold an inquest to establish the claim of the heir. Records of some of these inquests have survived in the sheriff court records – but not all. Most will list the members of the assize, and sometimes the depositions of witnesses are recorded, which can provide a great deal valuable information. A case concerning the disputed retour of an aunt as heir to Duncan Hendry, an eighteenth-century Argyllshire shipmaster, brought to light information on Duncan's father and grandfather, Duncan's sisters and nephews, and about relatives not only in Scotland but in North Carolina. In straightforward cases the verdict just confirms the claims of the heir.

Precepts of *clare constat* can be found in collections of family papers but often the only reference to such a document is found in the following sasine, which quotes it. If you come across papers called 'progress of writs' in family muniments, these may list in chrono-logical order all the legal documents concerning the past ownership of lands – charters, precepts, retours and resulting sasines.

Not every owner of lands completed title and there may therefore be some missing links in the ancestral chain (which you should be able to fill in from the sasine registers). Some retours have been lost and sometimes the verdict of the sheriff court where the inquest was heard does not seem to have been returned to Chancery.

Retours to lands in the royal burghs are not included in the Chancery registers of services of heirs. Some royal burghs have their own registers of retours and these records may be rich in family infor-mation. A retour recorded in Peebles burgh court on 9 October 1789 spelled out the following relationships:

> George Nielson, eldest lawful son of deceased Abraham Nielson tailor in Peebles, eldest lawful son of John Nielson writer there, who was son of James Nielson merchant there, who was brother german to the deceased John Nielson senior, burgess of Peebles who was great grand uncle of the said George Nielson, heir male of tailzie to his great grand uncle.

Tailzies

If a landowner wanted to dictate to the generations to come who should inherit the estate, his wishes (under an Act of Parliament of 1685) could be recorded in a deed of tailzie or entail and entered in the register of tailzies (in the NAS – class RT1). Sometimes a copy of the tailzie is also recorded as a deed in the Books of Council and Session.

Tailzies could include any named heir or series of heirs, substitut-ing these for the heirs who would legally be entitled to succeed, includ-ing illegitimate children, but usually tailzies were drawn up to secure the succession to a heritable estate where there might be doubts as to who should succeed and to prevent it being sold. If there were likely to be no male heirs, then it was often laid down that a daughter might be the next heir, but on condition that she retained her maiden name, and if she married, that her husband would take the family name and bear the arms of the family concerned.

The register of tailzies is indexed from 1688, when the register commences, up to 1833. There is a further manuscript index which covers the period up to 1938. The register can be a source of useful information as tailzies may cover many ramifications of the family when nominating heirs – 'whom failing A, then B' and so on – some of whom may be only distantly related. An Act of 1848 allowed entails to be broken.

Court actions

The settling up of the affairs of the deceased was not always conducted with harmony, a fact which may be reflected in court records. There were disputes over the making of dispositions, over inheritance and, in many cases, concerning the payment of debts due by the deceased. Because of the number of different courts in which an action might be heard and a lack of searching aids, you need to have at least some inkling that trouble was brewing to make it worth beginning a search for litigation. If you think this might have been so, start by checking whether a case was heard in the Court of Session. A growing number of indexes to Court of Session cases are being put onto the NAS electronic catalogue (class reference CS) and can be searched online. The actual papers are in the NAS West search room. A catalogue of productions, the material evidence produced to support a case, is also online. If you do find an ancestor involved in such a court action, you may learn a great deal about that forebear's family and business associations. The death of John Ogilvy of Inshewan *circa* 1765 resulted in a court case, at which time a rental was produced for his estate for the years 1765–83, there were executry accounts including notes of his debts, funeral expenses, servants' wages and farm expenses. Following the death of George Cheyne, who was serving in the East India Company and died in India in 1813, the process documents included papers concerning a legacy and accounts for clothing and education of his illegitimate son, Edward Cheyne, later a farmer in Aberdeenshire.

IV *Profiling the Ancestors*

Finding sources

Birth, marriage and death are the focal points for research on family history and many people feel that once they have exhausted the information given in statutory registers, census returns and OPRS, they have come to the end of the line. The internet, however, has opened new lines of enquiry and made people aware that there are many sources which, though they may not have a direct bearing on these three 'facts of life', will produce evidence of the lives and families of our forebears and provide opportunities for identifying and linking earlier ancestors.

The internet is bringing more and more opportunities for research within the reach of family historians, including the facility to find out about almost any topic from the comfort of home. One often hears the query: 'Can I now do all my research through the internet?' Without doubt, the answer should be 'No'. Such a concept of research at the best is likely to be limiting, and at the worst may lead to wrong conclusions and dead ends. Information found on websites is very useful but it often constitutes the 'fast food' of genealogy (occasionally even the 'junk food') and the study of family history will be the poorer and less interesting if other source material is disregarded.

The internet does, however, open up the chance to explore a wide range of sources of genealogical value. In the excitement of the chase in finding transcripts of censuses and other listings and extracts from a range of records online, the facility to search catalogues of archives, libraries and institutions online is often overlooked. Catalogues provide the 'maps' for genealogical journeys and open up the 'freedom to roam' in a wide range of source material, not all of which may be accessed online. But in setting out to explore unfamiliar country, one needs guidance in which direction one should go and what is worth seeing.

Sightings and scents

All researchers will have found that some references in documents are more useful than others. The occurrence of a name in a document may only indicate the existence of someone bearing the right surname, living in the expected place at around the right time. This is what can be termed a 'sighting'. It is not always possible to determine immediately whether this individual is your quarry but the reference may provide a clue which leads to something more significant and several 'sightings' can make a substantial contribution in building up the profile of the ancestor. Further research may turn up additional details – the name of a spouse, an occupation or place of residence, a reference to a parent – which, when added to your original sightings, provide positive identification. You can then term this a 'scent' – information which not only confirms that this is a member of the ancestral family but which may provide a base or clues to take you further.

Primary and secondary sources

Source material is divided into two categories – primary and secondary. The term 'primary sources' can cover a wide range of material such as diaries, letters, rentals, legal papers, testaments or court hearings. Marwick, in his contribution to a handbook on sources and methods for studying family and community history (Drake and Finnegan, 1994) defines primary sources as those which derive naturally or in the ordinary course of events from people going about their business. Accounts, inventories and minutes of proceedings are certainly covered by this description, but there are other records such as narrative accounts of current events, private letters, autobiographies, even evidence given in court, which contain a more subjective element as the author or person concerned is interpreting what is seen or has happened or presenting a particular view. Secondary sources are those which involve an intermediary and give the author's interpretation of what has been found in primary sources or in other secondary works (such as histories, biographies or other commentaries).

The discovery of primary sources is the basis of all good research but Marwick issues a warning – 'Handle with care'. They cannot be taken at face value and must be evaluated, a process which raises a number of considerations. An autobiography or public report, for example, is a primary source but each has to be weighed up. Was it compiled to enhance a reputation, to prove a point or act as a justification for a certain course of action? The work may have involved the selection (or biased presentation) of facts and must always be regarded as a subjective view of a situation.

Similar – and even more stringent – assessments have to be made when studying secondary sources. Secondary sources are too often afforded value just by being in print. The reasoning given is: 'If it is printed, it must be true.' Unfortunately in recent times this dangerous – and often erroneous – assumption is spreading to information found on websites, with dire results.

Using catalogues

The level of online information provided about the holdings of an archive varies from institution to institution and also within that catalogue. You may find that every item or bundle of documents in a repository is described: for others there is as yet only a broad outline of subjects on which there is information. In the case of a detailed catalogue such as the online NAS catalogue, the problem is often that having keyed in a particular name or topic, you are faced with an enormous number of entries referring to references occurring in various classes of records. Such a choice can be overwhelming as you may not know what to expect in these records, what the terms mean and how easy or productive a search will be. On the other hand, your search may be negative. If, for example, you know that your ancestor was a tenant of a particular farm, there may be no catalogue entry under the name of either tenant or farm – but there may be information in a rental of the whole estate. Prior knowledge of the proprietor of the lands is therefore necessary if you are to make a successful search.

A wrong instruction given to a computer can result in a negative search and a certain amount of trial and error is necessary in exploring the system of cataloguing used for a particular archive. If you want to discover what kirk session records there are in the NAS for a particular parish, you can, for example, key in 'North Berwick ' and you will find that the class reference is CH2/285 and that there are records spanning the years 1608–1909 but that there are also some relevant records in the Biel muniments (GD6/1221–6). If you then enter CH2/285 a more detailed list will come up, showing that there are minutes, collections, a roll of male heads of families and other papers, while the GD6 references refer mainly to sixteenth-century records concerning the medieval hospital there.

The NAS online catalogue contains useful notes on each class of records held by them. Key in the class reference (see Appendix 4) and the catalogue of records under that class will come up on the screen. By clicking on the first entry, the notes will appear.

It is important to remember that though a great many catalogues of archives can be accessed online, archives may also have additional and valuable databases which can only be consulted in the archive concerned. If, therefore, you are visiting an archive, check what is available.

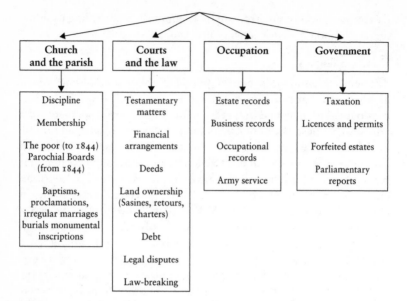

Figure 5   Route finding

Route finding

In 'Profiling the ancestors' the aim is to help you find your way. The challenge of choosing research routes will be viewed from three angles. The often asked questions 'Where do I go next?' and 'Can I go any further?' can be countered by finding the answers to three further queries about your ancestors:

Where did they live?
When did they live?
What did they do?

1. Where did they live?

There are two aspects of this question which need to be considered:

The 'habitat' of your ancestor has a bearing on occupation and on social conditions – for example, whether the district was rural or urban, highland or lowland. In genealogical research, social history is not an irrelevance but is an important constituent. Knowledge of the environment will help you to select sources which may be relevant to a particular family and throw light on their background.

It may also help to answer questions as to where, when and why a family moved and what they did and is linked with the consideration as to the period of time when they lived (see 'Timelines 1560–1900', pp. 149–54).

Records relating to individuals are made by the relationship of one person with another, with a group of people or with an authority – whether it is the local minister, landlord, employer or representative of government at local or national level. Knowledge of the administrative 'map' of any area is therefore important as it will provide an indication as to where references to a particular individual are likely to be found. Who was the landlord? What courts had jurisdiction there? Was the town a royal burgh? All such matters (among others) will influence a choice of what records are likely to be worth searching.

The locality

Maps

Maps are an essential part of family history research – whether you want to visit the places where your ancestors lived, identify old settlements now lost or study boundaries and the lie of the land. Some will say that they are as important as a family photograph or portrait – certainly they are a valuable adjunct and they enable you, literally, to put your ancestor on the map.

Many maps are held in local archives and libraries but the largest collection, covering the whole of Scotland, is held in the National Library of Scotland map library in Edinburgh. They date back to the sixteenth century, and include maps of counties and towns, as well as marine charts, road maps, canal and railway plans and military plans. A *Guide to the early maps of Scotland to 1850* has been published by the Royal Scottish Geographical Society in two volumes (the first volume covers maps of the whole of Scotland, the second deals with local and specialised maps or plans) and describes what there is and where copies can be viewed. Access (without charge) to many of these maps is now possible through the NLS website (www.nls.uk/maps). Searching on the website for maps of Perthshire, for example, brought up a list of thirty maps which could be viewed online, dating back to the end of the sixteenth century and coming forward to the Ordnance Survey maps of the late nineteenth century and a twentieth-century Bartholomew's atlas. There are also a number of other online sites for maps.

From the mid-nineteenth century onwards, work was carried out on a national mapping survey of Britain. A controversy over the scale to be used was resolved and by the end of the century a series of maps were issued on a scale of one inch to the mile, known in Scotland as the 'parish edition'. Ordnance Survey maps were also produced on a scale of six inches to the mile for the whole of Scotland, with the detailed twenty five inches to the mile scale maps being reserved for the more cultivated part of the country.

Accompanying the one-inch scale maps for much of central Scotland and the Borders, lowland areas of the Highlands and Perthshire, are books of reference which give acreages of parcels of land indicated on the maps and notes on land use. Unfortunately, Fife, Midlothian, East Lothian, Wigtownshire and Kirkcudbrightshire are not covered. The surveyors also compiled name books to accompany the two series of larger scale maps, arranged by county and then by parish, which give information on place names, spelling variants and descriptions of features and buildings. The name books can be consulted on microfilm at the NAS (reference RH4/23).

Ordnance Survey maps are now being produced on DVDs which provide a three-dimensional aerial view of particular districts, showing mountains, valleys, rivers and settlements, as well as a flat map of the area. This is an excellent and interesting way of looking at the geography of an area, and assessing routes of access.

Information given on maps – particularly the older ones – does need evaluation. What was the reason for drawing the map? Is it likely to be accurate or representational? How many places are shown? Is it based on an earlier survey or the result of a new one? These are all factors which will have a bearing on the interpretation of the map. The names of places included are usually selective. They may have been included because they fitted in the space available on the map, not because one place was more important than another. You will also find many variants in the spelling of place names. It was common for some cartographers to use an earlier survey as a base, adding a few variations. Drawings of towns were often representational rather than accurate but on the other hand, after detailed research, it has been concluded that Pont's individual representation of important buildings in parts of sixteenth-century Scotland is carefully and accurately depicted.

Plans

Disputes over boundaries, mapping of estates by landowners, plans for agricultural change, surveys for the building of roads, canals and railways have all resulted in plans. The National Archives of Scotland holds a very large collection of plans originating in collections of deposited papers and extracted from Court of Session processes, most dating to the period 1750–1850. These plans can be studied in the West search room of the NAS. The catalogue of all their plans is on the NAS electronic catalogue (search under the name of the parish in which lands were situated). There is also a card index in the NAS West search room (arranged by county and then by parish). Four volumes titled *Descriptive list of plans in the Scottish Record Office* (the older name for the NAS) – each arranged by county – have been published and can be consulted in various archives and libraries but these published lists do not include the whole of the archive's holdings. Plans will also be found in local libraries and archives and in many private collections.

Within the royal burghs, the authority responsible for looking after matters affecting buildings was the Dean of Guild. Many of the pre-1975 records have disappeared but *A Guide to Dean of Guild court records* has been compiled by Gray (1994) and he notes where surviving plans are held. Most of the records are not earlier than the nineteenth and twentieth centuries.

The Royal Commission on the Ancient and Historical Monuments of Scotland incorporating the National Monuments Record of Scotland holds information about listed archaeological sites, ancient monuments and historic buildings, including drawings, plans and photographs. Access to the database of their collections is through CANMORE at www.rcahms.gov.uk or you can see the collection at 16 Bernard Terrace, Edinburgh.

Photographic collections and postcards

Many local collections of photographs are now being digitised or put on CDs, as well as catalogued. Libraries also often hold old postcards and some have been published in book form. These are of great interest to family historians, showing houses which no longer exist, views of town and country in the past and portraits of local people. Local Studies Group (Scottish Branch) has published a guide to *Photographic collections in Scotland's local studies libraries* but their guide should be read in conjunction with Cox (1999) and online searches of holdings of local archives, libraries and universities will provide up-to-date information on what is available. Local libraries may also have scrapbooks of newspaper cuttings and other material.

Statistical Accounts

The two *Statistical Accounts* are important primary sources for local history. In 1790, Sir John Sinclair of Ulbster launched a project to produce an account of every parish in Scotland. He sent a list of 160 questions to every minister. Realising that he was setting his correspondents a big task, he ended by saying: 'It is not expected, that all the inclosed Queries should be answered by any individual; nor is minute exactness looked for.' This latitude has resulted in each account in the *First* or *Old Statistical Account* (published 1791–99 as each return was submitted) being a very personal one, reflecting the character, interests and sometimes bias of the minister concerned. Comments are found on wages, the morals of the local inhabitants, dress, agriculture, natural history and parish matters. In the 1980s the accounts were republished, then arranged by county. The *New Statistical Account* was compiled between 1834 and 1845 on the same lines as the previous one but each volume was concerned with the parishes in one county. Both *Statistical Accounts* can now be read online at http://edina.ac.uk/stat-acc-scot/. A *Third Statistical Account* of each county has been produced between 1951 and 1992 and the *Fourth Statistical Account of East Lothian* is now being published – the first project to bring the Statistical Accounts up to date.

Gazetteers and directories

The *Ordnance gazetteer of Scotland* edited by Francis H. Groome (1882–85) is widely available in libraries and contains a great deal of useful information. (Entries are online at http://www.visionofbritain. org.uk/descriptions/index.jsp). It identifies where places are and comments on their history and any particular features or points of interest. In the case of towns and cities, notes are included on churches (all denominations) and when they were built, as well as on schools and industries. County maps and some plans of large cities are included.

Many larger towns are covered by directories and almanacs, sometimes issued annually and some dating back to the early nineteenth century (see Torrance, 1998). Later directories were produced for smaller towns and country areas. Their arrangement and content vary but they usually contain lists of landowners, tradesmen, professional people and farmers, with their addresses. The additional material in the publications is also sometimes useful in giving an interesting insight into life at the time, throwing light on such matters as regulations for chimney sweeps, fares for hackney carriages and plans for school education, and the advertisements may throw light on the style of funerals, design of kitchen and bathroom equipment or the latest bicycles and tricycles. Some directories are now being issued on CD-ROM and local directories will usually be found in a library.

Local histories

Many histories of parishes have been published – some good, some less reliable. Consult the online catalogue of the National Library of Scotland to find out what has been printed on a particular place. The *Bibliography of Scotland* – a database of books, serials and major periodical articles mainly written after 1987 – is presently being put online. Mitchell and Cash (1917) and Hancock (1960) are out of date but list many useful older works. Most libraries have a good local section. Look for books which quote the sources, which can then lead you back to the primary sources – and do not believe all you read.

Newspapers

Every aspect of life is reflected in newspapers and work is currently being undertaken to microfilm and preserve old Scottish newspapers. The *Scotsman* digital archive was launched in 2004 and for a small fee you can read every edition of *The Scotsman* from its launch on 25 January 1817 onwards. Access to the index is free. The website is http://archive.scotsman.com. Work is already complete on editions up to 1900. *Directory of Scottish Newspapers* compiled by Joan P. S. Ferguson (1984) lists known Scottish newspapers, noting when they ceased to publish or amalgamated with other publications, and indicating where copies can be found.

The British Library Newspaper Library catalogue contains details of the national archive collection of British and overseas newspapers. Their main catalogue of British newspapers is now online at www.bl.uk/catalogues/newspapers and can be searched under a key word such as place name or title of the publication. *The Times* has been digitised from 1785 to 1985 but is only available to institutional users – though you may be able to access it through a subscribing library. Work is going ahead in indexing a number of local newspapers, and local libraries or family history societies will have information about such undertakings, and some hold microfilmed copies of local papers.

Parliamentary reports

The value of parliamentary papers has been highlighted by Haythornthwaite (1993) who comments on the 'buried treasure' in these reports. From the eighteenth century onwards, parliamentary commissioners have produced reports on a very wide range of subjects including, among others, on the poor, prostitution, religion, emigration, education, industry, housing and agriculture. The main 'treasure' in the reports is the evidence taken down from hundreds of ordinary people, as well as from professionals and landed members of society. *Hansard's catalogue and breviate of parliamentary papers 1696–1834* and *Select list of British parliamentary papers 1833–99*, both edited by P. and G. Ford, cover both English and Scottish material. A guide to Scottish material for the same period is provided by Haythornthwaite. Finding copies of parliamentary papers is not always easy but a number of larger libraries and university libraries hold copies and microform copies can also be consulted in some places.

Local government records

From the first half of the nineteenth century onwards there was a dramatic expansion in urban development which resulted in the formation of new administrative bodies to deal with health issues, law and order, sanitation or planning. Many of these duties were carried out by the old county councils (abolished in 1974). Moody (1986) gives a brief overall view of local government functions 1832–1975 and this may lead you to some of the records (many of which are still in the hands of district councils). A selection of records taken from public health papers, town council minutes, parochial board minutes, police records and other bodies has been selected by Levitt and published by the Scottish History Society (Levitt, 1988). This illustrates the wealth of information which can be found on social conditions in the nineteenth century and later.

The administrative 'map'

In making up your menu of sources to search for information on an ancestor, you need to have some idea of the administrative functions of various authorities – at parish, county or national level – so that you can assess whether it is likely that their records might have had a bearing on the lives of your forebears.

There are various practical matters to be considered in making your choice – the bulk of the records, availability of indexes or other searching aids, any likely difficulties in understanding or reading the documents (Latin, Old Scots or difficult handwriting, for example) and above all, what sort of information you may hope to gain from studying them. Where the records are kept may influence your decisions as to what should be studied. Are they held locally, or can you study copies in a family history library or archive, for example? Can you visit the archive yourself or will it be worth employing a professional to do some work for you? Only after making such assessments can you develop a strategy in approaching the vast range of material which is listed in online or paper repertories and catalogues.

Further references will be made to these authorities and the records which result from their administrative duties when discussing sources which are applicable to people of various occupations or classes of society (see 'What did they do?', pp. 154–201).

The parish

The parish as a unit of ecclesiastical administration goes back to medieval times and by the beginning of the fourteenth century it seems that the whole of Scotland was divided into parishes. The parish boundaries were fixed but in some places the parish included some areas of land which were separated from the main part. This persisted in some places till 1892. Over time, boundaries – and names – of parishes changed. Some large parishes were split, while in other places two old parishes were joined in one. Glenorchy and Innishail in Argyllshire were originally two separate parishes but joined in 1618, were disjoined in 1650 and reunited again at the time of the Restoration. By the second half of the nineteenth century, Scotland was divided into 887 parishes.

In some large parishes, missions or preaching houses were built to administer to the people in outlying parts and a few kept their own records of baptism and marriage. The huge Argyllshire parish of Ardnamurchan which included Acharacle (sometimes spelled Aharacle), Sunart and Kintra, was probably divided in earlier times into three parishes – Kilchoan, Island Finan and Kilaria. After these had been joined into one parish, Aharacle, Ardnamurchan and Sunart continued to keep their own registers and there was a mission at Kintra which also had records. The larger cities – such as Edinburgh, Glasgow, Dundee and Aberdeen – had a considerable number of churches but Edinburgh was divided into just three parishes for the purpose of keeping parish registers – Edinburgh, St Cuthberts and Canongate – while Glasgow was made up of the parishes of Glasgow, Gorbals, Barony and Govan.

As the population grew and the size of towns increased, more churches were needed to serve the people. A number of Chapels of Ease were built and parliamentary acts of 1823 and 1824 provided for the building of new churches and manses in the Highlands. In some urban areas in the nineteenth century, ministers were appointed to serve in new churches within existing parishes, known as *quoad sacra* parishes. No registers of baptism, marriage or burial were kept for these congregations, the registers still being the preserve of the original parish.

Location of church records

Unlike the old parish registers of baptism, marriage and burial which, under the Registration Act of 1854, were deposited in the keeping of the Registrar General in Edinburgh, there was no such legal directive regarding other church records. The NAS hold many kirk session records as well as presbytery, synod and general assembly records. It also has microfilm copies of some (but not all) collections which are in local archives. Some church records still remain in private hands. All kirk session records are being digitised and it will be possible to search them (without charge online) in the NAS search rooms and also on the ScotlandsPeople website (some charge may then be involved). The huge task of indexing these records is also in hand but browsing through these records is possible and always rewarding.

Details of the NAS holdings are now included in their online catalogue and can be accessed by keying in CH2 and the name of the parish or just the name of the parish followed by 'kirk session' as the search request. You will then have to key in the number given to the CH2 collection to read a detailed description of what is there. Presbytery and synod records also come under CH2 but each collection has a separate number. The online entry gives a brief description – minutes, communion rolls etc. – and includes beginning and end dates of runs of records. There are also some informative notes about the church or presbytery and the availability of further searching aids in the NAS.

As more catalogues of archives and libraries in Scotland come online, it will become possible to carry out much wider searches. The National Register of Archives provides information on records in archives and other repositories throughout Britain and on collections which have been catalogued but are still in private hands.

Content of church records

Till about the middle of the nineteenth century, the Church played an important role in local life – both socially and morally. Knox in his *Book of Discipline* emphasised that the kirk was there to reprove and correct 'those faults which the civil sword doth either neglect either may not punish'. These included drunkenness, excess, fornication, licentious living and slander. There was, in fact, a close co-operation between the civil authorities (through the courts) and the Church, particularly in earlier times. The other matters in which the kirk session had responsibilities were education and the care of the poor. Whether episcopacy or presbyterianism was in the ascendancy, the influence of the Church and its authority changed little in relation to the parishioners. It was only from the mid-eighteenth century onwards that the role of the kirk became of less importance. The drift of population to urban areas and the growing number of adherents of dissenting congregations weakened the hold of the kirk, while the Poor Law Act of 1845 transferred the kirk's responsibilities for care of the poor to parochial councils.

Records surviving for each parish vary enormously in content and period covered. They may include minutes (including disciplinary cases for fornication, adultery, breaking of the Sabbath and many other matters), accounts, records of the poor, testimonials, communion rolls and other listings. Some kirk session minutes go back to the time of the Reformation (St Andrews kirk session minutes commence in 1559), many are very incomplete and some have been lost. They are a source of great interest in providing information on individuals, both in putting 'flesh on the bones' and in giving genealogical information. Their value is that they deal with the whole community and particularly with the 'ordinary' people – labourers, tenants and cottars. Your ancestor may appear accused of some misdemeanour or perhaps as an elder or witness, whose age, occupation and perhaps relationship to the accused may be given. (See also 'What did they do?', pp. 154–201 for their relevance to certain classes of person.)

Presbytery and synod

The presbytery, whose members were the ministers of a group of parishes and an elder representing each parish, acted as the higher ecclesiastical court. The presbytery's remit was to make parish visitations, look after schools, churches and manses, and deal with the supply of ministers. It heard cases which had been referred from the kirk session (the referral will be minuted in the kirk session minutes), usually those regarded as more serious, such as frequent moral lapses, or witchcraft. Cases of incest – due to the strict laws of consanguinity these were not uncommon – also came before them. Some selections of presbytery records have been published (see Stevenson, 1987 for those which have been published in serial publications).

The third church court, the synod, was attended by the ministers and representative elders of the presbyteries forming it and heard cases referred from the presbytery. Being more remote from the parish, the records of this court are rarely of prime importance in family history research.

The General Assembly

The General Assembly, an assembly of ministers and representative elders, acted as the highest church court and its legislative arm. The papers of the General Assembly (class reference CH1/2) contain some most interesting – and commonly overlooked – material. Disputed vacancies resulted in lists of heads of families in the parish and there were hearings concerning the misdeeds of ministers and of their parishioners – excommunications, irregular marriages, petitions by parishioners and grievances against a minister. The appointment of missionaries in remote areas and listings of Roman Catholics in various parts of Scotland in the early part of the eighteenth century are also there.

The General Assembly papers are not indexed but there is a detailed annual list of cases in the NAS which is easy to search if you know the approximate year in which the event happened. It can also be searched online.

Dissenting churches

Congregations such as the Associate Session, Relief Church and Free Church were also organised in sessions, presbyteries and synods. The records kept by these congregations are usually less varied than those of the Established Church of Scotland but for many there are surviving session minutes, lists of members, communion rolls and seat rents, as well as some baptismal, marriage and burial records. The fact that many dissenting church congregations have joined with others often makes it difficult to trace in whose hands the records remained. Many are in the NAS, others in local archives or still with the churches concerned.

A search of the NRA catalogue can sometimes be rewarding. On searching under 'Organisations', you can then look for records of a particular religious denomination. On selecting the category 'Nonconformist and other churches', and the sub-category 'Scottish secession churches', a list of twenty four holdings comes up. Clicking on the entry produces a more detailed description. An entry for St Andrew's Erskine kirk session, Dunfermline shows that there are minutes, accounts, lists of baptisms, communicants' roll books, miscellaneous correspondence, and architectural plans and drawings covering the period 1745–1974. This holding is in private hands and permission to search it will have to be gained through application to the NRA.

For notes on episcopalians and Roman Catholics, see 'From birth to death', pp. 71–2.

Heritors

The heritors were the proprietors in the parish who, up to 1925, were responsible for contributing financially to the upkeep of church, manse, school and, before 1845, for the care of the poor. Tenants were not heritors. In the burghs, the magistrates acted as the heritors. They worked closely with the kirk session and up to 1845 heard claims by the poor and distressed for assistance. Heritors' records may sometimes include lists of tenants on their lands who were assessed for contribution to poor relief funds. The heritors of each parish are usually named in the *First* and *Second Statistical Accounts*.

Few heritors' records are extant before the eighteenth century. Some are held in the NAS – class reference HR – and indexed under the parish name. The NAS repertory also refers to heritors' records held elsewhere, such as among the papers of a local landowner or with the kirk session records. Some heritors' records are in local archives.

The royal burghs

From the time of David I (1124–53) onwards, some towns (often very small communities) were erected into burghs. Under their charters of erection, they had administrative rights and trading privileges within their boundaries. Those who held charters from the Crown became royal burghs. Burghs of regality had rights which were similar to those of royal burghs. There were also burghs of barony, whose charters were granted not by the Crown but by subject superiors (see 'Understanding legal documents – Land ownership' p. 208) and they had fewer privileges. Some burghs of barony were later erected into royal burghs. Pryde (1965) gives a list of all burghs with the dates of their erection. No new royal burghs were created after 1707, at which time they numbered sixty six, but in 1833 the Parliamentary Burghs (Scotland) Act created police burghs which had full rights of local government.

Records of the royal burghs

Royal burghs had various duties and privileges. Through their courts they administered both civil and criminal justice. They elected their own town councils (whose actions were recorded in town council minutes), they had a monopoly in overseas trade, could collect taxes, create burgesses, have craft guilds and send representatives to Parliament. They kept registers of sasines for property within their precincts and the courts were competent to register deeds.

There are large holdings of records of royal burghs in the NAS, but for many burghs the collections are split, with some in the NAS and others in the relevant local authority archives, in university collections (St Andrews University archives hold many of the Fife burgh records) or in libraries. SCAN (www.scan.org.uk) provides connecting links to online catalogues of most of these archive collections but you should also search the NRA. Many extracts from burgh records have been printed (see Stevenson, 1987).

The following is a list of the royal burghs for which there are some records in the NAS, with the relevant NAS class reference number:

List of the royal burghs

Aberdeen (B1)	Edinburgh (B22)	Maybole (B50)
Annan (B2)	Elgin (B23)	Montrose (B51)
Anstruther Wester	Falkland (B25)	Musselburgh (B52)
(B3)	Forfar (B26)	Nairn (B53)
Arbroath (B4)	Forres (B27)	Newburgh (B54)
Auchtermuchty (B5)	Fortrose (B28)	New Galloway
Ayr (B6)	Glasgow (B29)	(B55)
Banff (B7)	Haddington (B30)	North Berwick
Brechin (B8)	Hawick (B31)	(B56)
Burntisland (B9)	Inveraray (B32)	Paisley (B57)
Campbeltown	Inverbervie (B33)	Peebles (B58)
(B82, see below)	Inverkeithing (B34)	Perth (B59)
Cockenzie and	Inverness (B35)	Pittenweem (B60)
Port Seton (B74)	Inverurie (B36)	Prestonpans (B76)
Crail (B10)	Irvine (B37)	Queensferry (B61)
Cullen (B11)	Jedburgh (B38)	Renfrew (B62)
Culross (B12)	Kinghorn (B39)	Rothesay (B63)
Cupar (B13)	Kintore (B40)	Rutherglen (B64)
Dingwall (B14)	Kirkcaldy (B41)	St Andrews (B65)
Dornoch (B15)	Kirkcudbright (B42)	Sanquhar (B67)
Dumbarton (B16)	Kirkintilloch (B43)	Selkirk (B68)
Dumfries (B17)	Kirkwall (B44)	Stirling (B66)
Dunbar (B18)	Lanark (B45)	Stranraer (B69)
Dundee (B19)	Lauder (B46)	Tain (B70)
Dunfermline (B20)	Leith (B47)	Whithorn (B71)
Dysart (B21)	Linlithgow (B48)	Wick (B73)
Earlsferry (B24)	Lochmaben (B49)	Wigtown (B72)

Campbeltown burgh court processes for the years 1754–74 and deeds for the years 1765–68 have recently been found among the sheriff court processes and are indexed and catalogued in the sheriff court papers of Inveraray – SC54. The town council minutes are in the Argyll and Bute archives.

The sheriffdoms

The office of sheriff dates back to the reign of David I (1124–53) when sheriffs were given administrative and military duties, acting as the representatives of the king within designated parts of the kingdom. They had wide administrative remits and judicial powers, both civil and criminal. At an early date in many places the office of sheriff became heritable – this was abolished in 1747 under the Heritable Jurisdictions Act. After that time, sheriff deputes (qualified lawyers) were appointed, with sheriff substitutes and clerks under them. After 1823, the sheriff courts took over the responsibilities of the commissary courts and of the admiralty court (after 1830).

Up to 1974, Scotland was divided into counties. Until the nineteenth century, the term 'sheriffdom' was in many areas almost the same as 'county', though the boundaries of sheriffdoms varied a little from time to time and after 1853 there were some further boundary changes. In some parts of the country (such as Lanarkshire) there was more than one sheriff court within a county, though in most cases only one of the courts would deal with commissary business or keep a register of deeds.

It is sometimes confusing that the sheriff court is sometimes referred to by the town in which it was held and sometimes by the county – Duns sheriff court in Berwickshire, for example. Some counties used to be referred to by the name of the county town – Forfarshire for Angus, Haddingtonshire for East Lothian, Edinburghshire for Midlothian, Elginshire for Morayshire and Linlithgowshire for West Lothian.

Sheriff courts

The following table shows the sheriff courts within each county and where each was held, with the 'main' court in each county in bold. The last two columns indicate which courts dealt with post-1820s commissary business and show the courts which kept registers of deeds. These vary considerably in dates covered. With the exception of the sheriff court records for Orkney and Shetland which are kept in the Orkney and Shetland archives, these records are all housed in the National Archives of Scotland.

County	Sheriff Court	NAS ref.	Commissary business (post 1820s)	Deeds
Aberdeen	Aberdeen	SC1	Yes	Yes
	Peterhead	SC4		
Angus	See Forfarshire			
Argyll*	Dunoon	SC51	Yes	Yes
	Tobermory	SC59		
	Inveraray	SC54		Warrants
	Campbeltown	SC50		
	Fort William	SC52	See Inverness-shire	
	Oban	SC57		
Ayr	Ayr	SC6	Yes	Yes
	Kilmarnock	SC7		
Banff	Banff	SC2	Yes	Yes
Berwick	Duns	SC60	Yes	Yes
Bute	Rothesay	SC8	Yes	Yes
Caithness	Wick	SC14	Yes	Yes
Clackmannan	Alloa	SC64	Yes	Yes
Dumfries	Dumfries	SC15	Yes	Yes
Dunbarton	Dumbarton	SC65	Yes	Yes
East Lothian	See Haddington			
Edinburgh	Edinburgh	SC39	Yes	Yes
	Leith	SC69		
Fife	Cupar	SC20	Yes	Yes
	Kirkcaldy	SC23		
	Dunfermline	SC21		
Forfarshire	Forfar	SC47	Yes	Yes
	Dundee	SC45	From 1832	
	Arbroath	SC43	From 1975	
Haddington	Haddington	SC40	From 1830: earlier Edinburgh	Yes
Inverness	Inverness	SC29	Yes	Yes
	Fort William	SC28		
	Portree	SC32		
	Lochmaddy	SC30		
Kincardine	Stonehaven	SC5	Yes	Yes
Kinross	Kinross	SC22	From 1847	Yes
	Alloa	SC64	To 1847	Yes
Kirkcudbright	Kirkcudbright	SC16	Yes	Yes
	Dumfries	SC17		

County	Sheriff Court	NAS ref.	Commissary business (post 1820s)	Deeds
Lanark**	Hamilton	SC37	Yes	Yes
	Lanark	SC38	See Glasgow	Yes
	Glasgow	SC36	Yes	Yes
	Airdrie	SC35		
Linlithgowshire	Linlithgow	SC41	From 1830	Yes
Midlothian	See Edinburgh			
Moray	Elgin	SC26	Yes	Yes
Nairn	Nairn	SC31	Elgin to 1838: Nairn from 1839	Yes
Orkney	Kirkwall	SC11	Yes	Yes
Peebles	Peebles	SC42	Yes	Yes
Perth	Perth	SC49	Yes	Yes
	Dunblane	SC44	Yes	Yes
Renfrew	Paisley	SC58	Yes	Yes
	Greenock	SC53		Yes
Ross and Cromarty	Tain	SC34		Yes
	Cromarty	SC24		Yes
	Dingwall	SC25	Yes	Yes
	Stornoway	SC33	To 1850	
Roxburgh	Jedburgh	SC62	Yes	Yes
	Hawick	SC61		
Selkirk	Selkirk	SC63	Yes	Yes
Shetland	Lerwick	SC12	Yes	Yes
Stirling	Stirling	SC67	Yes	Yes
	Falkirk	SC66		
Sutherland	Dornoch	SC9	Yes	Yes
West Lothian	See Linlithgowshire			
Wigtown	Wigtown	SC19	Yes	Yes
	Stranraer	SC18		

*Inveraray was formerly regarded as the town in which the principal sheriff court sat but this was later changed to Dunoon. In looking for Argyllshire records, the repertory of Inveraray sheriff court should always be checked, as well as that for Dunoon.
**Lanarkshire is divided into three wards – Upper (Lanark), Middle (Hamilton) and Lower (Glasgow). See also Glasgow Sheriff Court.

Records of the sheriff courts

Studying the repertory of a sheriff court can be daunting. If you are searching the NAS website, key in SC, followed by the number of the sheriff court in which you are interested and you will get up the 'menu' for that sheriff court – which is the same as that given in the paper catalogues available in the NAS historical search rooms. The repertories of the sheriff courts in the NAS contain user-friendly explanations of the content of each section of the records and these are also accessible online. The arrangement of each sheriff court catalogue is not standardised and the headings for the various classes of record may vary but the sections you are most likely to find are:

Ordinary court including civil actions, processes, sequestrations for debt and improvements to entailed estates

Workmen's compensation

Small debt court

Debt recovery court

Commissary business including testamentary deeds, register of confirmations, inventories, wills and edicts of executry (after *circa* 1823)

Criminal court – roll books, minutes, processes and productions

Juvenile court (twentieth century)

Register of deeds and protests (there may also be warrants, the original documents later copied in to the register)

Services of heirs

Diligence records – actions at the instance of creditors

Other sheriff court business – freeholders' minute books, electoral matters, public utilities such as harbours and turnpike roads and licensing

Commissioners of supply (these are sometimes held in the local archives)

Miscellaneous

The sections most likely to be worth consulting are the commissary records, registers of deeds and protests, services of heirs and, in certain circumstances, court records. The 'miscellaneous' section of sheriff courts often contains a fascinating and very varied collection of papers. In Ayr sheriff court they include poor law applications, in Inveraray papers for McEachern of Tangie, in Forfar militia papers 1799–1823, in Banff trust records of James Longmore, merchant and shipowner. Once the complete catalogues of the NAS are online, it will be possible to find these papers by keying in a subject, place or personal name.

Justices of the Peace

Justices of the Peace were introduced into Scotland by James VI under an Act of 1587 but many of the surviving JP records start later and are often rather fragmentary, if they have survived at all. They persisted till 1975 but with limited powers. Under an Act of 1609, the appointment of the justices was by the king but from 1707 onwards this was made by the Lord Chancellor, and later by the Secretary of State for Scotland. Their jurisdiction was both criminal and civil and their remit covered local breaches of the peace, maintenance of roads and bridges, settlement of wages, small debt, illicit distilling, licensing, recruitment for the army and militia, vagrancy and payment of duties.

Guide to the National Archives of Scotland (SRO, 1996) includes a list of most of the known JP records and where they are kept – some in the National Archives of Scotland, others in local archives. Malcolm (1931) gives a useful introduction to the work of the JPs in his edition of the minutes of the JP records for Lanarkshire 1707–23, while the flavour of JP court records can be sampled by studying the catalogue of processes of JP courts in Argyll 1723–1825 compiled by Bigwood (2001d). As in the kirk session records and town council minutes, the JP records provide a picture of life in local communities, as well as naming many local inhabitants.

Commissioners of Supply

Within each county, Commissioners of Supply, who were owners of property above a certain value, were first appointed in 1667 to collect cess – a land tax. Later they were also employed to draw up valuations of land and their duties were extended to include oversight of highways, bridges, ferries and harbours. They also had responsibilities for supervising the police forces and seeing that militia quotas were met. In 1889 their duties were passed to the elected county councils.

Generally these records will be found amongst the old county council records, most of which are now in local archives or district council offices but a few are still in the NAS. Not all records for a particular county are in the same place.

Lieutenancy

The formation of a permanent lieutenancy, headed largely by the influential landowners, was instituted as a means of raising a militia and also volunteers to fight in defence of the country in the eighteenth century. Each county had a lord lieutenant who was appointed by the Crown, with several deputies whose duty it was to direct and organise these units.

Some lieutenancy records are with the sheriff court records, others can be found with burgh records, in the muniments of the landowners or elsewhere. By searching the NAS online catalogue under 'lieutenancy', you will see a list of records relating to this office such as minute books, correspondence and other matters.

Franchise courts

Under the feudal system, the Crown, at various times, granted heritable rights of jurisdiction in designated lands to certain vassals – usually the important landowners – to encourage the enforcement of law and order. A regality had a similar jurisdiction to that of the Crown, only the crime of treason being excluded from its criminal jurisdiction. Stewartries and bailieries were royal lands administered by an appointed or hereditary steward or bailie, and within their bounds (set out under a Crown charter) the sheriff had no jurisdiction. The barony court was a lesser court, mainly concerned with the keeping of 'good neighbourhood', having civil jurisdiction for petty debt and minor crimes and criminal jurisdiction for theft and murder if the criminal was caught red-handed. Appeals from this court were to the regality court or sheriff court. Under the Heritable Jurisdictions Act of 1747, regalities, stewartries and bailieries were abolished. Only the baronies continued, with diminished responsibilities.

It is not always easy to determine where the lands of these franchise courts were situated. The index to places in the published *Registers of the Great Seal* (1314–1668) is a good place to start such research as you may find a crown charter granting the franchise, and defining the boundaries. Groome's *Ordnance gazetteer of Scotland* is sometimes helpful.

The records which have survived for the franchise courts are fragmentary. *Guide to the National Archives of Scotland* (SRO, 1996) provides a list of the records held in the NAS, some being listed with the sheriff court records, others as part of family papers (GD) or in a class of miscellaneous records (RH11). Searching the NAS electronic catalogue under RH11 will only bring up references to some franchise court records but does not list those which are kept with sheriff court papers or form part of family muniments. Collections of papers held in local archives or privately may also include some of these records – check the NRA catalogue.

Several court books have been published by the Scottish History Society (SHS), while the Stair Society has produced *Court Book of the barony and regality of Falkirk and Callendar* (1991), all of which have good introductions. Records include court books, rentals or rolls of vassals and, with the exception of the baronies, the franchise courts were competent to register deeds and protests. There may be diligence records (actions for debt) and the records for the regalities of Dunfermline and Dunkeld include some services of heirs. Franchise court records are not indexed (unless published) and may be difficult to read but they may contain valuable material for both family and local history.

Admiralty courts

Criminal and civil jurisdiction in maritime cases was the concern of the admiralty courts. Under the Act of Union of 1707 all admiralty jurisdictions belonged to the Lord High Admiral of Great Britain, who appointed a vice-admiral for Scotland. Before 1707, there was a Lord High Admiral for Scotland appointed by the Crown. In 1830 admiralty court civil jurisdiction was transferred to the Court of Session. There were also some inferior admiralty jurisdictions – Argyll and the Isles, Caithness, East Fife, Kirkcudbright, St Andrews, and Logan and Clanyard, Wigtownshire but few records survive. The admiralty court catalogue in the NAS (class reference AC) lists what is extant.

Cases heard in the admiralty courts concerned freights, salvage, wrecks, collisions and war-time prizes. Criminal jurisdiction covered cases of mutiny, piracy and other offences at sea. The most useful records of the courts are the decreets and processes. In the NAS West search room there are chronological lists of cases giving names of pursuer and defender. There is also an indexed catalogue of processes, bonds of caution and deeds registered in the Vice-Admiral Court of Argyll for the years 1685–1925 (Bigwood, 2001e).

Commissary courts

Before the Reformation, the Scottish bishops exercised a wide jurisdiction through the commissary courts. They were responsible for appointing executors, confirming testaments, dealing with cases of divorce, legitimacy, marriage and desertion, and also for actions for slander and any matters concerning contracts made under oath. These courts were abolished in 1560 but reconstituted as civil courts in 1563, dealing with much the same matters as before. Their business was transferred to the sheriff courts by an Act of 1823.

The head court was in Edinburgh and it had responsibilities for the whole of Scotland in such matters as dissolution of marriage, legitimacy and confirmation of testaments of those dying outside the country but leaving moveable property in Scotland. It also acted as the local court for most of Midlothian, East Lothian and West Lothian (see Appendix 1) and anyone had the option to register a testament in this commissary court, rather than in their local court.

The jurisdiction of the local commissary courts was not based on sheriffdoms but on the bounds of the old episcopal dioceses. This has resulted in some apparently strange results as the pre-Reformation bishops sometimes owned property which was scattered. Thus, the parish of Aberlady in East Lothian was under the jurisdiction of Dunblane commissary court. During the Commonwealth and Protectorate periods only, the bounds of the inferior commissary courts were changed to concur with the limits of the sheriffdoms but at all times there was sometimes a rather grey area on the edges of the commissariots. Fortunately, as all registers of testaments are now indexed online on the ScotlandsPeople website, this is less of a problem. Appeals from local commissary courts might be heard by the head court and later by the Court of Session.

Only the registers of testaments have been indexed online. Other records include edicts, petitions, inventories, processes and deeds (see 'From birth to death – Other records of the commissary court', pp. 108–11). There is a manuscript index covering at least some of these other records in each commissary court. These can only be consulted in the NAS.

National administration

With very few exceptions, the records which come under this section are in the National Archives of Scotland in Edinburgh. The range and bulk of material which has resulted from national administration is enormous but there are many records which involve the 'ordinary' inhabitants of the country – through taxation, regulation of trade, civil and criminal jurisdiction and other matters. The classes of records listed below are only some of those of value to the family historian.

The Privy Council

The Privy Council probably dates back to the thirteenth century but it was not till 1489 that its functions were defined by statute, when it was declared that the Council was 'for the ostensioun and forthputting of the King's autorite in the administracioun of justice'. It was abolished in May 1708. The Council also came to exercise legislative, administrative and executive functions, though at various times the duties varied.

The records are voluminous but abstracts of the *Register of the Privy Council of Scotland* have been published (and indexed) for the years

1545–1691 and these volumes are a source of much interesting information. References are made to a wide range of matters such as the
control of plague, the regulation of trade, cases of counterfeiting coin,
Catholic disaffection, lists of Covenanters and the taking of oaths of
loyalty to the House of Hanover after 1689. Many cases are quoted
relating to ordinary people. The printed volumes can be found in many
archives and larger Scottish libraries and elsewhere round the world.

The Court of Session

The Court of Session is the highest civil court in Scotland. It keeps a
register of deeds known as the Books of Council and Session, and as
a civil court hears appeals from the lower courts, as well as dealing
with cases which had their first hearing there. (See 'Understanding
legal documents – Registers of deeds', p. 202 and 'Civil jurisdiction:
the Court of Session', p. 223).

High Court of Justiciary

It is often not easy to determine in what court a criminal case might
have been heard but those who committed serious crimes were likely
to be tried in the High Court of Justiciary, the supreme criminal court
in Scotland. This includes cases where the accused was later transported. (See 'What did they do?', pp. 197–8.) When sitting in
Edinburgh, it heard cases from the Edinburgh area and some from
elsewhere, but it also went on circuit. (For a fuller description of the
workings and records of the High Court of Justiciary, see 'Understanding legal documents – Criminal cases: the High Court of
Justiciary', p. 221.)

Chancery

Chancery is the department responsible for dealing with official acts
done in the king's name including the issuing of Crown charters
(under the Great Seal), brieves to courts to hold inquests concerning
retours, services of heirs (see 'Understanding legal documents'
p. 211), gifts of offices, patents, and remissions.

Exchequer

Records for the work of the Exchequer (listed in the NAS as class E)
cover a wide and complex range of subjects concerned with the
country's finances – taxes, trade, accounts, receipts and revenues.
Some of the early financial records for Scotland have been published
by the HMSO – *The Exchequer rolls of Scotland 1264–1600* and
Accounts of the Lord High Treasurer of Scotland 1473–1566. The

Exchequer rolls can be a useful source of information about owners of property, as on the death of a vassal of the Crown, the new heir had to pay a certain amount for 'entry' to his lands, the payment being accounted for in the rolls. The *Accounts* deal with such matters as upkeep of royal palaces but contain references to various persons who worked for the Crown.

Valuation rolls

Valuation rolls (E106) are arranged by county, compiled at various dates between 1643 and 1835, and provide differing amounts of information. Sometimes the rolls name only the larger landowners but, in a few cases, give the names of principal tenants. *A directory of landownership in Scotland c. 1770* (Timperley, 1976) is based on the valuation rolls for 1771 but it is important to remember that ownership of land was constantly changing and the 1771 valuation only presents a picture of ownership at a particular point in time.

Muster rolls

The class reference number is E100. These records refer to soldiers before 1707, mostly concerning the period *circa* 1680. They are arranged by regiment but are unindexed and unless you know the name of a regiment in which your ancestor was serving, you are unlikely to find him. There are also later records for payments to the families of militia men during the Napoleonic Wars (see under 'What did they do?', pp. 194–6).

Forfeited estate papers

The estates forfeited by those who took part in the two Jacobite rebellions of 1715 and 1745 were administered for some years by Commissioners of the Annexed Estates, appointed by the Crown. The documents concerned with the management of the estates annexed after the 1745 rebellion are a particularly valuable source of information about the lands and their occupants and a number of projects were undertaken in improving the estates and developing their industry and agriculture. The papers include rentals, reports, claims, correspondence and other matters. The NAS class references are E601-63 for the 1715 uprising and E700-88 for the 1745 rebellion. (See also 'What did they do?', pp. 167–8).

Hearth tax 1691

In 1690 Parliament levied a tax on every hearth in Scotland payable by all landowners and tenants in 1691. The returns were handed in by the collectors between 1691 and 1695. Some persons were exempt through poverty, a considerable number did not pay, many returns being registered as 'deficient', and often the heritor collecting the tax from his tenants returned a lump sum without including names of individuals. Even when listed by name, it is not always easy to be sure of the identity of the taxpayer as the only details given concern the name of the person and their place of residence. Adamson (1981) has published the returns for West Lothian and includes an abstract of hearth tax collections made in other counties, including comments on the nature of the records (names of individuals or not, names of places and likely accuracy of the returns). Most of the returns are in the NAS (E69), but a few are in family estate records. The whereabouts of the records – in the NAS or elsewhere – is noted by Adamson.

Poll tax 1694–99

In 1693 the Scottish Parliament needed money to pay the army and navy and in 1694 a poll tax of six shillings, followed by another the following year, was levied on all persons except the poor subsisting on charity and children under sixteen if they lived in households where the total tax did not exceed 30 shillings. A higher tax was paid by some persons such as merchants, well-off tenants, proprietors and professional people. By no means all the returns have survived. Some are in the NAS, mostly with the Exchequer records (class reference E70) but a few are among the burgh records, sheriff court records or in family muniments.

To find what poll tax returns are held in the NAS, search their online catalogue under E70. This list includes most of the surviving returns, as well as records related to the collection of the tax. Keying into the search field 'poll tax' will bring up a few additional records among the burgh records but then, by searching the catalogue under 'pollable persons', a number of further returns are listed which are part of burgh records, with the sheriff court records or part of collections of family papers. This is an illustration of the complexities of searching online catalogues to locate all the records you require.

The information given in the poll tax returns varies from place to place. Steel (1970) provides a useful guide to the nature of the return – those that include the name of the head of household's wife, names of children, occupations, location of houses or whether the return gives very few names or is imperfect.

Eighteenth-century taxes

As a result of the need for finance for the army and navy between 1747 and the first half of the nineteenth century, taxes were levied on a wide range of commodities, sometimes on assessments made over a series of years, sometimes only once. The taxes levied were: window tax 1748–98 (E326/1); inhabited houses tax 1778–98 (E326/3); shop tax 1785–89 (E326/4); male servants' tax 1777–98 (E326/5); female servants' tax 1785–89 (E326/6); cart tax 1785–92 (E326/7); carriage tax 1785–98 (E326/8); horse tax 1785–98 (E326/9); farm horse tax 1797–98 (E326/10); dog tax 1797–98(E326/11); clock and watch tax 1797–98 (E326/12); aid and contribution tax 1797–98 (E326/13); income tax 1801–2 – incomplete (E326/14); consolidated tax 1798–99 – only a few counties are covered (E326/15).

There is a useful introduction to the whole group of taxes listed on the NAS electronic catalogue. Key in E326 and click on the first entry. If you then want an introduction to a particular set of records – window tax for example – key in E326 followed by the number given to that set (in that case 1) and click on the first entry on the list. Many of these tax returns are not informative, either because people claimed that the tax was not applicable to them or because the information given throws little light on the person or household concerned. The most valuable returns are the farm horse tax and the consolidated tax.

Trade

The Exchequer was responsible for collecting customs due at the various Scottish ports on goods imported or exported. Some of these records go back to the fourteenth century but many are incomplete. From 1498 to 1707 there are incomplete customs accounts (E71–E74) but the most useful are the collectors' quarterly customs accounts (E504) for the years 1742–1830. These are arranged by port (small ports came under the administration of the main ports, being known as creeks) and document every ship entering or leaving Scottish ports carrying dutiable cargo either coastwise or overseas.

Some industries (such as linen or fishing) were offered encouragement by the government and bounties were paid under certain conditions. The most interesting records for the family historian are those relating to the buss fishing (herring fishing carried out on decked vessels of a certain size) 1752–96 and for whale fishing 1750–1825 (E508). The 'customs cash vouchers' as they are officially known, give details of the ships, their equipment, catch and names of the crew (see 'What did they do?', p. 196).

Customs and Excise

The Board of Customs and Excise was responsible for administration at the ports in taking action against smuggling, dealing with wrecks and supervision of trading activities (NAS class reference CE51–CE87). Outport records in the form of letter books have survived for many ports, covering much of the eighteenth century and for some places going on into the nineteenth century. These letters are in two series – from the central board to the collector of each port and from the collector to the board – the latter being the most interesting. The letter books mention many local persons (including smugglers), include personal details of the members of the revenue service and provide a detailed and graphic picture of certain aspects of life round Scotland's coasts. Some of the records are held in the NAS but others are kept locally. (See also 'What did they do?', p. 185.)

2. When did they live?

Most family historians are interested in more than the bare bones of genealogy and want not only to find out who their ancestors were but to discover how they lived. This involves exploration of social and economic history and sources have been noted throughout the book which may be valuable in this context.

It is, however, important to stand back and look at the wider picture. What was going on in the country as a whole? Was it a time of peace or war? What were the trends – social and economic? Agricultural improvements or industrial advances are the catalysts for change and for movements of population, which include emigration. And within a certain period, were there any particular happenings which might have had a bearing on the lives of ordinary persons in the short or long term? War, civil unrest, religious movements, inventions, plague and crop failure have far-reaching effects on the lives of individuals.

An examination of this background is important on two counts, which often interact:

Events create records of varying kinds involving people and also may have repercussions which result in economic change.

Economic trends may provide clues as to why people moved, changed jobs, went up or down in the world or emigrated, and this knowledge can be of assistance in retracing the steps of earlier generations.

The subject is a huge and interesting one and the intention here is only to arouse an awareness of the need to look beyond the immediate milieu of your family circle to what was going on in the outside world.

Events

War is the prime example of an event which affects the lives of those involved in it but which also spreads ripples through the economic ponds thereafter. Many battles are well documented and lists have been compiled of combatants and casualties. Those who served in the militia often travelled away from their home areas and sometimes found wives in the places where they were stationed. Some who served abroad – such as in the Seven Years War or American War of Independence – settled there and never returned to Scotland. For those who fought on the 'wrong side' of uprisings, records are made as they are branded as rebels, taken prisoner or tried, while administration of the forfeited estates after the 1745 rebellion resulted in a wealth of records relating to certain lands and the people who lived on them (see 'Forfeited estate papers', p. 167).

There are often far-reaching results of war which impinge on the economic field. One example is the kelp industry. The Napoleonic Wars encouraged the growth of the already expanding kelp industry (seaweed was used in the manufacture of soap and glass), as barilla, the foreign substitute, could not be imported. The industry was very work-intensive and was financially advantageous to the Highland landlords, as well as providing a livelihood for many. The local population expanded – the Laird of Ulva was said to have trebled his income and doubled the population on his estate on this account – but after 1815 the manufacture of kelp ceased to be economically viable, thus resulting in a redundant workforce. This proved to be one of the factors which resulted in emigration from the West Highlands. Other 'events' might be natural ones such as bad harvests, famine or changes in the movements of the herring shoals – all of which affected the lives and livelihoods of people.

Enterprises such as the disastrous Darien expedition left records of all those involved. Some papers have been published by the Scottish History Society and some by the Bannatyne Club but there is more documentation in the NAS collections. There is, for example, a list of persons who died in the Darien expedition, with designations, causes and dates of death, dated 1699 (GD45).

From the time of the Reformation onwards, the formation of new religious congregations has had a big impact on society, sometimes being the cause of war and rebellion (such as the Covenanting wars) or contributing to the gradual erosion of the influence of the Established Church of Scotland (the formation of the Associate Session of 1733 and of the Relief Church of 1761, for example). The growing number of dissenters throughout the eighteenth and nineteenth centuries resulted in the diminution of number of entries in the parish registers.

Economic trends

In whatever century people lived, economic events have affected their standards of living, what they did and where they lived. The agrarian and industrial revolutions taking place in Scotland from the eighteenth century onwards resulted in vast changes. In the countryside, the abolition of joint tenancies and runrig and the consolidation of smallholdings into bigger farms produced a growing landless population. Subsistence farming ceased to be acceptable to landlords living in a cash-flow society and as the population had grown during the eighteenth century and continued to grow, this resulted in a stream of persons moving to the towns where industries were now needing a workforce – or in emigration, forced or voluntary.

Some of the catalysts for economic change were 'events' of varying kinds, possibly spread over many years as developments took place, such as the introduction of the potato, coming of the railways, building of canals, introduction of machinery and growth of factories. Many of these trends and events have resulted in a push/pull factor – moving people from one place to another, usually in search of work, drawing them into urban environments.

The problem of the family historian is that research is taken back in time and the question of the mobile population has to be considered in reverse – not 'where to?' but 'where from?' The question can, however, often be resolved by taking into account the 'timelines' involved and where economic stresses may have been felt or events occurred which might have influenced movements of members of a community.

The following 'timelines' from the time of the Reformation to the beginning of the twentieth century are only intended to provide a framework within which to explore further the past history of Scotland. More information can be found by studying one of the many histories of Scotland (see Bibliography under 'Histories of Scotland').

Timelines 1560–1900

(The main events in Scottish church history are given in bold.)

| 1542–67 | Mary, Queen of Scots |
| 1560 | ***Parliament accepts Knox's Confession of Faith: the Reformation*** |

| 1561 | Queen Mary returns to Scotland from France |
| 1567 | Mary, Queen of Scots abdicates |

1567–1625	**James VI and I of England**
1587	Execution of Mary, Queen of Scots
1598	Highland lairds ordered to prove rights to land titles Lowland adventurers settled in Lewis
1599–1609	Secretary's Register of Sasines introduced
1600	Scotland accepts Gregorian calendar
1600	Formation of the East India Company
1603	Union of the Crowns: James VI of Scotland also becomes James I of England
1609–17	Plantation of Scots in Ulster
1617	General and Particular Registers of Sasines introduced
1618	*Five Articles of Perth – Bishops imposed on Presbyterian Church of Scotland*

1625–49	**Charles I**
1638	*The National Covenant signed (upholding presbyterianism and abolishing Episcopalianism)*
1639	First Bishops' War: start of Covenanting wars
1643	*The Solemn League and Covenant signed: Presbyterian Church in Scotland allied with English parliamentary party*
1644–46	Campaigns of Marquis of Montrose
1649	Battle of Philiphaugh: defeat of Montrose by General Leslie's Covenanters
1649	Execution of Charles I
1650–51	Battles of Dunbar and Worcester: imposition of Cromwellian rule on Britain

1651–60	**The Commonwealth**
1651	Imposition of Cromwellian rule on Britain
1653	*Formation of Quaker meetings*
1653	*Cromwell abolished the General Assembly: religious toleration enforced*

| **1660–85** | **Charles II** |
| 1662–90 | *The Second Episcopate: 300 ministers forced to give up their parishes Persecution of the Covenanters: the 'killing times'* |

1666	Defeat of the Covenanters at Rullion Green
1670	Foundation of Hudson's Bay Company
1679	Battle of Bothwell Bridge: defeat of Covenanters

1685–88	**James VII and II of England**
1685	Revocation of the Edict of Nantes in France: persecution of the Huguenots in France
1685	Rising of the Earl of Argyll: Argyll executed
1688–1708	*Persecution of Catholics intensified*
1689	James VII leaves Scotland

1689–1702	**William III (of Orange) and Mary (Stewart)**
1689	Uprising of 'Bonnie Dundee' for the Stewart cause: John Graham of Claverhouse killed at Killiecrankie
1690	National Convention of Estates: presbyterianism restored
1692	Massacre of Glencoe
1694	Death of Queen Mary: William continues as king
1695	Foundation of Bank of Scotland
1695–1702	The Seven Ill Years (bad harvests and famine)
1698	The Darien Expedition set sail – the colony was abandoned 1700

1702–14	**Queen Anne**
1701–7	Growing Anglo-Scottish tension
1707	Treaty and Act of Union: joining of Parliaments of Scotland and England
1709	Formation of the Society in Scotland for Propagating Christian Knowledge
1712	*Patronage restored* Methods of agriculture improving from the first half of the century onwards

1714–27	**George I**
1708	Jacobite rising (with French assistance) failed
1715–16	Jacobite rising – the '15 (Old Pretender): ended with stalemate at battle of Sheriffmuir
1720–	Rise of the tobacco trade
1725–36	General Wade constructing military roads in the Highlands
1727	Board of Trustees for Manufactures set up to encourage Scottish industry

1727–60	**George II**
1733	*First Secession (Ebenezer Erskine): formation of Associate Session*
1743	Potato introduced into the Hebrides: cultivation becoming more widespread
1745–46	Jacobite rising – the '45 (Bonnie Prince Charlie)
1746	Battle of Culloden: defeat of the Jacobites Pacification of the Highlands – persecution of Catholics and Episcopalians
1747	Abolition of Heritable Jurisdictions (except baronies) Pacification of the Highlands – persecution of Catholics and Episcopalians
1747	*Split of Associate Session – Burghers and Anti-Burghers*
1747–84	Commissioners for the annexed estates administering forfeited Jacobite estates
1752	The Appin murder (Colin Campbell of Glenure murdered)
1756–63	Seven Years War (Canada and India): many disbanded soldiers remained in North America after 1763
1759	Formation of Carron Ironworks
1760–1820	**George III** Agricultural and industrial revolutions gathering momentum Population rising rapidly
1760–1830	The Enlightenment: Edinburgh's 'Golden Age'
1760–	Emigration growing
1761	*Second Secession: formation of the Relief Church*
1767	Work begins on building the New Town in Edinburgh
1776–83	War of American Independence
1777	Collapse of the tobacco trade
1780–1800s	Trading opportunities for Scots with East India Company
1782	Bad harvests and famine in the Highlands
1784	Restoration of forfeited Jacobite estates
1787–1868	Transportation of convicts to Australia
1789	The French Revolution
1790	Opening of Forth and Clyde Canal

1790–1840	Rapid growth of textile industries
1791–99	Publication of *First Statistical Account*
1793–1815	French Revolutionary and Napoleonic Wars
1793–1816	Board of Agriculture – publication of county surveys of agriculture
1793	*Catholic Relief Act (limited relief)*
1797	Militia Acts
1799	*Burghers split into Old Lights and New Lights*
1801	First national decennial census (mainly numerical)
1802	Start of weaving of Paisley shawls
1804	Construction of Caledonian Canal begins
1805	Battle of Trafalgar
1806	*Anti-Burghers split into Old Lights and New Lights*
1807–21	Sutherland clearances
1815	Battle of Waterloo
1815	Start of decline of the kelp industry; economic depression; Highland and Lowland clearances
1815	Corn Laws passed forbidding import of foreign corn till domestic corn cost 80 shillings a quarter. Increase in cost of food and distress among working classes
1815–19	Collapse of the cattle market
1820–30	**George IV**
1820	*Formation of United Secession Church*
1820–40	Decline in handloom weaving; distress of weavers
1822	Union Canal from Edinburgh to Glasgow opens
1823	Removal of import tax on barilla and collapse of kelp industry
1823	Commissary Court Act – jurisdiction transferred to sheriff courts
1829	*Catholic Emancipation Act*
1830–37	**William IV**
1831	First passenger railway opens, Glasgow to Garnkirk
1831–33	Cholera epidemic
1832	Scottish Reform Act: franchise extended
1833	Factory Act limiting hours of employment of children in cotton mills
1837–1901	**Victoria**
1840s	Railway 'mania' beginning

1841	First decennial census giving names for the whole population
1843	*The Disruption: formation of the Free Church of Scotland*
1842	Employment of women and children underground in the mines ceases
1845	Poor Law Act: setting up of Parochial Boards Publication of *Second Statistical Account*
1846	Famine relief in the Highlands: failure of potato harvest Repeal of the Corn Laws
1847	*United Presbyterian Church (joining of Relief Church and United Secession Church)*
1848	Jute cloth first produced in Dundee
1852	Formation of Highland Emigration Society
1854–56	Crimean War
1855	Introduction of statutory registration in Scotland
1857–58	Indian Mutiny
1858	India Act (end of East India Company)
1861	American Civil War
1868	Scottish Reform Act; franchise extended to all male burgh householders
1872	Education Act: universal education from age of five
1874	Lay patronage abolished
1875	Factories Act: minimum age for child workers – ten
1878	Opening of Tay Bridge
1879	Tay Bridge disaster
1884	Manhood suffrage introduced (nearly all)
1886	Crofters' Commission set up
1892	Women admitted as undergraduates in Scottish universities Report of the Boundary Commission – many parish and county boundaries changed
1899–1902	Boer War
1900	*United Free Church (union of Free Church and United Presbyterian Church)*

3. What did they do?

Statutory registers, census returns and parish registers relate to everyone – whether pauper or professional, labourer or landowner – but there are many other sources which have a more specific relevance to persons at certain levels of society or working in particular areas. When exploring possible avenues of research it is, therefore, important to take into account both the person's occupation and their place in society. These considerations, taken in conjunction with where and when he or she lived, will help when selecting records which may throw light on life and ancestry. (See notes on the various classes of records mentioned, where they can be found and how easy it is to access them, under 'Where did they live?', pp. 122–47.)

Labourers

Country dwellers

'My ancestor was just a labourer' is often said as if this was the end of the quest – but in fact our labouring forebears left many records. The term 'labourer' is an open-ended description and can refer to a range of workers. Sub-tenants would not have legal leases of the land they worked. They were often referred to as cottars, pendiclers or grassmen, and worked a small area of land on which they kept a few cattle, paying rent by working for a tenant farmer. Grassmen might only have a house and garden. From the late eighteenth century onwards, as smallholdings were joined to form large farms, sub-tenants often became landless employees. They were usually given a cottage as part of their employment or, if unmarried, they were housed in bothies or in the farmhouse.

Labourers moved frequently from farm to farm, signing on with a new master at a feeing fair every six months or year. This is shown in census details of where a labourer's children were born. Farm servants in the more fertile parts of Scotland such as East Lothian often had more permanent jobs and might remain on one farm for the whole of their lives. Payments made to labourers and sub-tenants were occasionally recorded in estate accounts but references to wages in the form of a pair of shoes or allowance of meal are not of great genealogical significance.

Labourers and the courts

If your ancestor lived on the lands of a proprietor whose lands formed a barony, there may be minutes of the barony court, which was mainly responsible for the keeping of 'good neighbourhood'. In this context a great many local persons, both men and women, appeared before the bailie or steward to account for stealing green wood, poaching, failing to do duty in bringing in the new millstone, or breaches of the peace. Members of the family might be called to give evidence and names of accused and witnesses are usually accompanied by details of occupation, residence and sometimes age.

People of every rank of society in the past seem to have had access to the law and labourers, among others, appear in the records of all the courts, accused of misdemeanours or bringing accusations against others – for theft, breaking the peace, unpaid wages or debts due. The commissary courts dealt with many cases of scandal, when one person in the community was accused of miscalling another – regarded as a serious offence. The processes which record what happened not only throw light on relationships but through evidence heard in court illustrate behaviour and afford a picture of living conditions. Records of JP courts, burgh courts and sheriff courts provide similar information.

Time spent in looking through such records is never wasted from the point of view of a study of social history but unless you have particular information regarding the appearance of a forebear in a particular court, you are unlikely to be lucky enough to find a reference relevant to a particular person.

Parish and parishioners

Even those who moved frequently still came under the surveillance of the local kirk session. Cases heard by the session concerned accusations of fornication and adultery, illegitimate births, irregular marriages, slander, Sabbath breaking, swearing and breaking of the peace, among others. Evidence was given not only by the guilty but by the accusers and witnesses. In more serious cases, the case would be referred to the presbytery for a hearing.

What records have survived for each parish vary a great deal. Records listed for the parish of Liberton, Midlothian are an example of the wide range of administrative matters with which the Church was concerned and on which information may be found. There are minutes from 1639 to 2001 (with gaps), testimonials 1690–1700, cash and account books 1755–1913 (with gaps), poor's accounts 1773–89, rogue money society minutes 1811–31, a book of statute work in the parish 1784–1808, Liberton Board of Health sederunt book 1831–32, volunteer fund cash book 1802–79, communion rolls 1849–1908, baptisms 1855–1923, proclamations 1877–1909, sabbath school teachers and missionary collector's association minutes 1880–84, congregational committee minutes 1881–83, poor's fund 1802–8, and miscellaneous papers.

The value of any of these records in relation to a particular individual can often only be judged by sampling. Rogue money was a local tax levied to cover the expenses of arrest and detention of criminals and the society minutes were only concerned with the election of a local representative. Records of statute labour dealt with raising money and labour to mend the roads. In this context, the Liberton records include lists of heritors within the parish and give their residence, as well a list of persons who paid above 20 shillings yearly as rent and were therefore liable to pay for road labour. There is also an accompanying list of carters, giving their residence.

You may also come across school logbooks, pew rents and matters concerning lairs. In some places there are references to mortifications. These were funds, sometimes left by a local landowner, which could be used for the welfare of certain members of the community (often scholars or the poor) and applications for grants may throw light on the circumstances of that individual. Records of mortifications will also be found in burgh records, heritors' records and papers of landed families.

Testificates were supposed to be brought by those who moved into a new parish to be handed to the minister on arrival. Some came with a slur on their characters already on record. In Dalmeny in 1709 Mathew Houstone and his wife produced a certificate from Torphichen but it was noted that 'ther wer very gruff presumptions of theft laid to there charge though ther was never any thing judiciously proven against them.' Some entries are much briefer, such as this one from Largo: 'Agnes Herd from Scoonie March 1770'. Only a few testimonials have survived but where they exist, they can show where a family had lived earlier.

A much more detailed record of population movements in or out of the parish was kept by the minister of Greenlaw over the years 1839–42. Names of those arriving and those leaving were put down, with occupation, age, marital status and number of children, name of master or landlord, residence, parish to which they went or from which they came, as well as place of birth.

It is important to assess the circumstances motivating the compilation of listings. In 1798 there is a note in the kirk session minutes of St Cyrus (also known as Ecclesgreig), Kincardineshire: 'The Minister informed the Session that he was just now making out a full and exact List of all the Inhabitants of the Parish' which was to be inscribed in the session minutes. This resulted in what appears to be a complete census of the population, giving residence of each family, occupation of the head of the house, maiden name of wife, names of children and a note as to whether the family belonged to the Established Church or whether they were seceders or Episcopalians. Few ages are quoted except for the very old. Other parish listings often only concern members of the Established Church or of a section of the community.

The work of the minister generated many lists – of male heads of families, examination rolls (for catechism) and communion rolls, usually giving names, residence and occasionally occupation. These only refer to members of the Established Kirk and the evidence must be evaluated accordingly. Omission from such a listing may be an indication that the family belonged to another congregation. Sometimes general remarks on the lists provide valuable details, such as 'Christina Baigrie, Eskbank, married, now Mrs. Handyside', and a few supply proof of emigration: 'William Henderson, Hyvots Mill, Liberton, miller. Admitted June 1849. From Dalkeith. Left in May 1850 to America'. Death of a parishioner is also occasionally noted. Most communion rolls do not pre-date the nineteenth century.

Further listings of heads of families can sometimes be found in the General Assembly papers (NAS – class reference CH1). There were a considerable number of disputed appointments of new ministers, particularly in the first half of the eighteenth century, a period when the parish registers are often missing or incomplete. The lists contained the names of all those who supported one or other candidate, usually only giving name and sometimes residence. It is, however, not always possible to link up the person listed with the person for whom you are searching on the basis of this 'sighting'. Another problem is that from a failure to find an entry under the surname in which you are interested, you cannot assume that the family did not live in the parish at the time as there is no guarantee that every head of household signed a petition. Consult the entry in the *Fasti ecclesiae Scoticanae* for any particular parish, note when the ministers changed and then check to see if there are records of a disputed call in the catalogue of the General Assembly papers. Any reference to a surname which you are researching may provide valuable clues.

There are usually fewer surviving records for dissenting congregations but check the electronic catalogues of the NAS under CH3, the NRA and holdings of local archives.

At the time of the wars with the French at the end of the eighteenth century and early nineteenth century, many labourers (both in towns and in the country) served in the militia (see p. 194) and these records of the 1790s and early 1800s may produce a great deal of useful information.

Labourers may also fall into the category of the poor (see p. 161). Poverty exempted some labourers from the poll tax and hearth tax of the seventeenth century but if you have traced the family back to that time, it is worth checking whether their names are included. (See 'Where did they live?', p. 144–5.)

Testaments

A number of labourers did leave testaments. A search of the ScotlandsPeople index to testaments registered in commissary courts over the whole of Scotland between 1750 and 1800 produced eighty entries of persons described as labourers – and this did not include those who were indexed as 'in' a particular place, some of whom were probably tenants but many others may have been labourers. (See 'From birth to death', pp. 100–7.)

Labourers in the towns

From the middle of the eighteenth century onwards, there was a vast rise in the urban population of Scotland. Agrarian reforms, a rising population, a huge growth in industrialisation and various economic pressures meant that there was a widespread movement of people to the towns, especially from the Highland regions. The influx of new inhabitants into a crowded and alien environment meant that contact with a community and church was often lacking and it becomes more difficult to trace a labourer in Glasgow or Dundee, for example, than in a country district such as Glenorchy or Durness.

Census returns or entries in statutory certificates and the parish registers may provide clues as to where the family lived and their occupations – perhaps working in a factory, as a weaver or coalminer. A gazetteer such as *Groome's Gazetteer* or a local history of the town will identify any large industries in the district in which your ancestor may have been employed. Local directories and detailed contemporary maps of the area (many can be viewed on the NLS website) will pinpoint such places. If you can identify a church in the area to which the family might have belonged, check the NAS holdings of records of both the Established Church and secession churches (CH2 and CH3) to see if there are session minutes or communion rolls. The catalogues of district archives should also be searched. Glasgow City Archives hold records of a number of congregations of different denominations in the city.

Employment records

Many collections of business papers have survived but most of these relate to the nineteenth and twentieth centuries and only a few include wages books. There are, for example, muniments of Cox Brothers, jute spinners, Dundee, in Dundee University Library which include wages records for 1811–12. Most of the surviving records are likely to tell you more about the business than about those who worked in it and references to individuals will, in many cases, consist only of a name and payment made for wages.

Glasgow University Archives have a large collection of records for businesses over the whole of Scotland. Searching the SCAN website (which has a link to their catalogue of business records) under Ailsa Shipbuilding Company, for example, shows that there are workmen's house rent rolls for 1925–38.

The NAS holds many coalmining records, both in their private collections (GD) and in the records of coalmining companies before nationalisation (CB). In some industries, such as coalmining, schemes were run under which employees contributed a small sum of money as insurance against accident or death – though details given in the books may not be sufficient to identify an individual with certainty. The catalogue of *Labour records in Scotland* (MacDougall, 1978) provides an extensive list of records relating to workers in all trades and business sectors, indicating where the papers can be found. Many friendly societies were set up all over Scotland which looked after the mutual benefit of its members for particular trades or classes of person. Some date back to the middle of the eighteenth century. Unfortunately, in only a few cases are there lists of members but, for example, the Strathbogie Ploughmen's Society has a list of members for 1833, and the Glasgow Printcutters Friendly Society includes a list of members and returns of sickness and mortality for the years 1845–50.

If your ancestor worked on the railways, what you may find will depend on what he did. It is unlikely that you will find references to those who built the lines but the NAS hold a large collection of Scottish railway records (class reference BR) which include some relating to the staff of particular railways. They are listed according to the individual company and you need therefore to know (or guess) for which company a person was working. A directory of railway records which is useful to family historians has been written by Richards (1989). *Tracing your Scottish ancestors* (NAS, 2003) also has useful guidance in locating relevant records in the NAS.

Parliamentary papers

From the eighteenth century onwards, Parliament generated a vast mass of published material covering almost every aspect of life. Some of the information referring to Scotland is buried in papers dealing with the whole of Britain: other reports deal solely with conditions north of the border. The reports appear as sessional papers or reports of select committees and royal commissions which included the findings of specialists appointed by the Crown. Evidence was collected – both oral and written – and included the testimonies of persons of all ranks of society. The material is of enormous value both to social historians and genealogists as many case histories are quoted giving detailed accounts of the family circumstances. Academic books published on particular subjects, such as fishing, weaving or coalmining, for example, usually draw on this material and a bibliography should indicate what parliamentary reports have been published on the subject. (See also 'Where did they live?', pp. 127–8.)

The poor

The old poor law

The poor fell into two main categories – those who could not support themselves – the old, infirm, handicapped or orphans – and those who were in distress through some disaster such as crop failure, or the burning of a house or boat. These might include merchants, craftsmen or the well-to-do who had fallen on evil times, as well as labourers. There were also those who lived on the edge of destitution for most of their lives – often termed the general labouring poor – who needed occasional assistance but at other times were self-supporting. Finally, there were those termed 'the undeserving poor' – beggars, thieves and other undesirables.

Up till 1844 the chief responsibility for looking after the poor lay with the kirk session and the heritors. Lists of persons to whom help was given were kept by the kirk session, their names recorded either in the minutes or in the kirk session accounts. Occasionally these lists formed part of the heritors' minutes.

From an entry reading 'To George Mills 6s.' it is difficult to deduce very much or to assume a positive identity for the recipient of relief but sometimes more details are given – age, residence and frailty – and death may also be recorded. A more revealing entry was one in Rothesay in 1721 when the session gave Elspeth NcTaylour money for shoes, adding 'if she pawns them for drink, she'll get no more.' On the other hand, additional evidence may provide a great deal of information. In 1793 Melrose kirk session granted an allowance to Isabel Young, wife of George Mabon, a Chelsea pensioner, lately called from Melrose to Chatham Barracks. She was left destitute and her husband claimed that he could make her no allowance out of his pay. This reference opened up the possibility of tracing the records of George as a Chelsea pensioner in army records in the National Archives in London. The discharge papers (class reference WO97) can be searched online and an entry will give the parish of birth, regiment, age at discharge and years of service.

There were sometimes disputes as to which parish was responsible for paying out maintenance for a poor person, as proof of residence for a certain number of years was a condition of support. In such cases the heritors were often involved in deciding the outcome. James Dickie was born in Kilmaurs, Ayrshire in 1798 and went to sea at a young age. His parents lived in Irvine but he lodged in Greenock and when he later became ill, there was an argument as to which parish was liable for his maintenance. It was decided that proof of residence rested on where he kept his clothes and had them washed. A complete potted biography of this unfortunate sailor was the result of this disputed claim. Inter-parish disputes were occasionally taken to the sheriff courts but unless you have some details of where and when the case was heard, it is not worth looking for such records.

Relief on account of occasional distress (such as harvest failure) often took the form of employment in public works or supply of cheap meal arranged by the kirk session or heritors. Lists recording the names of those who required employment (twenty two in number) and those who needed both employment and assistance (seven) were made in Crichton kirk session minutes in 1817. Adam Manderson, labourer, Pathhead required aid even after being put in employment but Peter Cockburn, nailer, Pathhead only needed to be provided with work. Such information can be of value in identifying an ancestor.

A number of charitable institutions were set up at various times which helped the deserving poor of a particular place (such as the King James VI Hospital in Perth) or took in orphans. Records for the Dean Orphanage and Dr Guthrie's Schools (in the NAS) can provide family details of applicants but there are no indexes, which can result in a long search.

Following the failure of the potato crop in 1846, boards were set up to help those living in the Highlands by providing meal, work or financial aid. These records are listed in the NAS catalogue for Highland Destitution (HD). The lists give residence, name of the head of the family and a note of how many adults and children made up each family.

The new poor law (post-1844)

By the middle of the nineteenth century, it was clear that the parish funds were insufficient to cope with demands made upon them and the growing numbers of the poor and unemployed exacerbated the problem. In 1845 the Poor Law (Scotland) Act was passed which transferred the responsibility for care of the poor to local parochial boards under a Board of Supervision in Edinburgh. There was, however, an overlap in the transfer of responsibility from the kirk session to the parochial boards and therefore it is important to check whether there are documents relating to the poor with the kirk session records for some years after 1845, as well as looking for records of the parochial boards. In Longniddry, in East Lothian, there is, for example, a visiting book of the registered poor kept with the kirk session records in which an inspector made his half-yearly remarks:

> Margaret Fairley, Setonhill, Longniddry, admitted 13 May 1837; 19 May 1855 blind and confined to bed: died 27 December 1856.

The records of the parochial boards are a source of much valuable information about the poor, though not all have survived. The most rewarding are the general registers of the poor for each parish (referring to successful applications) and the record of applications for parochial relief (some of which may have failed). The minutes of the boards are more concerned with administrative matters which are mainly of interest from the point of view of social history. There are some separate registers relating to children.

Details given for applicants vary from place to place but often include age, place of birth (particularly useful in the case of Irish immigrants), religion, marital status, occupation and particulars of the family, with ages and occupations. Widow Herkis in Dunbar was aged fifty five in 1861, born in Dunbar, partially disabled and had children: one daughter at school; Robert, aged twenty four, a fisherman (married with a family); John, twenty six, a sailor (married with a child); and three daughters in service.

Sometimes you may find on a post-1854 death certificate that a member of a family who had seemed to be reasonably self-supporting died in the poor-house – a place which sometimes seems to have fulfilled the need of a hospice – but the resulting admission records may be very useful.

Most poor relief records are kept in local archives or libraries but the NAS hold a collection of those for some parishes in Wigtownshire, East Lothian and Midlothian. (See Forbes and Urquhart, 2002 for a full description of the NAS holdings.) The NAS class reference is CO. Most of the records are unindexed but there are a number of on going projects in this field. There is a database index in the Glasgow City Archives for poor relief registers for parishes in Lanarkshire, Renfrewshire and Dunbartonshire. Check the internet under the parish in which you are interested to see if any transcriptions or indexes for poor relief have been made. The register of poor for Liff and Benvie 1854–65 and the register of Dundee East Poor-house (1856–78) are online at www.fdca.org.uk/.

Tenants

Proprietor or tenant

The term 'tenant' may refer to a farmer of many acres, a joint tenant holding a piece of land in common with several others or to sub-tenants and crofters, living on very smallholdings. The first problem, however, is to ascertain whether someone owned their land or was a tenant. Census returns will usually only describe a person as 'farmer' or 'crofter', sometimes providing information as to the acreage of the farm. Statutory certificates and entries in the OPRs are equally lacking in information. If, however, someone is described as 'of' a place, this almost always indicates ownership, while 'in' denotes a tenancy or place of abode. A person described as 'possessor' or 'occupier' was a tenant, not the owner of the lands. Some proprietors of land were also tenants – the Maxwells were always termed 'of Southbar', their property in Renfrewshire, but from the late seventeenth century onwards the family lived in Kintyre, Argyllshire, as tenant farmers.

There are several routes you can follow to separate the owners from the tenants and in that case, to find out who was the proprietor of the property. From 1855 to 1974, the annually compiled valuation rolls covering the whole of Scotland provide a useful source of information in this matter, naming the proprietor, tenant and occupier of each property. (See 'From birth to death – Valuation rolls', p. 53). As the rolls are not indexed by name, it can take time to search urban areas but smaller country districts present no problems. Pre-1855 valuation rolls were compiled from time to time but may not cover every area nor list every place. They are not nearly so informative, usually giving only the names of the proprietors, the principal lands (but often not all) they held and the valuation.

Between 1781 and 1830 and from 1870 onwards you can use the Index to Places which accompanies the abridgements of the registers of sasines, arranged by county (see 'Understanding legal documents – The abridgements to the sasines: 1781 onwards', p. 216). Look up the name of the farm or piece of land in which you are interested and check the sasine abridgements to see who owned the property. If the name is not that of your ancestor, then it is probable that he or she was a tenant. Before 1781, if the particular register of sasines for the county is indexed, you can check under a surname to see if there was a landowner of that name. The *First Statistical Account* (1791–99) and the *Second Statistical Account* (*circa* 1845) usually name the heritors who were the landowners, in each parish. If you have found a reference in a testament to money owed by the deceased to his 'master' for rent – this can be taken as a proof that the person was a tenant, and details of rent paid may be found in the muniments (if any) of the 'master'.

Tenants and tacks

Many tenants held their lands from the proprietor without a formal lease and sub-tenants, holding their lands from a tenant, rarely had a written agreement. Leases (referred to as tacks) could be recorded in any register of deeds (see 'Understanding legal documents – Registers of deeds', p. 202), but without some knowledge of when such a lease was registered and where, a long search may be involved – and the information given in a tack often provides little of interest. It may state the length of the lease, the rent payable and possibly outline various requirements in working the land which had to be fulfilled by the tenant. In 1714 Robert Adam signed a lease with Sir Francis Grant of Cullen for land in the parish of Monymusk. He was to pay as rent a certain amount of meal, as well as one hog, three geese, six capons and twelve hens per year. The tack also laid down that he was not to take more than five crops from the outfield land without intermission and to keep the buildings in good condition. Many tenancy agreements are only found in the muniments of the proprietor concerned.

Tenure of tenants was often precarious and in court processes there are frequent references to 'removings' when the landlord officially warned tenants that their present agreement concerning occupation of their land would end. (Sub-tenants were liable to remove at the same time as the tenants.) This could be on the grounds that the rent had not been paid, as a means of raising the rent or to 'clear' the tenants. It is often impossible to know whether the tenants did quit the land or if, on agreeing to pay a higher rent, the lease was renewed. The names of a great many small tenants in Highland townships are recorded in these records but determining identity from a name and a place of residence may not be easy. Work is being undertaken in indexing some of the eighteenth-century Argyllshire removings, but without the aid of an index research time is unlikely to be rewarding.

Tenants with more extensive rights to the occupation of land were those termed 'kindly tenants', whose claims to occupy certain lands were passed down from generation to generation – but these were not very common.

Crofters

Particular attention was paid to Highland crofters in the 1880s as there was serious destitution at the time. Crofters paid a small rent to a landlord for a few acres of land, while cottars tenanted a house but had no land. Their rent was often so low that they were not listed in the post-1854 valuation rolls. In 1883 a Royal Commission on the Highlands and Islands (known as the Napier Commission) listened to the evidence of 775 people in sixty one places and in many instances the evidence refers to conditions prevailing many years earlier. The report of the Commission is printed with other parliamentary papers and reports but there is additional manuscript material which was collected when the evidence was being taken, giving details of tenants and crofters – their names, residences and families. The returns are in the NAS – class reference AF50. These are listed on the online catalogue but the documents have to be viewed in the NAS. The sections of most value are AF50/7/1–19, giving the names of all crofters on certain estates and AF50/8/1–17, dealing with cottars.

Rentals

In any collection of papers belonging to an influential landowner, there are likely to be rentals and some have been published – a number are listed in *Scottish texts and calendars* (Stevenson, 1987). The NAS holds many collections of family papers (class reference GD) and estate papers can also be found in the National Library of Scotland, in local archives or libraries, and some are still in private hands – many have been catalogued and are listed through the NRA.

The NAS catalogues of deposits of family papers – all of which are being put online – usually include a section devoted to estate management. The catalogue entry is unlikely to mention every farm but will probably refer to lands in a particular parish or on a named estate. A few rentals can be found in records of the franchise courts. The regality of Argyll records (in the NAS), for example, include rentals from 1595 to 1608 and 1633 to 1643.

The amount of personal information in rentals is very variable. Some rentals only list the lands and the rents paid: others list each tenant and the lands they held, as well as the rent – in earlier times usually in kind, as chickens, geese or grain. In the eighteenth century this was mostly commuted to a money payment.

If there is a long series of rentals for a particular estate, it may be possible to trace several generations of a family following each other in a farm but it is often difficult to determine the identity of tenants from a rental which gives only their name and their holding. On the other hand, you may be lucky. The survey of the estate of Assynt made by John Home in 1774–45 (Adam, 1960) includes 'a consolidated list of tenants and inhabitants' which names the farm, the tenant, marital status, number of children and servants. At Store, a township in Assynt, John Kerr, carpenter, had a wife (unnamed) and three children. His son, another John, was also living there, with a wife and six children. The survey is an interesting source of information about the farms and shielings, describing the type of agriculture carried out and acreages of cultivation.

The changes in agriculture which took place from the mid-eighteenth century onwards resulted in many landowners making surveys of their estates which contain varying amounts of detail. The Duke of Argyll in 1779 listed the inhabitants of parts of his estates but for some districts this was only a numerical return (Cregeen, 1963). A later survey of part of this estate – *List of inhabitants upon the Duke of Argyle's Property in Kintyre in 1792* (Stewart, 1991) gives the names of all those living in each place, with ages, but omits any indication as to relationships within the household. A very detailed listing of persons on an estate relates to the inhabitants of Blair Drummond Moss in Kincardine parish, Perthshire in 1814 (NAS, GD1/321/1). This was land which was cleared of peat, drained and settled from about 1790 onwards, mostly by Highlanders from Callander and Balquhidder. Each family was granted a holding of about six acres – some arable and some land needing reclamation. Details include the names of former possessors, the present possessor with wife, named children and ages of each person, details of any members of the family who had died and cause of death, years settled in the moss, where they came from, farm equipment and stock – including cats and dogs.

Forfeited estate papers

After the Jacobite rebellions of 1715 and 1745, a number of estates were forfeited and administered on behalf of the Crown. In the case of the estates forfeited after 1715, almost all of these were sold off by 1725, a number being bought in 1719–20 by the York Buildings Company. Both sets of forfeited estate papers (NAS class reference E601–E663 for the '15 and E700–E788 for the '45) contain a great deal of material, valuable from the point of view of social and economic history, as well as providing information on people who lived on the estates. The records include rentals, examination of claims by creditors, factors' accounts and papers relating to the administration of the estates, improvements in buildings, schools and churches and projects to encourage manufactures and fisheries.

Names of the estates forfeited after the '15 are given by Livingstone (1905). After the '45, the estates administered by the Barons of Exchequer were: Abernethy, Aldie, Ardsheal, Arnprior, Asleed,

Balmerino, Barrisdale, Burnfoot, Callart, Clanranald, Cluny, Cromarty, Dungallon, Dunipace, Elcho, Gask, Glastullich, Glenbucket, Glencarse, Glencoe, Gordon, Graden, Hamilton, Hay, Henderson, Keppoch, Kilmarnock, Kinloch and Nevay, Kinlochmoidart, Lethendy, Lindsay, Lochgarry, Lochiel, Lovat, McIntosh, KcKinnon, McLauchlan, Monaltrie, Nairn, Nicholson, Park, Perth, Pitscandly, Pitsligo, Redhouse, Row, Strathallan, Struan, Terpersie and Watson. To find what material is available, search under the name of the estate on the NAS electronic catalogue

The NAS has published two books of material taken from the records relating to the forfeited estates of the '45, *Reports on the annexed estates 1755–1769* (Wills, 1973), which includes factors' reports on a number of the estates, providing a detailed contemporary account of life in the Highlands at the time, and *Statistics of the annexed estates 1755–1756* (SRO, 1973), referring to the possessors (tenants) on seven of these estates, where they lived, numbers in each family, the stock on their lands, and crops sown. A study of the work carried out by the factors has been published by Smith (1982).

Estate plans

(See also 'Where did they live?', pp. 124–5.)

Surveys of estates with a view to improvements have resulted in the production of an enormous number of plans, many of which are in the NAS collection of plans at West Register House. The catalogue entry gives the reference number of the plan, its date and a brief description of the plan. Other plans can be found in local archives and libraries or are still in private hands. All are interesting in providing information about boundaries, whereabouts of farms, buildings and farm towns (many of which may now have disappeared), land use in the past, and field names, and occasionally the plans will include the names of the tenant farmers as well as the owners. A plan of the farm of Upper Coullie, part of the Monymusk estate in Aberdeenshire, dated 1798, was drawn up in connection with the abolition of runrig. Each rig is shown with the name of the tenant who cultivated it, the type of land (pasture, infield or outfield), and the size of the plot. Sketched over it are lines indicating the new consolidated holdings. Some plans are illustrated by vignettes of buildings or of the countryside.

Listings of tenants

There are a number of sources in which tenants are listed. Personal information given is rarely detailed but 'sightings' of an individual in a particular place can be useful. Under the old poor law (prior to 1845)

tenants were sometimes liable for a contribution to funds for the care of the poor of the parish, and assessment rolls, giving the names of tenants under each proprietor and the size of their holdings, may be found in either the kirk session minutes or the heritors' records. (This was not a popular assessment and an entry in the JP records for East Lothian in response to a request for an extra contribution to the poor-rate in 1623 stated: 'Every contribution is odious and smellis of ane taxatioun.')

In the nineteenth century the obligation to pay money to provide statute labour on the roads was levied from tenants paying over £6 in rent (as well from cottagers and young persons over sixteen, who paid a reduced levy). This can provide yet another list of names, with their place of residence. Such records may be with the kirk session records or in the JP records.

In the second half of the eighteenth century, the government raised money through a whole series of taxes on various commodities. The farm horse tax, levied in 1798–99 (NAS, E326/10) is useful as the returns identify a great many tenant farmers in every parish in Scotland. In the Argyllshire parish of Glenorchy and Inishail, sixty four persons were listed, each with their place of residence, owning between one and ten horses each. Most people only claimed to have one horse or perhaps two.

The hearth tax (NAS, E69) was levied on both landowners and tenants (including cottars) in 1691 but not all the records have survived and in some parishes the landowner gave in a return for tenants' hearths on his lands without stating individual names. At best the list will only provide a name and a residence. The poll tax returns (1694–99) are often much more informative, if they have survived. One of the most complete and detailed returns is that for Aberdeenshire in 1696, published in two volumes by the Spalding Club. The lists are arranged by presbytery and by parish within the presbytery and provide details of tenants, sub-tenants, children over sixteen and names of servants and tradesmen in the township. This detailed information may link up with parish register entries.

It is sometimes possible to follow up information given in the hearth tax by finding the same person listed in the poll tax records. Robert Cochran was listed in the hearth tax return for Newbattle in 1694: 'In Cockpens lands – Rot Cochran yr . . . 01'. Then, in the only surviving fragment of the poll tax return of the same parish, we find a receipt for tax paid: 'From Robert Cochrane cupmaker, and Janet Douglas'. The additional information giving the name of the wife of Robert Cochrane and his occupation, cup maker, meant that it was possible to find the marriage of this couple in the adjoining county of East Lothian and to trace the family back further in the burgess records of Haddington, where Robert was a wright.

Local research

A great deal of work has been done and is being undertaken to research the people and history of various localities in the past. Research by the late Allan Begg on the deserted settlements in Mid Argyll draws on rentals, oral history, census returns and monumental inscriptions and provides much valuable information about places which are now just a pile of stones and the people who had lived there. Similar work has been published by the Kilmorack Heritage Association. Details of such research and local publications can be found by contacting a library or history society in the relevant area.

Tenants and testaments

The fact that the term 'tenant' can be applied to persons from such a wide range of economic backgrounds – ranging from subsistence farmers (sometimes also working as weavers or shoemakers or in other occupations to make ends meet) to those of considerable means – makes it difficult to generalise about what other records are likely to document them and their families. Tenants often appear in the barony courts (or in other courts) and in the kirk session minutes. Many left testaments. A search of the Brechin commissary court register of testaments between 1780 and 1823 showed that there were over 130 registered testaments for those termed 'tenants' and this does not take into account the many more who are described as 'in' a particular township or place, some of whom may have been inhabitants or labourers, others tenant farmers. In many cases, these documents will supply much information about the family – surviving relatives, the name of the landlord and interesting details in the inventory about the stock on the holding and crops grown there.

The more prosperous tenants sometimes made arrangements for the disposal of their moveable goods or for the taking over of the remainder of a lease by a son, in the form of a deed, often recorded in the local sheriff court or commissary court registers of deeds. In 1823, James Pullar, tenant of the Mains of Turin in the parish of Rescobie, agreed to assign the remaining years of the lease of the farm to his son Charles, but he drove a hard bargain, laying down that the latter should pay his parents a yearly annuity, and certain sums of money to his brothers, who were named and described. His parents were to have the right to choose any two rooms in the farmhouse in which they might live, and Charles was to maintain a cow for them and grow half an acre of lint for their use, and James and his wife were to be allowed to keep six hens and some chickens 'not exceeding sixteen at a time' in the farm steading. Such a document is not only valuable for the amount of family information it contains but interesting in providing a picture of life on a prosperous farm in Angus at the time.

Landowners

Printed works

If your ancestor was a landowner and connected to a well-known family, you may be able to find out quite a lot about the family from printed books. Check whether a family history has been published. Stuart (1978) lists families on whom there is published information and includes references in serial publications. This guide should be read in conjunction with the work by Ferguson (1986), as the books include different works and Ferguson brings the listings up to a later date. Ferguson includes some manuscript material in the National Library of Scotland. The catalogue of the National Library of Scotland (a copyright library) is now online (www.nls.uk) and there is a separate section of the catalogue for manuscript holdings. Local libraries often have interesting local collections, including privately printed works.

Burke's Peerage (the 107th edition was published in 2003) and *Burke's Landed Gentry* (19th edition, 2001) have been published in a number of editions. Not all families appear in every edition but there is a supplementary volume which is an index, showing in which editions a particular family is written up. The information on each family is usually contributed by the family concerned and is not always correct. There are omissions and mistakes and some wrong links. Sir James Balfour Paul's *Scots peerage* (1904–14), which can be purchased on CD from the Scottish Genealogy Society, covers the ancestry of the leading families in Scotland and has the advantage that references are quoted for the sources used.

Biographical details of the careers of the illustrious may be included in the *Dictionary of National Biography*. There is a one-volume concise edition but it is always worth consulting the multi-volume work. The latest edition (2004) runs to sixty volumes and can be consulted online on payment of an annual subscription. Many libraries will have copies of the large, older edition. Do not expect to find everything there about a person's life or career and, as in other published works, you may uncover conflicting or additional information in your own research. You may be right and the published material wrong. The same is true of the many publications giving details of the background and careers of persons in various categories – former pupils of schools, university graduates, lawyers or ministers. They are useful but neither infallible nor necessarily comprehensive.

From the nineteenth century onwards a great deal of work relating to families and their history has been published by societies such as the Spalding Club, Maitland Club, Stair Society, Scottish History Society and Scottish Record Society and others. The material includes a wide range of original sources such as legal and historical documents, account books, family letters, and genealogical memoirs, with commentaries or introductions by the editors. These serial publications can be found in many larger libraries and some family history centres such as the Scottish Genealogy Society Library. *Scottish texts and calendars* (Stevenson, 1987) is a guide to serial publications (it does not include official Scottish publications) and updates and largely replaces two older reference guides – *A catalogue of the publications of Scottish historical and kindred clubs and societies, and of the volumes relevant to Scottish history issued by His Majesty's Stationery Office 1780–1908* (Terry, 1909), continued by Matheson (1928), covering the period 1908–27.

Many articles on particular families or individuals have been published in the *Scottish Genealogist* (1953 onwards) and in historical and local family history society publications. The Scottish Genealogy Society magazine periodically issues indexes to all its published articles. To find out what research has been published by local societies, contact the family history society in the area where the family in which you are interested lived. (See Appendix 3.)

Information given in printed works should never be regarded as infallible unless it can be confirmed by reference to primary sources. Most family histories are secondary sources – narratives or commentaries written by a third party, often after the elapse of some time, and even narratives written by a member of the family may have a bias or even depend on dubious evidence. Some family histories are compiled as a celebration of the family or are written to support a particular view of history, attitudes which have a value but which may lead to discrimination in the selection of facts and result in a slant on the interpretation of events. (See 'Where did they live?', p. 120.)

Much can be gained from reading what has been published or put online about a particular family or individual but everything should be checked and tested against your own research.

Family muniments

Family muniments often include a fascinating collection of material. There may be correspondence (both personal and connected with public service), papers concerning legal matters including titles to lands or administration of the estate, accounts, cookery books, memoirs, genealogies and much else. Detailed catalogues of the Gifts and Deposits collections of the NAS are being put online. If you are searching for papers concerning a titled family, remember that the reference may be either under their territorial title or under the family surname. Many archives (including the NAS) hold manuscript genealogies (which may be separate from collections of papers for a family) and reference to these can be accessed from website catalogues of holdings under the name of the family concerned. By no means all manuscript family charts or histories are to be trusted.

Maps and plans found in a family's muniments are an important and interesting source of information. These may define the bounds of lands held by the owner, show land use, names of adjacent proprietors, and give details of buildings. The Royal Commission on the Ancient and Historical Monuments of Scotland holds details of a great number of old and listed buildings, with drawings, manuscripts and photographs. A summary of information on the holdings relevant to a particular site or building can be accessed on their online database CANMORE.

Titles to land

(For detailed information on charters, sasines and retours, see 'Understanding legal documents – Land ownership', pp. 208–21.)

Records relating to the acquisition, possession and disposal of heritable property constitute a major source of information on a landowning family. You will need to find out whether the person in whom you are interested held land as a vassal of the Crown or of a subject superior. The abstracts of the Register of the Great Seal (published 1314–1668) include a great deal of information about those who were Crown vassals. In 1664, for example, the lands of Innerdeviot in Fife were to be granted to James Hamilton of Innerdeviot, second son of the late John Hamilton of Muirhouse and the late Anne Elphinstone his wife, whom failing to Thomas, brother of James, and then to Henry, John and Frederick in turn. Crown charters include grants of land to a wide range of persons, from small 'bonnet' lairds to the great magnates of Scotland, and in the view of Hamilton-Edwards (1972) 'there is probably hardly a family of any note in Scotland which does not appear somewhere in this register.'

Lands held of a subject superior were also granted under a charter. There is no register of these charters but many have survived in family charter chests, usually in those of the superior. The charters themselves are not always very interesting, naming the granter and the grantee, the lands concerned and the terms under which they are conveyed and any payments to be made for feu duty or other services. There may be a reference in a catalogue of family muniments to 'a progress of writs'. This is always worth studying as it will list documents validating the various transactions concerning the transfer of property at various times – charters, precepts, sasines, retours.

Land was transferred from one person to another through inheritance, by purchase or as security for a loan (the terms usually found are 'under reversion' or as a 'wadset'). All these transactions are common. Particularly from the eighteenth century onwards many landowning families felt the pressure of economic circumstances and either mortgaged land temporarily or disposed of it through sale (alienation). In the case of a wadset, the person who lent the money was infeft in the land and once the debt was repaid, another sasine was recorded whereby the lands were redeemed and reverted to the original owner.

Sasines are an important source for family history, but unfortunately, except during the Commonwealth period, they are written in Latin till well on in the eighteenth century. The post-1780 abridgements in English are, therefore, a life-saver for many. It is important to read the sasine (or abridgment) carefully, to check the terms of the transaction. The sasine indexes will not indicate the terms under which the land was being conveyed – whether this concerned inheritance, sale or a wadset. Wadsets can result in apparent complications. The original owner may continue to be termed 'of' the lands and the same lands could appear as security for several different loans. Sometimes a sasine was registered long after a new owner took possession and occasionally title was not completed by going through all the legal processes for many years.

Deeds

(See 'Understanding legal documents – Registers of deeds', pp. 202–8.) Deeds such as marriage settlements, dispositions, settlements and trusts have already been mentioned in relation to sources in connection with marriage and death but many other transactions are recorded in registers of deeds. Deeds have been described by Maitland Thomson as 'an inexhaustible store of information about the private life of our forefathers'. In a register of deeds – whether in the Books of Council and Session, in the registers of a sheriff court, burgh court, commissary court or franchise court – you may find agreements concerning trade, tacks, factories, bills, bonds and protests, as well as dispositions, trusts and settlements, all of which fill out what is known about the family – the people and their lives. In 1677, Sir John Falconer of Balmakellie made a contract with an Edinburgh mason to build him a house in Angus and this deed included a detailed description of the proposed building. In 1711 Lord Hay, who had rights over the Bass Rock, a precipitous island off the East Lothian coast, agreed with two poultrymen in Edinburgh that they might catch and sell 'all and haill the young solan geese and oyer fouls to be brought furth in the island' – the flesh of the geese being a delicacy in Edinburgh. George, Marquis of Huntly in 1684 wanted to be sure that he had the services of a personal physician and signed a contract with Robert Smith that the latter was to serve the Marquis in 'chirurgery and physick'. Bills and protested bills are concerned with financial matters and often contain little of interest, but contracts, factories and heritable bonds are likely to contain useful genealogical information.

Although many landowners had testaments registered in the commissary courts (and later included in the sheriff courts), it is as likely that their wishes for the settlement of their affairs after death will be found recorded as a deed – a document which could concern the disposal of both heritable and moveable goods.

The decision as to which register of deeds to search for evidence of your ancestor will often depend on which registers of deeds are indexed over the relevant period. You may find information on a landowner in any register of deeds – the Books of Council and Session contain documents relating to the affairs of many persons of social standing – but if these registers are not indexed and you have no exact reference to the date of registration of a particular document, it is unlikely to be worth taking the time to search this huge series. On the other hand, if there are indexes, searching annually under the name of your ancestor will not take very long and you may come across some interesting information. Sheriff court registers of deeds are not so bulky and with the aid of minute books or, if you are lucky, indexes, they can be searched more easily. Burgh registers of deeds will only be a hunting ground if your ancestor lived in a royal burgh. Very few registers of deeds of the franchise courts have survived.

Court cases

(See also 'Understanding legal documents – The courts', pp. 221–5.) Our ancestors were a litigious lot and much can be learned about them through the records of the law courts. Many got into financial difficulties or engaged in disputes with others. Without specific knowledge as to time and place of a case, it may be difficult to decide in which court an action was heard and the records of the various courts are so voluminous that it is unwise to embark on a blind search. There are, however, a growing number of records which can be searched online and these can yield interesting results. A database relating to Scottish criminal trials before the High Court of Justiciary can be consulted in the NAS West search room. It is also always worth searching the NAS online catalogue under the family surname, which may bring to light material in criminal or civil cases. As part of an action heard before the Court of Session, the highest civil court in Scotland, a great deal of material of various kinds might be produced in evidence. The Court of Session productions (volumes produced as evidence in the case) are now catalogued as CS96 (the NAS electronic catalogue can be searched by person or place) and the documents can be studied in the West search room of the NAS. Most of these cases deal with business concerns (many of them the result of bankruptcy) but there are a number which throw light on the private and public lives of landowners – concerning disputed trusts, and administration of estates, for example. In 1756 the judicial rentals of David Hay of Leys appear in a production; there is a genealogy of the Earls of Glencairn in another; and between 1669 and 1676 the Earl of Winton was engaged in litigation, resulting in a Court of Session action. The productions for this case include a rental book of his estate – and rules for feeding horses! There is also evidence produced in a legitimacy case concerning the Udny family which reveals a great deal of family history and includes title deeds of Udny from 1407. The productions also reflect the business interests of landowners. Clerk of Penicuik, for example, had considerable interests in coalmining and paper manufacture, and such undertakings resulted in many legal actions.

Merchants

The term 'merchant' is one which is not always easy to interpret. Someone described as a merchant may be little more than a peddler, trading goods from horseback or carrying them on his own back or, on the other hand, a merchant may be a very rich entrepreneur. At the top end of the scale were those involved in overseas trade and large-scale enterprise. There were also those running smaller businesses such as shopkeepers.

There have always been merchants in Scotland but with the growth of industrialisation in the eighteenth century, a growing number made money at home or overseas, set up manufactories and bought land, often becoming first-time landowners as well as merchants. The records relevant to landowners therefore also apply to many merchants. Merchants are found recording deeds in the Books of Council and Session or in any other court. Their property transactions will be found registered in the general, particular or burgh registers of sasines and not a few appeared in court.

The testamentary dispositions of merchants appear in the commissary courts and in sheriff courts, as well as in registers of deeds in the form of settlements, trusts and dispositions. As there were often a great many matters to clear up after death, merchants of any standing usually left a settlement of some kind.

Burgesses

(For a list of the royal burghs, see 'Where did they live?', p. 134.)
Until the Burgh Trading Act of 1846, only burgesses or freemen of a burgh were entitled to engage in trade overseas and thus you will find many merchant ancestors admitted as burgesses. There are comparatively few instances of women becoming burgesses though occasionally a widow of a burgess might put in a supplication to trade as a burgess. There was a rather surprising request in 1673 by the widow of Andrew Kinnear, the deceased minister at Calder, that she should be allowed to trade as a burgess during her lifetime.

Burgesses were admitted on the basis of being the son of a burgess, by marrying the daughter of a burgess (a means of raising the value of unmarried daughters of a burgess, so it was said), having served an apprenticeship, on payment of a sum of money or as an honour. Burgess entries are often very informative, stating the trade, reason for admission and in cases where this was on account of the father being a burgess, giving his name. If the man was married to the daughter of a burgess (and through her gained his right to be admitted), her name and that of her father will be supplied. Some admissions provide mini-genealogies and others say very little. When Frederick Augusta Campbell was admitted as burgess of Inveraray in 1768, the following entry was put in the town council minutes:

> Frederick Augusta Campbell, Esq. merchant in Venice, son to Dr. James Campbell of London who was son to the Reverend Mr. George Campbell, Professor of Divinity in the University of Edinburgh, who was a brother to the deceased Colin Campbell Esq., sometime of Ottir and son to George Campbell Esq. of Kenochtrie, Sheriff Justice General and Vice-Admiral Depute of

the Shire of Argyll and Western Isles of Scotland and a cadet of the Noble and Illustrious family of Argyll.

At the other end of the information scale, in 1767 there is a brief statement concerning this admission: 'John McColl, tailor in Inveraray'.

Evidence of admission as a burgess may sometimes enable you to draw up a genealogical chart covering several generations. If someone was admitted burgess by right of their father, a burgess, you can then look for the admission of the father. On the negative side, you can make certain assumptions from the fact that a man was admitted a burgess on account of having married the daughter of a burgess or because he had served an apprenticeship. In these cases, it is probable that the man could not claim the right to become a burgess through a burgess father. He may perhaps have moved into the burgh from another district and become a first-generation burgess there. Such deductions can be useful in knowing where to look next.

Many burgess entries (in Edinburgh, for example) are followed by the letters B. & G. B. This stands for 'burgess and guild brother'. Particularly in places which were trading ports (but also elsewhere), merchants (as well as the crafts) formed themselves into guilds. The composition of the guilds varied from time to time and from place to place and might include both merchants and craftsmen. Perth, Aberdeen, Stirling and Elgin had merchant guilds from the thirteenth century onwards. Members of the guilds were concerned with the administration of the burgh and control of trade.

Each royal burgh kept a list of burgess admissions. Entries are usually inscribed in the town council minutes. Names have been extracted from these records and published for a number of burghs (including, among others, Glasgow, Edinburgh, Inveraray and Aberdeen). The index to *Scottish texts and calendars* (Stevenson, 1987) will identify many of those which have been printed but a great deal of work has been done recently in extracting entries and publishing them. If there is no printed list of burgesses, then locate the relevant burgh records (in the NAS or a in local archive), see if there is a separate register of burgesses and if not, go through the council minutes to look for admissions.

Council minutes

The records of the royal burghs are an important and interesting source of information about any forebears who lived within these communities. The most important class in the burgh was made up of those who were merchants and from these persons (if they were burgesses) were elected most of the town magistrates. Beneath them were the members of the crafts – shoemakers, wrights and so on – who might also become burgesses, and below them were the unfreemen, referred to as 'indwellers' or 'inhabitants'. The town council minutes record the results of the yearly election of members of the council and the office each held.

The council minutes provide a detailed picture of life in the burgh in their administrative functions, dealing with such matters as water supplies, plague control, disposal of dung, fire risk to buildings and vandalism, but they also include the names of many merchants. In Campbeltown in 1743 the minutes include the names of twenty one maltsters who petitioned that several 'skilful' men should be appointed to examine the grain brought in for sale by tenant farmers, to ensure that the barley was properly cleaned and measured. In 1783 there is another list of Campbeltown maltsters who agreed to stop steeping the bear for malt as there was a scarcity of meal in Argyll, which was needed to feed the people. Such references may not provide a great deal of genealogical information but in profiling your ancestor and looking for identity clues, such 'sightings' can be of value. There may be other detailed listings. Bound in with the first volume of council minutes for Campbeltown in 1700 is 'ane accompt of the ground drawght of Campbeltown, declaring how much every man possesseth of houses and yeards', which includes not only the merchants but also the better-off tradespeople.

Shipowners and traders

Merchants in ports are often found listed as shipowners. Ships over a certain tonnage had to be registered and it was common for shares in a ship to be spread among a number of owners, often nine or more, sometimes only two or three, rarely one. These shares frequently changed hands and the alteration in ownership had to be recorded. By no means all shipping registers have survived. Some are in the NAS, some are still kept locally. If you search the NAS electronic catalogue under 'shipping registers' a number of entries will come up under the class 'CE' with information as to where these registers can be found, but other registers will be found kept locally. The records will only give you the name of the persons who owned shares in the ship, the ship's name, her tonnage, and where and when she was built. An analysis of the names of Campbeltown shipowners in the second half of the eighteenth century, tested against other lists of merchants in the burgh, indicated that nearly every merchant in the burgh had shares in a vessel.

The import/outport records kept by each main port (NAS, class reference E504), known as the collector's quarterly customs accounts,
are of more interest. These returns are arranged by port and record
the arrival and departure of every ship carrying dutiable goods coastwise or engaged in overseas trade within the period 1742–1830. Each
entry gives the name of the ship, her tonnage, the name of her master,
details of her cargo, the port from which she had come or to which she
was bound and the name of a merchant responsible for the cargo. This
is usually one of the owners but the names of all the owners of the
ship are not given. Members of the same family sometimes appear as
merchant owner and as shipmaster. There are no indexes but the
records are clearly written and much can be learned about the trade
of the locality and the names of those engaged in it by browsing
through the pages. The amount of genealogical information about an
individual may be small but details of trading interests are often
interesting.

Business records

Once you have established in what business your merchant forebear was
engaged, you can then search further. There are a number of collections
in the NAS concerned with business records and overseas trade. Payne
(1967) includes surveys of records of various industries, and Glasgow
University Archives (as well as other local archives and universities)
hold a great many records relating to various enterprises and companies. A search of the online catalogues for the NAS, the NRA and of
local archives and libraries under either the name of the family (if they
owned the business) or under the type of business is often rewarding.
Records may include ledgers, journals, letter books, accounts, reports,
correspondence and agreements, as well as wage records.

Such collections are often large and you will have to decide what
you want to find – background details of the family's business enterprise or just genealogical details. You may find both. Catalogue entries
relating to collections in Dundee University for the Baxter Brothers,
linen and jute manufacturers, indicate that the records go back to the
end of the eighteenth century and include minute and letter books,
ledgers, wages books, order books, inventories and valuations but
there are also genealogical notes on the Baxter family from 1795 to
1986.

Many books have been written about various trades and industries
and if you know the particular trade in which an ancestor was
involved – such as weaving or the tobacco trade – a published work on
the subject may include a bibliography of primary sources and other

printed books on the subject. The NLS online catalogue can be searched by subject, as well as by author and title.

Merchants and the courts

Involvement in enterprise was risky and a great many businessmen either got into legal arguments or financial difficulties or went bankrupt (see p. 200). Court of Session productions contain references to an enormous number of business records of all kinds – inventories, work journals and ledgers, ships' logbooks, letter books, correspondence and accounts. The catalogue is indexed under name, place and subject, which makes it possible to use this as a source list in discovering background information on the management of various businesses, or on occupations and trades – apothecaries, artificial flower makers, calico printers, cattle dealers, papermakers, potters or upholsterers. When searching the NAS electronic catalogue, key in CS96 plus a family or business name or a particular trade.

Crafts and trades

Apprenticeships

Members of the crafts and trades – skinners, cordiners, wrights, weavers, hammermen and others – were the other important component in the make-up of the burgh. Though considered inferior to the merchant burgesses, they were represented on the town council. When Campbeltown became a royal burgh in 1700, there were eighteen members of council, of whom four were drawn from the trades – a maltman, a hammerman, a tailor and a joiner.

Admission to a craft was through serving an apprenticeship (an indenture), as son or son-in-law of a craftsmen or for good service to the community, and as burgesses they are listed with the merchant burgesses. A number of merchants, in fact, apprenticed their sons to crafts – this was one of the ways in which a merchant from outwith the burgh could gain his son's admittance to the ranks of the burgess elite of a burgh. The social system in Scotland was flexible and the younger son of a landowner was often trained in a trade.

The Scottish Record Society has printed and indexed the registers of apprentices for Edinburgh, covering the years 1583–1800. These volumes are available in most larger libraries and family history centres in Scotland and elsewhere. The name of the apprentice's father is given, the name of the person to whom he is apprenticed, his trade and the date of the start of the apprenticeship. There is also a series of indentures covering the years 1695–1934 in the NAS, (referenced

RH9/17/274–326) but they are not at present indexed. Once the whole catalogue of the NAS is online, it should be possible to identify a relevant document in this series by keying in the name of the person. Some Scottish apprentices (but by no means all) are listed in the English Stamp Board's apprenticeship books for the years 1710–1811 as stamp duty was levied on apprenticeships over these years. These books are in the National Archives in London but they are also indexed online at www.britishorigins.com. This is a subscription service. Each entry gives the name of the apprentice, a parent and master, as well as occupation. A number of local societies are working on extracting names of apprentices and publishing them. The records of the particular craft or incorporation if they have survived also include details of apprenticeships.

Apprenticeships were regulated according to the supply and demand for persons of a particular skill. A boy was usually apprenticed at the age of about fourteen but it could be later or earlier. The kirk session, who had the expense of maintaining an orphan, were often eager to rid themselves of their responsibilities and in Crichton there is a note in the session minutes referring to William Russell 'now about nine years of age' for whom they wanted to find an apprenticeship. The apprenticeship lasted between three and seven years, usually five, the apprentice then becoming a journeyman, paid by the day.

Some indentures are registered as deeds – usually in the burgh or sheriff court – but it may be difficult to find such a document and for a great many apprenticeships there is no surviving documentation. The deed will usually name the apprentice's father or person who is responsible for him, the terms of the apprenticeship and the name of the master. In 1748 James Sawers, son of Robert Sawers in Haddington, became indentured to George Roughhead, a glazier, and had to sign an agreement whereby he promised not to absent himself, to protect his master in all ways, not to play cards, curse or swear or 'idely mis-spend the Sabbath day' and 'god forbid' that he should be guilty of adultery or fornication. In return, his master had to uphold him in clothes, linen and woollens, give him bed and board and teach him fully.

Craft incorporations

Whenever there was a sufficiently large group of persons belonging to a particular craft in a burgh, an incorporation or guild was formed and there are records of various incorporations both in the NAS and in local archives. Look also at the index to the NRA under the name of the burgh or under 'guilds and incorporations'. In the NAS, the craft records are very scattered and appear in burgh registers (bakers of Haddington, hammermen of Burntisland), in deposits of private papers (carters in Leith, goldsmiths in Edinburgh) or in the Exchequer records (fleshers of Ayr and dyers of Aberdeen). The records of the Leith incorporation of coopers going back to the sixteenth century have just been acquired by Edinburgh City Archives. These are only a few of the records which have survived.

The craft records often include lists of members. Entries referring to admission of a craftsman to the incorporation may, like the burgess admissions, provide genealogical information in the grounds for acceptance – through his father or wife or having served an apprenticeship. *The history of the Incorporation of Gardeners of Glasgow 1626–1903* (McNab, 1903) includes a list of members up to 1903 in order of their admission 'with their craft genealogy'. Some of these lists cover a number of generations. On 12 September 1884 William Connell was entered as a member, being son-in-law of John Bryce, who was entered in 1864 as son of James Bryce, entered 1793 as son of William Bryce, entered 1766 as son of William Bryce, entered 1738 as son-in-law of William Hatridge. The incorporation of weavers in Glasgow has membership records showing the enrolment of apprentices and journeymen between 1717 and 1817.

Details of when the boy started his apprenticeship and when he made his final assay – the practical proof of his skills – are useful in providing genealogical information. In the Haddington fleshers' craft records it is stated: '4 September 1742: the which day Alexr. Fraser son to the deceast John Fraser gardner in Had^n is booked apprentice to David Dick flesher of the burgh'. Such an entry provides quite a lot of clues for further work on the family. The 'assay' for an apprentice to become a member of the fleshers' incorporation in Haddington was to kill and dress a sheep within three hours.

Many of the guilds acted in the capacity of friendly societies and their records include references to payment for funerals, pension rolls, assistance to the poor or other expenses relating to its members, who may be listed by name. The records also provide insight into social life at the time. By 1744 the fleshers of Haddington were already spending money purchasing newspapers from London – and there are regular annual accounts for the provision of music at their elections. MacDougall (1978) lists many of these records though they are often of little interest genealogically and contain few names.

Burgh sasines

Many of the craft members were well-to-do and owned property in the burgh. Even though most of the burgh sasines registers are unindexed and lack minute books, it is worth looking through the registers at the appropriate time. As the burgh registers of sasines are local in their coverage, this will not be too great a task. The sasines are in English unless you are dealing with a very early period and simpler in form than those in other registers. In the case of inheritance, you may find retours in a burgh register – documents which were much simpler than those which involved Chancery. Burgh registers of deeds should also be searched. (See 'Understanding legal documents').

Tradespeople

Many people who had a trade were not members of a craft (which was only applicable to the burghs). Some combined farming a smallholding of land with carrying out a trade such as shoemaking or weaving. The *First* and *Second Statistical Accounts* often include information on how many persons were working in a particular capacity in the parish at the time of writing – as masons, wrights or weavers, for example. A popular 'trade' was that of spirit seller. The sale of spirits was widespread – often illicitly distilled – and many cases concerning those apprehended by the excise officers were heard in the JP courts. The excise officers were not always unopposed in the execution of their duties. In 1729, an officer seized over five gallons of British spirits for which the changekeeper in Inveraray, Alexander Lambie, had no permit. His wife, Florence McKay, denied obstructing the officer when he attempted to gauge the cask but did admit obstructing him when he tried to remove it.

In the nineteenth century, licensing courts were held by the sheriffs. Lists may appear among the sheriff court records giving the name of the applicant to sell spirits and his address, the name of the landlord, names of persons recommending the applicant (sometimes, rather surprisingly, the minister or an elder of the kirk), the accommodation and whether the application was granted. There may also be a register of applications for publicans' certificates, giving the name and designation of the publican and the 'house' and its whereabouts.

Some directories for towns and cities giving names of merchants and tradespeople go back to the second half of the eighteenth century. Torrance (1998) gives a list of published directories. Nineteenth-century post office directories exist for a number of large towns and have sections covering trades, individuals and lists of those living in each street – but the directories do not cover everyone. The books also include advertisements, which are an interesting source of social history about goods sold and services offered. Whether the name of a person engaged in trade is in a directory will probably depend on his financial situation and size of business.

Some tradesmen qualified for the vote from 1832 onwards and their names may be included in voters' registers. The occupation of the voter will be given – but the fact that the person had the vote will tell you something about their station in life.

Testaments of tradespeople

The facility to search the indexes to testaments and inventories for the whole of Scotland up to 1901 under an occupation as well as under a name can produce some interesting findings and illustrates the fact that many people working in the various trades registered testaments. In Glasgow commissary court between the mid-sixteenth century and 1823, 305 weavers and 146 cordiners left testaments, while in the less populated area covered by the Dunblane commissary court, seventy five weavers and thirty five cordiners were listed over the same period. A study of these testaments can throw light not only on family members and individual circumstances but on the tools and trade of those following particular occupations.

Customs and Excise officers

The history of the board of Customs and Excise is on the NAS information sheet which can be accessed on their electronic catalogue under CE. The administrative structure of the boards of Customs and of Excise was different but officers from both boards were in many cases situated in the same places. The customs staff were stationed at out-ports (often having responsibilities for smaller ports or creeks), who reported to the board in Edinburgh, while excise was administered by local 'collections', then divided into districts. Staff records include lists of officers serving at each port, admissions to office, deaths, and details under records titled 'ages and capacities', which may include comments on general conduct and efficiency. Salaries paid to customs officers are recorded in the customs cash accounts – NAS class reference E502. The customs' letter books (collector to board) sometimes contain information about staff and are always worth reading as they give an insight into the daily workload of the officers, their struggles with Edinburgh's bureaucracy and their often unequal battle against smugglers. Wilkins (1993) provides a detailed introduction to these records. An indexed series of notes on excise officers covering the period 1707–1830 has been compiled by Mr J. F. Mitchell and can be viewed in the NAS search room on microfiche.

Lawyers

Members of the professions – including lawyers, doctors and others – were often sons of landed families but many belonged to an upwardly mobile class. As sons of merchants or craftsmen or even as 'lads o' pairts' (who sometimes became ministers) they frequently married into the landed classes or acquired property on their own account and records can therefore be found in registers of deeds and sasines, as well as in material relating to their own profession. Many attended schools (such as the Edinburgh Academy or one of the merchant company schools) for which there are printed records, or went to university.

There are several categories of lawyers in Scotland. The earliest lawyers were the notaries public. The notaries practised in a royal burgh or in a particular area, recording legal documents and instruments of sasine. The NAS catalogue for the records of the notaries (class reference NP) includes a guide to the district in which each worked. There are registers of admission of notaries (not always complete) from 1563 to 1903, and the registers are supplemented by warrants of admission (class reference NP2–NP6). Most entries give the name and designation but some, particularly the early ones, include age and the name of the notary's father and occasionally marital state.

Those who are described as 'writers' (now usually referred to as 'solicitors') acted as general law agents and could plead cases in the sheriff courts and other inferior courts. They may have served an apprenticeship, which would be recorded in a sheriff court register of deeds, but one rarely finds records relating to their training. From 1848 onwards there is a published *Scottish Law List* (originally published as the *Index Juridicus*), which can be consulted in many libraries. Some writers were also notaries public.

Writers to the Signet are lawyers who have been admitted as members of the College of Justice and add WS after their names. *Society of Writers to H. M. Signet* (McKechnie, 1936) gives the names of members from 1594–1890, including details of apprenticeship and often name of the father. Like many other secondary sources, it is very useful but not every WS is included. It is often assumed that an ancestor was a Writer to the Signet when in fact he was just a writer.

Advocates are the only lawyers who could plead in the Court of Session as well as in all other civil and criminal courts and before the House of Lords. In Aberdeen, solicitors working in the inferior courts also took on this title without having the same rights to practise (they are listed in *History of the Society of Advocates in Aberdeen*,

Henderson, 1912). A list of advocates in Scotland 1532–1943 has been published by the Scottish Record Society (Grant, 1944) and includes genealogical notes on members.

Judges of the Court of Session were known as Senators and their careers are described in *An historical account of the Senators of the College of Justice* (Brunton and Haig, 1832).

The medical profession

Chirurgeon apothecaries and barbers undertook a great deal of medical work in earlier times. A barber usually belonged to a barber's craft and may therefore be listed in such records in the relevant burgh. Registration of medical practitioners was introduced in 1858 and *The Medical Register* has been published annually from that date and is available in some public libraries. The name of the doctor is given, with address and qualifications. *The Medical Directory for Scotland*, also produced annually, gives rather fuller details. There was a separate *Medical Directory for Scotland 1852–60*, it was then continued as the *London and Provincial Medical Directory* up to 1869, and thereafter became known as *The Medical Directory*. There are published annual registers for chemists dating from 1869, for dentists from 1879, midwives from 1917 and nurses from 1921.

The Royal College of Physicians in Edinburgh, the Royal College of Surgeons of Edinburgh and the Royal College of Physicians and Surgeons of Glasgow all have archives containing information about their members. Their catalogues can be accessed through SCAN.

By keying in 'hospitals' or 'health boards' as the search word for all the SCAN sites you will find references to many hospitals in Scotland with records going back to the seventeeth century. These records may be held in the archives of a university, hospital or in a local archive and include information about nurses, doctors and patients.

Education

Teachers

The responsibility for appointing and paying the schoolmasters rested with either the burgh or the parish and in some cases with both – often with unhappy consequences for the schoolmaster if neither wished to pay his salary. References to appointments, fees, subjects taught and other matters concerning the burgh or parish school will be found in the council minutes of a royal burgh, in kirk session or presbytery minutes or in heritors' minutes. The presbytery was responsible for confirming the appointment of the parish schoolmaster. The school-master often acted as the session clerk of the parish and his name will therefore appear in the kirk session minutes, and after 1854 many took over the post of registrar. Many comments on their efficiency appear in the reports on the registrars made annually by the examiners (NAS class reference GRO1).

There are three manuscript lists of education sources in the NAS. The lists are not indexed but are listed by class of record in which the material is found – in gifts and deposits or heritors' records, for example. After the passing of the Education Act of 1872, school boards dealt with education in each parish and their minute books include references to the appointment of teachers and pupil-teachers. Most of these records are in the hands of local councils or local archives, though some (for Midlothian and East Lothian and a few others) are in the NAS. There are some records of teachers in the counties of Aberdeen, Banff and Moray (after 1832) in the Dick Bequest Trust records (NAS reference GD1/4) as Mr James Dick had left money for the maintenance and assistance of parochial school-masters in these counties.

In addition to the parish or burgh school, especially in the large cities, a number of schools, known as 'hospitals', were endowed by the merchant companies or through mortifications to educate orphans or those in need. The NAS holds the records of George Heriot's School in Edinburgh (GD421), Dr Guthrie's Schools (GD425) and the Orphan Hospital GD417). Scotland (1969) has references to many of these schools and printed works on them.

There were also private schools known as adventure schools or schools with a practical bias, teaching weaving or spinning, for example. It is not easy to find records of these schools though there are some references to their existence in the *Statistical Accounts*, where there are also comments on the state of the parish school, some-times with details of fees paid by the pupils and subjects studied. The commissioners responsible for the management of the Forfeited Estates were also concerned with education and there are a number of records relating to schools on the annexed estates (see Smith, 1982).

A considerable number of schools were run under the auspices of dissenting churches. At one time there were over 700 schools managed by the Free Church, and many episcopal schools. Information con-cerning these schools may be with the records of the church con-cerned. The appointment of teachers in Free Church schools, made by the deacons, can be found in the CH3 records in the NAS. For a long time, it was the policy for Catholics to attend the local schools, even after the Catholic Emancipation Act of 1829, but there were a growing number of Catholic schools during the nineteenth century.

In 1709 the Society in Scotland for Propagating Christian Knowledge (SSPCK) was granted letters patent 'to erect and maintain schools in such parts of the Highlands and Islands of Scotland, as should be thought to need them most'. There is a large collection of papers relating to these schools in the NAS (GD95) and the repertory can be consulted online. The records include details of all the schoolmasters, as well as reports on visitations of the schools. The Scottish Record Society has published a digest of all the information on the careers of the SSPCK schoolmasters between 1709 and 1872, including some personal details – not always complimentary (Cowper, 1997). John Campbell, who died in 1844, served as schoolmaster at Barr in Argyll for forty-two years. He had a wife and five children. It was reported that he was 'an irregular character' but his son, Peter, who assisted him, was 'more efficient'.

Pupils

Finding information on a particular scholar is rarely successful. Petitions for admission to the hospitals or orphanages can be very informative and provide full details of the family background, but, lacking indexes, a long and possibly negative search may be involved unless you know the date of admission.

School logbooks for many schools have survived for the period from 1872 onwards. A few are in the NAS but others are scattered round the country, many in local archives. Information about individuals is unlikely to amount to more than a name. Libraries and history societies may also have records for the local schools.

A number of schools, particularly (but not exclusively) the private schools such as the Edinburgh Academy, Fettes College and Loretto School among others, have published lists of former pupils (sometimes including details of post-school careers) and for many there are published Rolls of Honour recording those who have fallen in various wars (see Torrance, 1998).

Following the Reform Act of 1832, grants were made by Parliament towards the building of schools and this was followed by the appointment of inspectors to see how this money was spent. The first inspector was appointed in 1840 with the remit of visiting all grant-aided schools in Scotland. Reports compiled by a growing number of inspectors and reflecting the wider remit of their work are in the NAS (class reference ED16–ED18), covering the years 1859 onwards, though there are gaps. These reports throw light on conditions in schools in the nineteenth and twentieth centuries, their buildings and what was taught, but will not mention pupils by name.

During the nineteenth century a number of reports were compiled by parliamentary commissioners and select committees which include information and statistics on the education of the poor, parish and burgh schools and endowed schools. (See Haythornthwaite, 1993 and Ford, (1953)).

University students

There are published lists of graduates at the four oldest Scottish universities of St Andrews, Glasgow, Kings College, Aberdeen (and later Marischal College, Aberdeen) and Edinburgh but the information given is not always helpful from a genealogical point of view, nor is it always accurate. The matriculation lists for Glasgow University (Addison, 1913) are more helpful, giving parish of birth and name of father of each student. University archivists may hold additional material. Torrance (1998) provides a bibliography of published lists of students in Scotland and also of Scottish students studying elsewhere

Members of Parliament and electors

There are several printed works which deal with the careers of Members of Parliament. Up to the Union of 1707, Scotland had its own Parliament and brief biographies of the men who represented the burghs and counties up to that date are given in the two-volume work by Young (1992–93). Details are given of parliamentary career and on the family. References to the sources from which the information was taken are noted. *Who's who of British Members of Parliament* (Stenton and Lees, 4 vols, 1976–81) covers the period from 1832 to 1979 and again includes biographical details of members.

Before the Reform Act of 1832 a very few men had the right to vote but from this time onwards the number of persons entitled to vote expanded and by 1929 almost everyone over twenty one was on the electoral roll. Up till 1918, the annual registers had to record the qualifications of the voter – occupation, whether proprietor or tenant, description of property and occupation – but later rolls are valuable in providing an address.

County rolls are arranged by parish but there are also burgh rolls, sometimes with several burghs grouped together. Not all electoral rolls have survived. The NAS holds many kept with the burgh and sheriff court records (see *Tracing your Scottish ancestors*, NAS, 2003) but local libraries and archives will usually be able to provide information about what is available and where they can be consulted. Some very recent electoral rolls are online at www.192.com though you may have to pay to access them.

The Church

The Established Church of Scotland

Biographical details of the ministers of the Established Church of Scotland from the Reformation to the present are published in a series of volumes, *Fasti ecclesiae Scoticanae* (Scott, 1961). The volumes are arranged by synod and presbytery and by parish within the presbytery. Groome's *Gazetter* gives the name of the synod and presbytery within which each parish came. The *Old* and *New Statistical Accounts* also give this information. Each entry includes details of the career of the minister and usually personal details – names of parents, if known, children and publications – and there are references to some sources such as monumental inscriptions, testaments and written biographies. An enormous number of families seem to have a minister in their ranks at some time and the *Fasti* is a valuable reference book, though there are some errors and omissions. The period from the Reformation up to 1638 is covered by *Fasti ecclesiae Scoticanae medii aevi ad annum 1638* (Watt, 1969) but provides few or no personal details.

In the Highlands and Islands, itinerant preachers and catechists were often employed over the period 1725–1876 and information about them can be found in the records of the Royal Bounty Committee (NAS reference CH1/2/29/3). You need to have some idea as to when a forebear was acting in this capacity as the records are not indexed. Many ministers were university graduates.

Dissenting churches

There are a number of published books which provide biographical details on ministers of dissenting churches (see Bibliography). Most include personal information as well as an outline of the minister's career. The United Presbyterian Church (Small, 1904) gives details of ministers who had belonged to the Relief Church and the Associate Synods, with the subsequent splits in the congregations, most of whom who came together as the United Secession Church between 1820 and 1847 and were afterwards called the United Presbyterian Church. New College Library on the Mound, at Edinburgh, holds a considerable amount of material on the Free Church and United Presbyterian congregations, as well as on members of the Church of Scotland, including portraits of leading churchmen.

Roman Catholic Church

Roman Catholic doctrine and worship was abolished by Act of Parliament in 1560 though for a number of years the old organisation of the Church continued in many places. The names of Roman Catholic secular clergy for the years 1732–1878 are given in *The Innes Review* (Scottish Catholic Historical Association, Vols 17, 34 and 40). Some material may be found in the Scottish Catholic archives in Edinburgh.

The Episcopal Church

Bertie (2000) has published a *Fasti* of the Scottish episcopal clergy for the years 1689–2000, the parishes being listed by diocese. There is also a manuscript of list of episcopal clergymen extracted by E. W. Binning from the *Scottish Episcopal Church year book and directory*, which commenced in 1878.

Military service

The army

Before 1707 there was no standing army in Scotland and men were usually raised as need demanded. The result is that there are relatively few army records up to this time. Some muster rolls for the Scottish army in the seventeenth century are among the Exchequer records in the NAS (E100) but they are not indexed and few provide more than a name and usually rank.

After the Union of the Crowns in 1707, the army and the navy were administered from London and most of the records relating to the armed services (including later the Royal Air Force) are kept at the National Archives at Kew. There are a number of good guides to these records (see Bibliography) and TNA's online catalogue is accompanied by introductions to various classes of documents – the number of classes of records for which there are online indexes or which are digitised is growing rapidly.

World War I campaign medals have been digitised and the online index to soldiers' discharge records (WO97) is useful. This series covers the years 1760–1913 and concerns the service documents of soldiers (but not officers), many of whom were Scots, who became in- or out-pensioners of the Royal Hospital Chelsea. Details are given of the soldier's age, birthplace, service, physical description, occupation at the time of enlistment and reason for discharge. After 1883 the papers usually contain details of next of kin, marriage and children. The online indexes themselves include useful genealogical information.

Alexander Stewart served in the army between 1804 and 1827 and the index states that he was born in Dull, Perthshire, served in the 78th Foot Regiment and was discharged at the age of thirty nine. Copies of the papers can be ordered through the internet or viewed at Kew on microform.

Details of army officers can be found in the printed *Army lists*, issued annually from 1754 to 1879. The fuller lists compiled by Lieutenant-General Henry Hart commenced in 1839 (and continue till 1915) and contain more detail of an officer's war service. Most of these printed lists can be consulted at Kew. Kitzmiller (1987–88) has provided a useful guide to the movements of all regiments, tracing their service and where this took place – information which can be very useful both in locating where a soldier might have been at a particular time and indicating with which regiment he might have been serving.

If your ancestor was an officer, there may be information in a gazette, mainly concerned with the announcements of military promotions or awards of medals. Work is being carried out in putting the London, Edinburgh and Belfast gazettes online. The publications go back to the mid-seventeenth century and in time all will be available on the website www.gazettes-online.co.uk. The years 1900–79 have already been covered. You will need to know an approximate date in order to narrow the search.

The NAS has published a two-volume *Military source list* – a guide to military records which they hold, covering the period both before and after 1707. The first volume lists references to military matters found in private archives kept in the NAS. The volume is arranged by class of record and is indexed only by regiment and by battle and campaign but not by person. Later acquisitions are not covered. The second volume is a guide to documents dealing with military history in government sources such as sheriff court or Exchequer records but it is unindexed. Searching the NAS electronic catalogue under the name of the person (if important), by parish, sheriffdom, regiment or class of record (such as fencibles), by battle or campaign may now bring up useful references.

There are a number of museums in Scotland containing records and memorabilia of various Scottish regiments – for example, a room in the Dunkeld Cathedral Chapter House archives holds records of the Scottish Horse in the Boer War which list name, rank, enlistment date and names of next of kin. Cox (1999) includes references to a number of regimental museums including the National War Museum at the Castle, Edinburgh (previously known as the Scottish United Services Museum). *A guide to military museums and other places of military interest* (Wise, 2001) covers museums and historic sites over the whole of Britain.

Records of the East India Company Service, which was not only a trading company but until 1859 ran the army in India, and also had its own navy, are mainly in the British Library in London (Oriental and India Office Collections – website www.bl.uk). These include both civilians and members of the army and work is in progress to make these accessible by putting indexes online. There are also a number of online databases (see Stewart, 2004), as well as printed lists of such persons as officers in the Bengal army, and marine records. Hamilton-Edwards (1972) has an extensive bibliography of published material taken from the East India Company records.

There are a growing number of websites which provide information on men who fought or died in particular battles or campaigns.

Volunteers, fencibles and militia

After the Act of Union, there were occasions, most notably at the time of the Napoleonic War, when men were raised locally for military service as volunteers, fencibles and militia.

Volunteers – The volunteer corps (sometimes known as yeomanry) were raised to provide local defence in case of invasion. They were mostly led by local gentry. They signed on for an unspecified period and each corps had its own rules. They were regarded as the local 'home guard' and were often accorded little respect. Some corps remained even after the end of the Napoleonic Wars and were used to bolster up local policing.

Fencibles – A number of fencible regiments were raised by Scottish landowners over the period 1759–99. They were enlisted voluntarily, acting as full-time regulars but only during hostilities and usually only served in Scotland, occasionally in England or Ireland but never overseas unless all members voted for this action. From 1800 onwards these regiments were disbanded and their place was taken by the militia. A list of fencible regiments of the British army for the period 1793–1814 can be found on the website www.regiments.org/regiments/uk/lists/fen1793.htm.

Militia – The exigencies of the wars with France at the end of the eighteenth and beginning of the nineteenth century made it necessary to have a force of well-equipped and disciplined men who could be used for home defence and, if necessary, maintain civil order. Men could volunteer but most were raised under a ballot system. Service was primarily in Scotland.

Following the Scottish Militia Act of 1797, these forces became very important during the Napoleonic Wars and their records contain a great deal of genealogical information. Each parish was given a quota of men to be supplied for the militia. If there were not enough volunteers to make up the numbers, then the parish schoolmaster or constable had to compile a list of men within the parish who were liable for military service – able-bodied and between certain ages (the age limits varied from time to time but could be between eighteen and forty five, sometimes as young as sixteen). These lists usually state the name of the person, residence and occupation – occasionally a relationship such as 'son of'. Exemption was granted to certain categories of men – apprentices, ministers, schoolmasters, men with more than two children under the age of ten and those with a physical disability. Some of the lists of those within the age limits include comments – 'balloted', 'an apprentice', 'above age', 'wanting a thum', blind of an eye'.

From the numbers of those assessed as liable for military service, a ballot was taken to fill the quota required from that parish by the authorities. Some of the surviving lists refer to those balloted rather than to those who were liable for militia service and therefore only represent a small proportion of persons within the parish. It is important to try to ascertain which kind of list it is.

Service was not popular and there were many instances of a substitute taking the place of someone who was balloted. Sometimes a payment of money was made to the substitute and a number of insurance schemes were organised whereby each militia-liable person paid a subscription and if balloted, money was paid from the insurance fund to buy a substitute.

On joining the militia or fencibles, each man gave an attestation oath, naming the man concerned (or his substitute), and usually giving regiment, age, occupation, parish and county of birth, and signature or mark if he could not write. Occasionally personal remarks about the character or appearance of the soldier are included.

Once a soldier had enlisted, his wife might apply for dependant allowances. These applications normally name the soldier and the parish for which he served (which might not be his own parish of residence), give the name of his wife and names and ages of young children. When searching the parish registers for names of children born to a couple in the late 1790s and early 1800s, it is quite common to find a gap in the family and the reason may be that the father was away serving in the militia. Dependents' allowances may sometimes supply the names of children born during this period.

It is not always easy to track down relevant militia records and many have been lost. Some are in the muniments of landowners, others can be found with kirk session records, with sheriff court records (sometimes classed as 'miscellaneous records'), lieutenancy records (NAS reference CO), and a few are with the burgh records. The Exchequer made many payments to families of serving men during the Napoleonic Wars and there is a large collection of records there (NAS class reference E). Other records are in local archives (Edinburgh City Archives have a large collection) or are listed in the NRA. There are also a number in the Public Record Office at Kew as the army was an English responsibility. Arnold Morrison has compiled a valuable guide to Scottish sources for militias, fencibles and volunteers (1996). Searching the online catalogue of the NAS or of other archives and of the NRA under 'militia', 'fencibles', 'volunteers' or 'yeomanry' should bring to light many of these records.

Seamen

Information about those who served on Scottish ships is sparse. There are no official records for a Scottish navy and you should look for naval records (post-1707) in the National Archives at Kew (see Rodger, 1988).

Merchant seamen are also hard to trace (see Watts, 1991) and customs records name the master of a ship but do not include the names of the sailors. After 1834 it became compulsory for masters to make agreements with the crew but only a few of these documents have survived for Scottish sailors and you need to know on which ship your ancestor was sailing.

It can be very frustrating to find a good source of information about people but not to be able to access it. In an attempt to encourage fisheries and the training of seamen in the second half of the eighteenth century, the government paid out bounties on herring 'busses', which were decked ships of between 20 and 80 tons, but to qualify for the payment, the master had to put down the name of every member of the crew, with age, height, colour of hair and parish of birth. As the sailors (often landsmen) might sign on with a different ship each season, and in one year there might be several thousand men on the 'busses', without indexing it is impossible to make use of this source (customs cash vouchers, NAS class reference E508). Ships involved in whaling between 1750 and 1825 were also paid bounties and details of their crews are entered in the Exchequer papers (also E508) but the records are unindexed and are listed by ship. Unlike the hundreds of 'busses', however, there were comparatively few whalers, which makes it possible to go through the vouchers if you know your ancestor was a whaler.

Rebels

The names of many combatants have only survived because they were branded as rebels, were taken prisoner, transported or executed. It is important, therefore, to consider when an ancestor lived and to look for any clues as to where his allegiance might have lain. The Earl of Argyll's rebellion in 1685 and the Jacobite uprisings of 1715 and 1745 are only a few of the historical events which have left records relating to those who took part (usually on the losing side) and one has to bear in mind that surviving references to names of those involved are almost certainly incomplete. Due to the number of common Highland names, it is often difficult or impossible to determine with certainty the identity of the person concerned, but the information may provide at least a possible 'sighting' of an ancestor. The *Register of the Privy Council of Scotland* (published and indexed from 1545 to 1691), contains the names of a number of persons who were transported as prisoners during this time.

The disarming of the Highlanders after the 1715 rebellion has resulted in a most valuable document compiled at that time by James Campbell of Stonefield, sheriff depute of Argyll at the time (Maclean-Bristol, 1998). This probably names a good proportion (but not all) of the male population of Canna, Coll, Tiree and Mull, as well as of the nearby mainland of Morvern, Ardnamurchan and Sunart. The men in each township are named and described as 'not in the rebellion', 'out of the country' or 'confesses he was in the rebellion'. Many are named by their patronymics. At Drumfinn on Mull one of those listed was 'Neil McDhoil VcNeil alias McCraing' – Neil son of Donald, grandson of Neil alias McCraing – which takes the family genealogy back two generations.

The problem of finding out about rebels is illustrated by the difficulties of discovering the names of those who fought for Prince Charles Edward Stuart and what happened to them. About 3,500 prisoners were taken at or after the battle of Culloden but many were tried at Carlisle, Newcastle or London. Lots were drawn among the prisoners and one in twenty was selected for trial, thus representing only a small proportion of the total number. A great deal of research has been carried out and lists published of names of those who served under the various Jacobite commanders (see Livingstone, Aikman and Hart, 1984), but a reference to Daniel Smith or James Robertson serving in the Duke of Perth's regiment makes positive identification almost impossible and all that may be known about a person is whether he was taken prisoner or killed. Lists of prisoners taken in the '45 (Seton and Arnot, 1928–29) do contain more information.

If you can locate a history of the particular war or uprising in which an ancestor was concerned, this may include a bibliography of primary sources which can then be consulted.

Criminals

In genealogy circles, it pays to have a criminal rather than a law-abiding ancestor as there will almost certainly be records relating to the wrong doer, and the more heinous the crime, the more likely you are to find information on the case.

Petty crime could be dealt with in an enormous range of courts – in the commissary court, burgh court, JP court, admiralty court, sheriff court, franchise or baron court – and therefore unless you have an exact reference to the court in which a case was heard and the approximate date, it may not be worth taking time to trawl through such a range of records. Serious cases (including cases which resulted in transportation) came before the High Court of Justiciary which sat both in Edinburgh and went on circuit. All nineteenth- and twentieth-century High Court trials held before a jury are now indexed on the NAS electronic catalogue – and the indexing is being extended. (See 'Understanding legal documents – The courts', pp. 221–3.) These cases may contain a great deal of information about the person or persons concerned, though not all evidence given should be believed.

Emigrants

(See also 'Starting research – Emigrant links', p. 9–11.)
One of Scotland's biggest exports has been its people. There are a growing number of online databases dealing with emigrants. An index of the names of emigrants who were assisted by the Highlands and Islands Emigration Society to settle in Australia 1852–57 (NAS reference HD4/5) has been put online and can be consulted at scan.org.uk/researchtools/emigration.htm. A full transcript of the entry for a particular family or individual can be brought up on this site, giving names, ages, residences and family groupings. Stewart (2004) includes an interesting list of other online listings – US

immigration through Ellis Island 1892–1924, immigrants to Canada 1925–35, to the Australian states of New South Wales 1839–96 and Victoria 1839–1911, and names of children sent to work in Canada in the late nineteenth century. *Cyndi's List* contains links to a great many genealogy sites, a number of which concern immigration indexes. In Australia there are numerous websites dealing with immigrants and, in New South Wales, with convict records (see Stewart, 2004). *Ancestors* and *Family Tree* have published a number of useful articles on sources for emigrants. Work is in progress to put online an index to published articles in *Family Tree*.

Full details of the cases of those who were transported from Scotland, following a trial in the High Court of Justiciary, are contained in precognitions which include the statements of both witnesses and accused. Few precognitions have survived before 1812 but all are now indexed on the NAS online catalogue of justiciary records. Search under the name of the accused. The papers can be consulted in the NAS West search room.

The online catalogue for the NLS manuscript holdings includes references to early emigrants' guides to North America, Australia and New Zealand, as well as emigrants' correspondence held in the library. This material provides an excellent background to the subject. Nineteenth-century parliamentary reports and papers are also a source of first-hand information on reasons for emigration, conditions on board the ships carrying the emigrants and reports on living conditions of the emigrants on arrival (see Hawthornthwaite, 1993 and Ford, 1968).

Debtors

Court appearances

Debt (often for a very small sum) was endemic in all ranks of society at all times and cases were dealt with by all the courts – burgh courts, sheriff courts, commissary courts, Justices of the Peace and the Court of Session. Debt may also become apparent in the form of bonds and protested bills.

Court appearances can be very valuable in supplying genealogical information. Janet Campbell in Strontoiller, widow of John Campbell there, and her son John were summoned in 1725 at the instance of the collector of excise to pay money due for brewing, the record showing that at this date Janet's husband was dead but that she had a son. The petition was recorded in the Justice of the Peace records for Argyll but the case might well have been heard in any other court. This can make it very difficult to carry out research on this aspect of an ancestor's career.

Diligence records

If the creditor wished to enforce a court's decree that money should be repaid, a procedure known as diligence could be started. There were three main forms of diligence – hornings, inhibitions and apprisings (or adjudications). Letters of horning acted as a warrant to seize (poind) the debtor's moveable goods in payment of the debt. In cases where the debtor owned heritable property, an inhibition might be registered to prevent the debtor from selling his land before the creditor was paid. Apprisings and adjudications were actions by which the creditor made claims on the moveable estate of the debtor in satisfaction of the debt.

Diligence registers are in the NAS (class reference DI) with general registers for the whole of Scotland and particular registers for each county. The regalities (up to 1747) could also keep registers. There are indexes to inhibitions and adjudications from 1781 onwards but otherwise minute books have to be searched. These records can be very informative (but are time-consuming to search), particularly if the debt was passed on from one generation to another.

The financial embarrassment of a landowning ancestor often becomes apparent in the registers of sasines, as property was mortgaged (wadset) as security for a loan. After the money is repaid, the creditor renounces any rights to the property and the land is 'redeemed'. (See 'Understanding legal documents – Sasines', pp. 214–21.)

Bankruptcy

With the expansion of business enterprise in Scotland from the eighteenth century onwards and economic pressures being felt by many, both by those with large estates and those involved in small undertakings, bankruptcy was common. Cases of bankruptcy were heard before the Court of Session but from 1783 onwards there should be a reference to a particular case in the printed and indexed catalogues of the register of inhibitions. Some of these are now catalogued on the NAS electronic catalogue.

Many Court of Session productions concerned with these cases were in the form of business books, which provide a fascinating insight into the dealings and often the genealogy of the persons concerned. The list of such productions can be searched on www.nas.gov.uk. After 1839, there are three series of processes, CS280, CS318 and CS319, all of which are indexed on the NAS website. All the papers are in West Register House, Edinburgh.

Some bankruptcy records can be found in the sheriff courts, usually catalogued under 'register of sequestrations'. There are some sheriff court records of claims made for relief from legal actions involving possible imprisonment for debt known as *cessio bonorum*. In return for surrendering his 'whole means and estate' to the creditors, the debtor could raise an action in the sheriff court praying for interim protection. The debtor had to make a complete statement of debts owing and this sometimes included the narration of many personal details of past mishaps. In 1886 Thomas Tweedie, a farmer, applied for a process of *cessio bonorum* following a series of personal disasters – the death of his wife, expenses of her last illness, loss of cattle and failure of a turnip crop. Most of these registers date back to the nineteenth century but earlier cases can be found in the Court of Session and other courts. Searching the NAS catalogues online under '*cessio*' will bring up those which were recorded in the Carmichael and Elliot arrangements of extracted and unextracted processes recorded in the Court of Session, some dating back to the seventeenth century.

V *Understanding Legal Documents*

Scots law

Scotland has always had a separate legal system and this can cause difficulties in genealogical research in understanding the implications, form and also the terminology and meaning of Scottish legal documents. Some knowledge of Scots law is important as this may be the key to the interpretation of what you find in your research. Reference to some Scots legal dictionaries can cause as many problems as they solve as the explanations may be technical and complicated but *Bell's dictionary and digest of the law of Scotland* (Watson, 1882) is very helpful and relatively user-friendly. *Bell's dictionary* has been published in a number of editions, the earlier ones compiled by Robert Bell and then by William Bell, but the nineteenth-century editions are the most useful. Copies will be found in the NAS search rooms and in other main libraries or archives. For the enthusiast there is a six-volume *Legal history of Scotland* (Walker, 1988–2001) which includes a great deal of interesting general background to the law and its application. A *Student's glossary of Scottish legal terms* (Gibb, 1971) has been published by Green (various editions).

One of the problems in tackling legal matters is the length of many of the documents. If you understand the form of any particular class of record, this will enable you to pick out the parts which contain the 'meat', as there is often a great deal of repetition. In *Formulary of Old Scots legal documents* (Gouldesbrough, 1985) there is a brief introduction to a wide range of Scottish legal documents commonly used in family history research with examples of the documents included.

Registers of deeds

A deed is a document concerning any matter transacted between two or more parties on which information needed to be preserved or on which action might be required. It sets forth the terms of the agreement and contains in it a final clause in which the parties involved consent to registration in a register of deeds. In the fifteenth and sixteenth centuries the notaries used to keep a record of loans of money, agreements or contracts in their protocol books but there was no central system for registration of these books and it was claimed that the ability of the notaries was often dubious and their integrity doubtful. By the sixteenth century the need for formal registration of such documents was acknowledged and a number of courts were deemed to be competent to keep registers of deeds.

The interest of deeds lies in the wide range of subjects covered – marriage contracts, testamentary settlements, indentures, tacks, personal agreements, factories, financial matters such as bonds and bills, contracts to build churches or schools or charter a ship. They document both the public and private lives of our ancestors. Till 1809 any court could keep a register of deeds but after this date only the sheriff courts and Court of Session had this competence, though the courts of the royal burghs could register deeds relating to heritable rights. Unfortunately, finding out in which court a relevant deed might have been recorded is a matter of informed guesswork, trial and error and your choice will initially often be influenced by ease of access – existence of indexes and consideration of the bulk of the records – though the social standing of the person concerned and where they lived also have to be taken into account. (See also 'Profiling the ancestors – What did they do?', pp. 154–201.)

Books of Council and Session

The Books of Council and Session are also known simply as the 'register of deeds' (NAS class reference RD). Before 1660, some deeds were recorded among the Acts of the Lords of Council or Council and Session and among the acts and decreets, and there are some calendars and indexes in the NAS covering the years 1501–14, 1532–59 and 1542–81. There is also a calendar of the register of deeds itself for the years 1554–95, partly indexed. The deeds are written in Latin. From 1596 to 1660 the register of deeds is not indexed and the difficulties of the task of searching five series of concurrent minute books kept by five clerks' offices are almost insuperable unless you have some idea of the approximate date of registration and note of the clerk's office in which the deed was recorded.

From 1661 onwards, the register of deeds (written in the vernacular) offers a great deal of scope for research in the indexed years.

1661–1811: There are three series of deeds, each kept in the office of a different clerk – Dalrymple (referred to as DAL, RD2), Durie (DUR, RD3) and Mackenzie (MACK, RD4), and a deed might be registered in any one of these offices. Annual indexes (covering all three series) exist for the years 1661–1702, 1705–7, 1714–15,

1750–52 and 1770–1811. The indexes between 1661 and 1683 indicate the type of deed – bond, contract, disposition etc. – and indexes up to 1811 include references to all those mentioned in the deed (not just the principal parties) but not witnesses. The index gives the name of the clerk's office, the volume number and folio number. When ordering up a document, convert the office name to the relevant number – DAL to RD2, for example. From 1684 to 1715 the description of the nature of the deed is omitted. From 1770 onwards, when the annual indexing recommences, only the name of the granter is indexed, with the name of the grantee and type of document written beside it, date of deed and date of registration, which is usually soon after the date of writing but could be some time later.

1812 onwards: all the deeds are in one series – RD5. The annual indexes provide the same information as those for the period after 1769.

If there are no indexes, then minute books have to be searched. This can be a long task in the period before 1812 as all three clerks' registers have to be checked. An additional problem is that the entries in the minute books may be very short, stating the nature of the deed (bond, disposition etc.) and the surnames of the parties concerned. Copies of some of the indexes to the register of deeds may be found in local archives and LDS family history centres but the registers themselves and most of their searching aids can only be studied in the NAS.

Sheriff court registers of deeds

There is at least one sheriff court in each county which kept a register of deeds (see 'Profiling the ancestors – Where did they live?', pp. 136–7). The date of commencement of the registers of deeds varies and in some places there are gaps in the registers. These can sometimes be filled by searching the warrants, which are the original documents, later copied into the register. Warrants are kept in boxes, usually tied in bundles by year. There is a superscription on the outside of each document, stating its nature, date and the name of the granter.

There are very few indexes to the registers of deeds before 1809 but some minute books are in existence. Most of the registers are indexed over the rest of the nineteenth century. With the exception of the registers of deeds for Orkney and Shetland, which are held in their respective archives, these records are kept in the NAS.

Burgh court registers of deeds

The courts of the royal burghs were deemed competent to register deeds and there are a considerable number of surviving registers (including some registers of probative writs) though the dates they cover vary considerably. Few are indexed or have minute books but as they deal with a localised area, it is possible to go through the registers for a series of years in quite a short time. Many of the books have good side-heads stating the nature of the deed and the granter. Some registers are in the NAS, a few are in local archives.

Franchise courts: registers of deeds

Regalities, stewartries and bailieries were entitled to kept registers of deeds, though few have survived and even these are mostly very fragmentary. You can search the NAS online catalogue under RH11 for a list of records of the franchise courts. If you know the name of the franchise court, key in RH11 plus that name of the court and a detailed list of the records will come up. For example, in looking for the records for the bailiery of Cunningham, you will find that there are registers of deeds covering the years 1633–1735 with some gaps. A list of those which are in the NAS is given in *Guide to the National Archives of Scotland* (SRO, 1996). Other records may be found in local archives or among collections of family papers. Regalities, stewartries and bailieries were abolished by the Heritable Jurisdictions Act of 1747. Baronies did not have the right to register deeds.

Commissary court registers of deeds

Until 1809 commissary courts could register deeds and there are surviving deeds (as well as protests and probative writs) for all commissary courts, though some are extant for very few years. Most of these registers of deeds are catalogued in the manuscript inventory for each commissary court. These are all held in the NAS.

Form and content of deeds

Probative writs

After 1697 it became legal to record a deed in which there was no clause at the end consenting to registration. This is known as a probative writ. Some probative writs are included in a register of deeds (of the sheriff court, for example) but some are recorded in a separate register within a court titled 'register of probative writs'. These writs are in many forms – charters or often informal private letters, registered so that action might be taken on them – such a loan of money or proof of an irregular marriage.

Bills and protests

The 'paper-money' of the past was in the form of bills of exchange and promissory notes. There was no set form to make this a valid document which was often written in a coffee house or private house. It simply stated that a certain sum of money should be paid back to the creditor within a set time. Many bills were not registered, but if a bill had been registered, then legal action could be taken to recover the debt through a process of diligence.

A protest quotes the original bill and provides the evidence that a demand for repayment has been made, this being done in the presence of witnesses. The legal process to obtain repayment could then follow the protest. Bills and protests are rarely of interest to the family historian, though sometimes personal details are revealed in the nature of the debt – a bill for stockings, buttons or gloves, an unpaid fine due to a kirk session for fornication or – a rare example of a more interesting transaction – money due for a passage to America.

Bonds

Many bonds will tell you very little about your ancestors – except to indicate that they may have had financial difficulties, or sometimes to open a window on their business activities, but on occasion they do reveal important information, particularly heritable bonds (see below). Cautioners to bonds may be relatives and bonds of corroboration may indicate that an heir has taken over debts of a previous generation. Witnesses are always worth noting as relatives often took on this role. The date of registration is often some time after the date of writing the document.

A bond was a written undertaking by the granter of this receipt to repay a certain sum of money which had been borrowed. The document will state in the opening paragraph that the person has received a sum of money (under a loan) and that he is 'justlie adebtit restand awand' this amount and binds and obliges himself, his heirs and executors to repay it between certain dates. The clause consenting to registration is included, the date and the names of witnesses. In some cases the lender of the money (the grantee) might demand surety from a third party that the debt would be honoured. This was done under a *bond of caution* whereby a third party (sometimes a relative of the granter) stood surety for that person. The cautioner might then demand a promise from the granter (the debtor) that repayment would be made to the cautioner if he had to honour his responsibilities. This was done under a *bond of relief*.

If there was any need to renew the bond – on the death of the original granter or grantee, for example – then this could be done under a *bond of corroboration*, establishing that the debt was due by or to the heir of the original granter or grantee.

It was also very common for this right to receive payment under a bond to be passed from person to person. This was known as an *assignation*, the assignee, known as the 'lawful cessioner', then having the right to claim the original sum of money and to take legal action if it was not paid. If the assignee passed on the bond to a third party, then the deed was known as a *translation*. At this time the original granter of the bond (the person who had borrowed the money) had to be informed of the name of the person to whom he now owed money by an *intimation*. When the debt was finally repaid, the debtor demanded a *discharge* from the person who then held the right to be paid the money as proof that the debt had been paid.

Heritable bonds

The bonds described above were only concerned with moveable property but some bonds, known as heritable bonds, were loans secured on heritable property – land. The borrower promised to repay the money and offered land which he owned as a security or an annualrent from it, or both. This was known as a *contract of wadset*, the lender being known as the *wadsetter*. Under this contract, the wadsetter promised in a *letter of reversion* to give up all rights to the land or to the annualrent once the debt had been settled. Such wadsets also appear in registers of sasines, as ownership of the land under a wadset was deemed to have been transferred to the lender for the duration of the loan.

Bond of provision

This was was a partial settlement, not covering the whole estate, whereby a payment could be made to a widow or children. The arrangement may state that it is to take the place of the 'bairn's rights' or the rights of a widow to moveable property under Scots law. Reference is sometimes made back to the terms of a marriage contract.

Factory

If someone was about to go abroad or be absent for a while, he or she might appoint a factor to manage matters during this time. This might be a wife or member of the family – or an associate. It can provide clues as to overseas business interests or employment in the army or navy.

Contracts

Contracts, legally described as 'the voluntary agreement of two or more persons, by which something is to be given or performed upon one part, for a valuable consideration' (Watson, 1882), cover an enormous and interesting range of subjects. Marriage contracts are a useful source of genealogical information, usually registered on the death of one of the parties, not at the time of the marriage, as either an antenuptial or postnuptial agreement. (See 'From birth to death – Marriage contracts', p. 84.)

Other contracts may concern indentures of apprentices or agreements to serve someone in a particular capacity, partnership agreements, sale of rights in a certain undertaking, charter parties (agreement between the owner of a ship and the freighter) and contracts of excambion, involving the exchange of two pieces of land.

Arbitration

When there was a dispute, the parties involved sometimes voluntarily asked for arbitration to settle it. A submission was made setting out the nature of the disagreement and one or more arbiters were named. Sometimes an oversman was appointed to act as an umpire if the arbiters disagreed. The deed included a description of the powers given to the arbiters and both parties agreed to abide by their decisions. Pleadings and replies were then heard and once a decision had been reached, a decree arbitral was recorded. This narrated the nature of the submission and set forth their findings on the case. The decree arbitral was then entered in a register of deeds.

Dispositions, settlements and trusts

Such documents might be drawn up a few days or many years before death but were normally registered after the decease of the person concerned. They could deal with the settlement of both moveable and heritable property and include lists of personal bequests. In the case of trusts, property was conveyed into the hands of trustees, who were then responsible for carrying out the wishes of a person after death. (See 'From birth to death – Testamentary dispositions', p. 112.)

Land ownership

In Scotland, landholding was based on the feudal system and involved two kinds of interest in the land – the superiority and the land itself. The Crown was deemed to own rights to all lands in Scotland and was known as the *superior*. The Crown could then

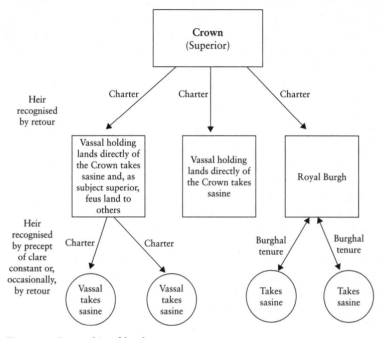

Figure 6 Ownership of land

grant permanent rights of lands to bodies such as religious founda-
tions (before the Reformation), to burghs, or heritably to individuals (known as the vassals) under charters which defined the terms
of the grant and laid down what was to be given as feu duty to the
superior.

The *vassal* (in whose favour the Crown charter had been granted)
could *sub-infeudate* the lands (again granting the lands heritably
under a charter) to someone else, the granter then becoming a *subject
superior* over his vassal. A vassal (whether holding 'of' the Crown or
of a subject superior) had the right to assign the lands to someone else
during his lifetime, to sell (alienate) the lands, or use the land as security for a loan (wadset), the new owner then becoming liable to pay
feu duty to the superior. The vassal's lands could be inherited by the
heir. It was also common for a proprietor to give his wife heritable
rights or a life interest in part of his lands. Whether as a result of
inheritance, assignation, sale, grant of life interest or wadset, confirmation of each transaction had to be validated by the superior
(whether this was the Crown or subject superior) and this was followed by the taking of sasine by the grantee.

Charters

The charter is the written evidence that a grant of heritable property has been made. An 'original' charter is the one under which the first grant of the lands is made. The charter names the superior (granter) and the vassal (grantee), followed by a description of the lands concerned and note of any special conditions of tenure set out by the superior. This is known as the *tenendas* clause.

The *reddendo* lays down the duty (feu) to be paid to the superior. The vassal might be asked to perform military service to the liege (ward-holding), make a nominal payment if asked (blenche-ferme) or pay feu ferme, which from the second half of the sixteenth century onwards became the most usual form of land holding. Feu ferme was originally usually paid in kind and later was almost always commuted to money. Feu duty persisted till the twentieth century but has now been phased out.

Certain dues were often payable to the superior by an heir on succeeding to the land, known as *casualties*. These were ward, marriage, non-entry and relief. Ward was payable to the superior if the heir was a minor, ending when majority was reached at the age of twenty one years complete. The casualty of marriage was due from an unmarried heir of marriageable age or on reaching marriageable age if a minor (twelve for a girl, fourteen for a boy). Payment of non-entry was due from the time of the death of the vassal until the heir entered as heir with the superior. If the heir was a minor, then non-entry was due till he or she was of age, but non-entry might also be due if the heir had failed to complete title in some way. Relief was money paid by the heir on entry with the superior. Gifts of these casualties were sometimes made by the Crown to others and were entered in the Register of the Privy Seal or in the Exchequer rolls.

Charters of lands held of the Crown as superior are entered in the Register of the Great Seal (*Registrum magni sigilli Scotorum*, known as the RMS) and abstracts (in Latin up till 1651) have been published in eleven volumes, covering the period 1314–1668. They are indexed by person (including all parties and witnesses) and by place but spelling of names and places has not been standardised. In most cases the abstracts include the necessary information – the name of the grantee, description of the lands, the previous owner, the terms of possession – whether through inheritance, sale or as security for a loan (under reversion) – the names of witnesses and details of the *reddendo*. At the bottom of each abstract there is a reference to the original in the records of Chancery, in the NAS. From 1668 to 1919, there are typescript indexes for these charters in the NAS, but they only name the grantee and the lands conveyed.

The published volumes of abstracts include charters taken from both the Register of the Great Seal and from the 'paper register'. The 'paper' register was established in 1596, but it has only survived from 1608 and continues till 1852. While the Great Seal register dealt with lands that were granted with lasting rights, the paper register was concerned with temporary grants – lands which were redeemable on repayment of a loan and liferent grants. Commissions, remissions and pardons are also registered in the paper register.

Signatures

The first step in drawing up a Crown charter was to make a draft (written in the vernacular) of the main clauses. It can be a bonus to find the signature of a charter, as reading the document in the vernacular is a much easier option than translating it from Latin. Not all signatures have survived. There is a collection of surviving signatures in the NAS, covering the period 1607–1847, indexed by grantee and noting the lands concerned, with the date. If the signature for the charter in which you are interested is missing, it may be useful to see if there is a later signature concerning the same lands as the terms may be very similar.

Charters of subject superiors

Charters granted by superiors other than the Crown (subject superiors) were not entered in a register and can usually be found in family muniments. Many are listed in the collections of papers catalogued in the Gifts and Deposits series in the NAS and there are similar collections in local archives and libraries or still in private hands (most of which are catalogued in the National Register of Archives). There is also a fifteen-volume catalogue (indexed) of early charters in the NAS (RH6) covering the years 1142–1600. For the majority of researchers, however, registers of sasines (from the seventeenth century onwards) prove an easier path to follow in tracing the history of a landowning ancestor and his territorial possessions. If you cannot find a particular charter, consider the possibility that it might have been registered as a deed.

Services of heirs (retours)

Under the Scottish laws concerning heritable succession, the eldest son inherited the heritable property. If there were only daughters, then they inherited equally and were known as *heirs portioners*. (The term 'portioner' is also used to refer to the owner of a small feu or portion of land.) If there were no surviving issue, then the brothers and sisters of the deceased were next in line to succeed, even if they had different mothers, sisters inheriting together as heirs portioners. If the deceased had both older and younger brothers, then the next heir would be the next younger brother, following a rule that heritage descends, but if the deceased had only older brothers, the next heir would be the eldest brother (Watson, 1882).

The term *apparent heir* is used for a person whose predecessor has died but who has not yet completed title. The term *heir apparent* is an English expression referring to one who will become the heir if he or she outlives the present heir. It is important to note which term is used as this has implications as to whether the previous property owner is then dead or still alive.

If lands were held of a subject superior and there were no problems concerning the inheritance, the subject superior would grant a *precept of clare constat*, stating that it was clearly known that A was the heir to B and had right to inherit the lands concerned. The bailie, an officer appointed to give sasine, was then instructed to do this. A copy of the precept may sometimes be found in the muniments of the superior but it is always quoted in the sasine. If, however, the lands were held of the Crown as superior or there was any dispute or complication about the succession of the heir to lands held of a subject superior, then it was necessary to go through the process of being retoured or served heir (alternative terms which are used). A brieve (or writ) of inquest (in Latin) was issued by Chancery, instructing a sheriff or other court to hold an inquest in front of a jury to establish that the deceased was not an outlaw, to examine what lands were involved and to establish the claim of the heir, who should be of 'lawful age' (twenty one years complete).

Some of the papers concerning the inquests heard in court by the sheriff or other judge have survived, but by no means all. The repertory of a sheriff court may contain a section titled 'services of 'heirs' or 'record of services'. The hearing was in English and the papers included a list of those on the assize and details of evidence heard. In most cases there was no argument but occasionally if there were conflicting claims a great deal of information will emerge concerning the family. A catalogue of the services of heirs for Roxburgh, covering the years 1636–1847, has been published by the Scottish Record Society (Macleod, 1934) and there is a catalogue of the services of heirs for Argyllshire 1683–1787 with the sheriff court papers of Dunoon in the NAS. In other courts it is necessary to go through the records.

The court which had heard the case returned (retoured) their verdict to Chancery who then issued a precept authorising sasine to be given to the heir. This retour was registered in the Chancery records of 'services of heirs' (in the NAS). There are three printed volumes of summaries of the retours in Latin (indexed by person and place) for the years 1544–1699, (also available on CD-ROM from the Scottish Genealogy Society), titled *Inquisitionum retornatarum abbreviatio*. From 1700 to the present day, there are printed indexes to services of heirs in Scotland, arranged decennially up to 1859 and thereafter annually. (These are also available on CD-ROM.) Each entry has brief details, giving the name of the person being retoured, the lands concerned, relationship of the heir to the deceased, sometimes the date of death of the previous heir and date of retour. There is a supplement in each volume indexed under the name of the deceased owner if this was different from that of the heir. In most cases the published entry will provide all the necessary details but if the heir was retoured to a grandfather, uncle or more distant relative, the full text will fill in the names of the intervening links. An heir sometimes did not complete title till many years after the death of the predecessor and therefore searches should be made for a considerable number of years after a known date of death.

The term 'heir' is usually used for an 'heir of line' – the person who would succeed to heritable property under the laws of intestate succession. An 'heir of conquest' is one who will succeed to lands acquired by the ancestor either by purchase or gift, as opposed to inheritance (the distinction was abolished in 1874). In some cases, the heirs of conquest and line might be different people. An 'heir of destination' is one who succeeds according to the provisions of the will of the proprietor. This may also be laid down in an entail (tailzie).

The terms 'general service' and 'special service' are also used in connection with retours. A 'general service' followed the claim to be acknowledged as heir to all a predecessor's heritable property, while a 'special service' concerned specific lands in which the deceased had been infeft.

Brieves were also issued by Chancery in connection with a retour of tutory or curatory. A retour of tutory concerned the appointment of a tutor for a fatherless girl under twelve or a boy under fourteen, the tutor usually being the nearest adult male on the father's side: a retour of curatory appointed a curator to look after the affairs of a minor or an insane person, again a relative on the father's side.

Burgage property

When burgage property was involved, the process of inheritance was simpler, completed by an instrument of cognition and sasine. When an owner of property in a royal burgh died, the heir asked one of the bailies of the burgh to examine a couple of witnesses on the claim to inherit. On the basis of their evidence, the claimant who was declared to be the heir took hold of the hasp (latch) and staple ('eye' on the gatepost for holding a hook) of the door and entering the house, bolted the door. On coming out, the heir was given an instrument of cognition and sasine. The proceedings are recorded in English.

Form of a retour

Retours are in Latin but for those with even a small amount of Latin, it is not too difficult to work out what is being said as there is a standard form for the document. The opening paragraph starts with the statement that 'This inquest was made in . . .', followed by a note of the court in which the inquest was held and the date. This information should be noted if a search is to be made for any surviving papers concerning the inquest. The names of the members of the jury are given – these did not have to be related to the heir and are usually fifteen in number. The next section is marked by the opening words, usually written in larger letters *Qui jurati dicunt* – 'who being sworn say' – after the administration of a great oath (*magno sacramento interveniente*) and then follows the central information of the retour, starting with the word *Quod* ('That '). It is then declared that the deceased (name and relationship to the heir given) died in the faith and peace of the Lord (not having lands that were forfeited) and that the bearer of the retour is heir to the deceased. The relationship is then explained in detail, naming any who may complete the chain of inheritance between the heir and the ancestor. In the case of a special retour, a description of the lands in which the deceased was 'vested and seised' is given. The date of death of the person to whom the heir is served heir is sometimes given. The heir is declared to be nearest and lawful heir and of lawful age (over twenty one).

Sasines

The charter was the authority for the giving of sasine, the written and registered proof of the act of handing over legal possession of property – originally by the symbolic giving of earth and stone or other appropriate symbols – on the lands concerned. The sasine recorded transactions resulting from inheritance, purchase (sale, alienation or disposition) or as security for a loan (wadset, the lands conveyed being under reversion), including under a heritable bond. If a husband at the time of his marriage gave his wife or wife-to-be a life-interest in certain lands which he held, this required sasine to be taken under a joint infeftment. In many cases a lender (known as the wadsetter) was seised in land as security for a loan, or a liferent of certain lands equal to the interest on the debt might be conveyed. In such cases, the lender promised to relinquish rights to the land or liferent once the debt was repaid. This repayment was officially recorded under a letter of reversion or grant of discharge and the fact that the lands were now disburdened of debt and had been returned to the original owner had to be recorded in a sasine.

Protocol books

Before the commencement of the registers of sasines – and in fact up to 1660, after which time, registration of sasines becomes more reliable – the 'taking of instruments' as proof of the transfer of land might be recorded in the protocol books of the notaries, either those working in a royal burghs or recording legal transactions in a particular area of Scotland. An instrument recorded by the notary will usually name the granter and grantee, the lands concerned, the grounds for the grant (inheritance, purchase or other reason) and the names of witnesses. The problem is that most protocol books are in Latin, many written in a very cramped style and unless you are motivated by a high degree of dedication (and possessed of palaeographical skills) or they have been published and indexed, they are best left alone.

A great many protocol books have not survived. The NAS has a manuscript list of those which they hold, indicating the part of the country where the notary was working. There is also a list in *Guide to the National Archives of Scotland* (SRO, 1996) and *Scottish texts and calendars* (Stevenson, 1987) lists many of those which have been published. The burghs kept their own series of protocol books and these are listed in the catalogues of the burgh records.

Registers of sasines

In late medieval times many protests were made against 'falsis notaris' and even after action had been taken to curb the fraudulent activities of the notaries, there were many doubts about their work in recording instruments (sasines being their most important business). An attempt was made to introduce a register of sasines in 1599, known as the Secretary's Register, but this was abandoned in 1609, having been termed 'ane cullor for ane extraordinarie intendit extortioun of his maiesteis subiectis'. Not all the Secretary's registers have survived (see table p. 217).

Another attempt to introduce a national system of registration of land transfer was made in 1617, which was successful, and in that year the general and particular registers of sasines were introduced. The general register referred to property in any part of Scotland and was often used for registration in cases where a proprietor owned property in several different counties. The particular registers of sasines concerned land in particular parts of the country, usually based on county boundaries but in some cases (such as Argyll, Bute, Dunbarton and Arran) covering a wider area (see table below). After 1868 there is no general register of sasines – all are recorded in the particular registers of the county concerned.

The registers of sasines (general and particular), indexes and minute books are all kept in the NAS. Some indexes and minute books have been filmed by the LDS and can be viewed in their family history centre libraries.

The royal burghs had the right to keep their own registers of sasines for burgage property. The date of commencement of such registers is very variable. Dysart register goes back to 1602 but many registers start much later. Burgh registers of sasines were discontinued at different times between 1926 and 1963. There are some indexes or lists of contents but most do not exist before 1809. As however each register covers a local area, it does not take too long to search it. Most of the registers are in the NAS but in a few cases (such as Aberdeen, Glasgow and Dundee) part of the registers may be in the local archives.

Searching aids prior to 1780

The general register of sasines is indexed from 1617 to 1735 but between 1736 and 1780 you will have to use minute books. Not all the particular registers of sasines are indexed before 1781 and if there are no indexes, again minute books act as a searching aid. Although it takes time to go through minute books, it is not an impossible task. The minute will name the person who is being infeft and describe the lands concerned. There are often side-heads which help the searcher.

Given opposite are the groupings of areas covered by the registers and details of indexes available.

The abridgements to the sasines: 1781 onwards

From 1781 onwards there are printed abridgements of all sasines, whether recorded in the general or particular registers, arranged under the county in which the lands are situated. If the sasine refers to lands in more than one county, there are cross-references. The registers are indexed by person from 1781 onwards (including the names of all those mentioned in the abridgement) and by place for the years 1781–1830 and from 1872 onwards. These indexes are in manuscript, beautifully written and arranged first in blocks of years but later annually.

Registers	Indexes
Aberdeen (from 1661 includes Kincardine)	1599–1609; 1617–60
Argyll, Dunbarton, Arran, Bute and Tarbert	1617–1780
Ayr, Kyle, Carrick and Cunningham	1599–1609; 1617–60
Banff	1600–9; 1617–1780
Berwick and Lauderdale	1617–1780
Caithness (from 1646 onwards; up to 1644 with Inverness)	1646–1780
Dumfries, Kirkcudbright and Annandale	1617–1780
Edinburgh and Haddington (Midlothian and East Lothian)	1599–1609; 1617–60; 1741–80
Elgin, Forres and Nairn	1617–1780
Fife (and Kinross up to 1685 only)	1603–9; 1617–60
Forfar (Angus)	1620–1780
Inverness, Ross, Sutherland, Cromarty	1606–9; 1617–1780
Kincardine (only till 1657; from 1661 with Aberdeen)	1600–8; 1617–57
Kinross (with Fife till 1685)	1603–60
Lanark	1618–1780
Orkney and Shetland (Zetland)	1617–60
Perth	1601–9
Renfrew and Barony of Glasgow	no indexes
Roxburgh, Selkirk and Peebles	no indexes
Stirling, Clackmannan and Menteith	no indexes
Linlithgow (West Lothian – up to 1760 with Edinburgh)	1700–80
Wigtown	no indexes

The index volumes in the NAS are arranged alphabetically by the modern name of the county but it is a little confusing to find the old names of some of the counties given on the spine of the books. Thus: Forfar = Angus; Edinburgh = Midlothian; Hadddington = East Lothian; Linlithgow = West Lothian; Zetland = Orkney and Shetland.

Each index entry gives a number which refers to the number of the sasine in the relevant book of abridgements. Make sure that you tie up the index entry with the abridgements covering the relevant block of years. At the end of each sasine abridgement there is a reference to the original sasine – PR (for particular register) or GR (for general register) followed by a volume number and folio number. When ordering up the register of sasines to see the full text, you will need to find the RS (register of sasines) number which refers to sasines in a particular county at that time. There is a list in the NAS historical reading room. If it is a GR number, then the volume number must be preceded by RS3. After 1868, sasines were only registered by county and there was no general register.

In most cases the abridgement will provide all the relevant information but sometimes it is necessary to order up the full text, either to elucidate the abridged version or to check whether the original includes some extra details of interest which can be the case.

The abridgements can also be viewed at some local libraries or archives. Copies are held on microfilm by some LDS family history centres. Work is in progress (2006) to digitise the abridgements and their indexes. Initially it will be necessary to view the computerised index and then look up the relevant abridgement. In time, it is anticipated that all sasine registers will be digitised.

The abridgements do not cover registers of sasines of the royal burghs.

Understanding the abridgements

The abridgements to the particular and general registers of sasines provide a valuable and easily accessible source of information. By 1781 people from a wide range of social classes were involved in property owning, sometimes as lenders of money secured on a mortgage (wadset) rather than as purchasers or heirs. In all cases relationships may be stated, addresses given (which can sometimes be followed up in census returns), clues provided as to times of marriage or death and indications given as to financial difficulties which might lead to cases of bankruptcy or diligence cases.

Because the information is abridged, it is not always easy to understand the content of these entries, particularly when determining who is getting land and who giving it and why. A number of shortened terms are used, the most common of which are as follows:

assig.	assignation
convey.	conveyance
disch.	discharge
disp.	disposition
eod. die	the same day
gen. disp.	general disposition
hr.	heir
inter alia	among others
not. instrument	notarial instrument
por.	portioner
pro indiviso	undivided
prov.	provision
qua	as
ratif.	ratification

sp. and gen. serv.   special and general service
vide   see

Someone who 'gets bond and disposition' for a certain amount of money 'over' a piece of property is the lender who is then infeft (an alternative word for 'seise') in the land as a security for the loan.

If a person 'grants discharge' of a bond and disposition and declares the lands disburdened, this refers to a sasine which has been registered in favour of the lender of the money, as security, showing that an original debt has been paid off and the creditor no longer has any claims on the land.

Some abridgements state that a person 'registers disposition' to himself or herself – showing that following the presentation of the relevant documents, that presenter is now infeft in the lands concerned.

The reference to special and general service in certain property shows that the sasine follows a precept of clare constat and concerns inheritance.

When a property transaction concerns more than one person (this often happens when several married women as heirs portioners are disposing of land held in common), each woman will 'grant ratification' of the disposition by her and others – giving assent to what was being done.

The form of a sasine

Most sasines till well into the eighteenth century are in Latin, except during the time of the Commonwealth and Protectorate. They are often long documents and their form is complicated. They do, however, follow set forms and, as much of the information is repeated several times, if you know the form this will help you to pick out the most important nuggets of information without necessarily reading everything.

At the head of the sasine is the date of registration – normally a few days after the date of writing the sasine. There is usually a brief heading (in English) which gives the name of the person getting the land (the grantee) and a note of the lands concerned.

The first paragraph gives the date of writing the sasine and names the three parties who 'compeared' (were present) – the notary (the lawyer), the person to whom the land is being given (the grantee) or his/her procurator acting as the representative of the grantee, and the bailie acting for the present proprietor. The procurator is referred to in Latin as *actornatus*. The bailie (*balivus*) has been authorised by the feudal superior of the lands under a precept in the charter to give sasine. The lands concerned are described, as well as the reason for the grant – as heir (under precept of clare constat), in conjunct fee (joint ownership, usually concerning a wife or wife-to-be), in liferent, in fee (full ownership), under alienation, or 'anneilzied' (by sale – the phrase is usually added 'irredeemably without any reversion'), or as a wadset (termed 'under reversion').

The grantee has in his hands a copy of the charter with the precept which contains in it the authority of the superior for giving sasine and he passes this to the notary.

The precept follows, which is then read aloud by the notary in the vulgar tongue (though in the sasine it will usually be quoted in Latin). This section begins with the words *'Insuper, dilectis meis'* and then follows the names of the men whom the superior (who is named) appoints to act as his bailies to see that sasine is given to the vassal of the lands – again described. The terms of the grant are again stated (under reversion, alienation or on precept of clare constat). The date of the precept is given (this can in some instances be some time before sasine was given) and the witnesses are named.

The final section is concerned with the giving of sasine of the lands ('heritable, real, actual and corporal possession' is the phrase commonly used) which are described again and the bailie to the grantee or the attorney gives earth and stone of the lands or any appropriate symbols for other rights such as clap and happer of the mill or coble of fishings. The grantee takes instruments (which are the legal written evidence of the proceedings) 'ane or mair' and the names of witnesses to the giving of sasine are noted, usually different from those who witnessed the precept.

In most cases just one of the three sections – the opening section, the precept or the giving of sasine – will provide most of the important details: the names of granter and grantee, description of lands conveyed and terms of transfer. It is, however, always worth at least scanning all three sections in case there are additional details, and names of both sets of witnesses should always be checked as they may be relatives.

Burgh sasines

The form of sasines concerning lands within the precincts of the royal burghs (which are defined in the charter of erection of each burgh) is much simpler and in the vernacular. When land is transferred from one person to another, the vassal last infeft under a written mandate (procuratory) resigns the feu into the hands of a bailie of the burgh, and at the same time asks for new infeftment to be given to the grantee. Full descriptions are given of the property, the reason for transfer stated and witnesses named.

The courts

The Scottish courts have been divided into three categories – superior, inferior and mixed.

The superior courts are the Court of Session for civil cases and the High Court of Justiciary for criminal cases. These courts hear cases which are referred from inferior courts but they also deal with cases which originate in these courts.

The inferior courts are the sheriff courts, burgh courts, barony courts (also known as bailie courts) and JP courts. Sentences passed here might be reviewed by the supreme courts. In the regality courts (abolished 1747), the lord of regality had a civil jurisdiction which was equivalent to that of the sheriff but in criminal jurisdiction this was more extensive as he had the same jurisdiction as the High Court of Justiciary except with regard to cases of treason.

The mixed courts were the High Court of Admiralty and the commissary court of Edinburgh. They reviewed cases referred to them from local admiralty and commissary courts but their decrees could be subject to a review by the Court of Session or High Court of Justiciary. The jurisdiction of the Admiralty Court was transferred to the Court of Session in 1830, and that of the Edinburgh commissary court, also to the Court of Session, in 1823.

Criminal cases: the High Court of Justiciary

The High Court of Justiciary is the supreme criminal court in Scotland. The Lord Justice General sat in Edinburgh but from 1672 onwards the court also went on circuit ('justice ayres') twice a year. The northern circuit was held at Perth, Aberdeen and Inverness, the southern circuit at Dumfries and Jedburgh and the western circuit at Stirling, Glasgow and Ayr. In Argyll there was a hereditary justiciarship of Argyll and the Isles but after this was abolished in 1747, the western circuit court also sat at Inveraray and at the same time Ayr was transferred to the southern circuit.

Procedure

On being informed of a crime, a *warrant* was issued on the authority of a JP, sheriff or burgh magistrate to bring the person named before a competent magistrate. The warrant had to be dated and signed by the magistrate concerned. A prosecution could be brought either by the Lord Advocate (the only prosecutor for public interest) or by the injured party, who had to be directly concerned in the case – not, for example, more remotely involved as representing the interests of a community.

The next step was the *precognition* – an examination of witnesses and of the accused to establish the facts of the crime. This was for the information of the public prosecutor, put in writing to enable him to lay a charge against the accused. Witnesses could be compelled to attend the precognition.

The accused, at the discretion of the Lord Advocate, could then be committed for trial on a written warrant, specifying the offence for which he or she was committed.

The trial proceeded before the Court of Justiciary either on *indictment* or *criminal letters*. An indictment (also referred to as the *dittay*) was usually used when the accused was in prison, criminal letters when still at large. The indictment or criminal letters (also known as the *libel*) addressed to the accused (the *panel*) state the nature of the crime and conclusions founded on the charge. A copy had to be executed by being delivered to the panel, requiring attendance at the trial on a certain day. The accused also received a list of the witnesses to be examined and of the names of the forty five persons from whom an assize was to be chosen.

The accused and the prosecutor (whether a private prosecutor or the Lord Advocate) then appeared at a *diet* or sitting of the court and both parties could voice any objections to the libel as stated (often called *informations*). These might be in the form of legal arguments or exculpations (such as insanity or pupillarity). The accused was then called on to plead guilty or not guilty. If the plea was 'guilty', then sentence was given: if 'not guilty', then the case was heard at the next diet of the High Court or circuit court.

If the case went to trial, a jury was chosen (by ballot from the forty five named persons) and sworn in. The prosecutor stated his evidence in support of the libel, other evidence was heard, there was a summing up and the jury then retired. A verdict could be on the vote of a majority of the jury and in cases where the verdict was 'not proven' or 'not guilty', the accused was dismissed. There was no appeal from the Court of Justiciary in criminal cases.

Records of the High Court of Justiciary

The records of the Lord Advocate include High Court and circuit indictments, trial reports, criminal informations and procedure books. The justiciary court 'paper' catalogues cover books of adjournal and minute books (both of which give quite a full account of the trial as it progresses), dittay books (these cover the indictments), remissions, appeals, processes and productions. The JC (High Court of Justiciary) records also deal with cases heard in both the High Court and the circuit courts.

Precognitions form part of the records of the Lord Advocate (NAS class reference AD) but only a few have survived for the period before 1812. There is a seventy five year closure on access.

The NAS are now creating an electronic catalogue of all High Court cases heard before juries which can be searched under various categories. Most nineteenth- and twentieth-century cases are now included and the work is being continued back in time. The index entry supplies name (plus alias if used), occupation, residence, age, nature of crime, and others involved. The catalogue will also bring up details of any other documents concerning the case and refer to relevant papers both in the AD records and in the justiciary court papers (JC). The catalogue is not yet (2006) available for consultation outside the NAS West search room but may later become available online.

Sheriff court cases

The jurisdictions and duties of the lesser courts varied over the years. By the later nineteenth century, in general the more serious crimes and those for which the punishment was death or banishment were heard by the High Court but the sheriff courts could deal with cases such as those of theft, robbery or bigamy. These cases could be conducted before a jury (solemn procedure) – usually done in the more heinous crimes – or in summary proceedings, when the presiding sheriff sat alone. This became a less common option.

The catalogues of criminal proceedings in the sheriff courts may contain references to roll books, which are brief 'diaries' of what went on in court on that day, while reports of trials may be termed 'criminal court books', 'criminal records' or 'criminal registers'. There may also be a section containing indictments and productions – objects or written documents (often in book form) used as evidence at the trial.

Criminal cases (usually the less serious ones) could also be heard by the burgh magistrates, JPs, by the bailies in the baronies and up till 1747 by the franchise courts.

Civil jurisdiction: the Court of Session

This was the supreme civil court in Scotland. It acted as the court of appeal from inferior courts but also had an original jurisdiction,

hearing cases which started in this court. In 1830 it took over responsibility from the commissary court of Edinburgh in dealing with all
consistorial actions (such as divorce, nullity and legitimation).

Its records are vast and daunting and, as is admitted in *Tracing your
Scottish ancestors* (NAS, 2003) 'undersupplied with straightforward
guides and arranged in a complicated manner'. However, this is an
area where electronic cataloguing is making an enormous difference
and is opening up access to new areas for research.

There is an introduction to the records in the West search room of
the NAS titled *Court of Session processes after 1660 – a searcher's
guide* and further information can be found in *Guide to the National
Archives of Scotland* (SRO, 1996), in *Tracing your Scottish ancestors*
(NAS, 2003) and *Tracing Scottish local history in the Scottish Record
office* (Sinclair, 1994). There is also a useful introduction on the NAS
electronic catalogue (key in CS96 and click on the first item).

The classes of records most likely to be of value are processes, productions, and registers of deeds known as the books of Council and
Session (see 'Books of Council and Session', p. 203).

Processes

Processes consist of the writs and pleadings concerned with a particular case. Processes are described as either 'extracted' or 'unextracted', the only difference being that in the case of extracted
processes, one of the parties had an extract made of the court's decision, and in an 'unextracted' case this did not happen. Many cases
'went to sleep' and were never completed and thus became listed as
'unextracted'. There are an ever growing number of indexes in the
NAS (you can search their electronic catalogue online under the name
of any of the parties concerned), including what are known as the
Carmichael and Elliot arrangement of processes.

Productions

Productions are the material evidence produced in actions heard
before the Court of Session. The NAS catalogue can be searched
online under CS96 for all productions under the name of a person,
organisation, place or occupation, to find relevant material.

Civil jurisdiction: inferior and mixed courts

Sheriff courts, admiralty courts (up to 1830), burgh courts, commissary courts (up to 1823), JP courts, franchise courts (up to 1747) and
baron courts all dealt with civil cases, much of the work being concerned with debt. The problem is that you may have no clue as to the

court in which a particular case was heard and there are very few indexes. There are also great variations in what has survived for each court and the years covered.

When searching sheriff court records, look for the section titled 'ordinary court': in the burgh courts, this may just be called 'court records'. In all the courts there may also be records listed under 'decrees' (or 'decreets') which are the judgments in the cases, and also processes, as well as diet books, act books and minute books. In the commissary courts, the processes are often very interesting and for many commissary courts there are manuscript indexes.

Court records are a valuable source of social history – even if you do not find the ancestor for whom you are looking.

Appendices

1 Parishes, with related sheriff courts, commissary courts and burghs

Table A1

Parish	No.	County	Local authority	Sheriff court		Commissary court		Burgh/town/village
Abbey	559	Renfrewshire	Renfrewshire	Paisley	SC58	Glasgow	CC9	Paisley, Johnstone
Abbey St Bathans	726	Berwickshire	The Scottish Borders	Duns	SC60	Lauder	CC15	
Abbotshall	399	Fife	Fife	Cupar	SC20	St Andrews	CC20	Kirkcaldy
Abdie	400	Fife	Fife	Cupar	SC20	St Andrews	CC20	Newburgh
Abercorn	661	West Lothian	West Lothian	Linlithgow	SC41	Dunkeld	CC7	Abercorn
Aberdalgie	323	Perthshire	Perth and Kinross	Perth	SC49	Dunkeld	CC7	
Aberdeen	168a	Aberdeenshire	Aberdeen City	Aberdeen	SC1	Aberdeen	CC1	Aberdeen
Aberdour, Aberdeenshire	169	Aberdeenshire	Aberdeenshire	Aberdeen	SC1	Aberdeen	CC1	
Aberdour, Fife	401	Fife	Fife	Cupar	SC20	Dunkeld	CC7	Aberdour
Aberfoyle	325	Perth and Kinross	Stirling	Perth	SC49	Dunblane	CC6	
Aberlady	702	East Lothian	East Lothian	Haddington	SC40	Dunkeld	CC7	
Aberlemno	269	Angus	Angus	Forfar	SC47	St Andrews	CC20	Balgavies

Parish	No.	County	Region	Sheriff Court	SC	Commissary Court	CC	Name
Aberlour	145	Banffshire	Moray	Banff	SC2	Moray	CC16	Aberlour
Abernethy	326	Perth and Kinross	Perth and Kinross	Perth	SC49	Dunblane	CC6	Abernethy
Abernethy & Kincardine	90a	Inverness-shire	Highland	Inverness	SC29	Inverness	CC11	
Abernyte	327	Perth and Kinross	Perth and Kinross	Perth	SC49	Dunkeld	CC7	
Abertarff (see Boleskine)	92	Inverness-shire	Highland	Inverness	SC29	Inverness	CC11	
Aboyne	170	Aberdeenshire	Aberdeenshire	Aberdeen	SC1	Aberdeen	CC1	Aboyne
Acharacle (see Ardnamurchan)	505	Argyll	Highland	Dunoon	SC51	Argyll	CC2	
Airlie	270	Angus	Angus	Forfar	SC47	St Andrews	CC20	
Airth	469	Stirlingshire	Falkirk	Stirling	SC67	Stirling	CC21	Airth
Alford	171	Aberdeenshire	Aberdeenshire	Aberdeen	SC1	Aberdeen	CC1	Alford
Alloa	465	Clackmannanshire	Clackmannan	Alloa	SC64	Stirling	CC21	Allloa
Alness	57	Ross & Cromarty	Highland	Dingwall	SC25	Ross	CC19	Alness
Alva	470	Clackmannanshire (Stirlings. c. 1600–1832)	Clackmannan	Alloa	SC64	Stirling	CC21	
Alvah	146	Banffshire	Aberdeenshire	Banff	SC2	Aberdeen	CC1	
Alves	125	Morayshire	Moray	Elgin	SC26	Moray	CC16	
Alvie	90b	Inverness-shire	Highland	Inverness	SC29	Inverness	CC11	Dunachton
Alyth	328	Perth and Kinross	Perth and Kinross	Perth	SC49	Dunkeld	CC7	Alyth
Ancrum	780	Roxburghshire	The Scottish Borders	Jedburgh	SC62	Peebles	CC18	Nether Ancrum
Annan	812	Dumfriesshire	Dumfries and Galloway	Dumfries	SC15	Dumfries	CC5	Annan
Anstruther-Easter	402	Fife	Fife	Cupar	SC20	St Andrews	CC20	Anstruther Easter
Anstruther-Wester	403	Fife	Fife	Cupar	SC20	St Andrews	CC20	Anstruther Wester
Anwoth	855	Kircudbrightshire	Dumfries and Galloway	Kirkcudbright	SC16	Kirkcudbright	CC13	Gatehouse of Fleet
Appin (see Lismore)	525	Argyll	Argyll and Bute	Dunoon	SC51	Argyll	CC2	

Table A1 (continued)

Parish	No.	County	Local authority	Sheriff court		Commissary court		Burgh/town/village
Applecross (incl. Shieldaig & Kishorn)	58	Ross & Cromarty	Highland	Dingwall	SC25	Ross	CC19	
Applegarth & Sibbaldbie	813a	Dumfriesshire	Dumfries and Galloway	Dumfries	SC15	Dumfries	CC5	
Arbirlot	271	Angus	Angus	Forfar	SC47	St Andrews	CC20	
Arbroath	272	Angus	Angus	Forfar	SC47	St Andrews	CC20	Arbroath
Arbuthnott	250	Kincardineshire	Aberdeenshire	Stonehaven	SC5	St Andrews	CC20	Arbuthnott
Ardchattan	504	Argyll	Argyll and Bute	Dunoon	SC51	Argyll	CC2	
Ardclach	120	Nairnshire	Highland	Nairn	SC31	Moray	CC16	
Ardersier	91	Inverness-shire	Highland	Inverness	SC29	Inverness	CC11	Campbelltown
Ardrossan	576	Ayrshire	North Ayrshire	Ayr	SC6	Glasgow	CC9	Ardrossan, Saltcoats
Arngask	404	Fife (also Perth and Kinross)	Fife	Cupar	SC20	Dunkeld	CC7	
Arrochar	492	Dunbartonshire	Argyll and Bute	Dumbarton	SC65	Glasgow	CC9	Tarbet
Ashkirk	781	Roxburghshire	The Scottish Borders	Jedburgh	SC62	Peebles	CC18	
Assynt	44	Sutherland	Highland	Dornoch	SC9	Caithness	CC4	
Athelstaneford	703	East Lothian	East Lothian	Haddington	SC40	Edinburgh	CC8	Drem
Auchindoir & Kearn	172	Aberdeenshire	Aberdeenshire	Aberdeen	SC1	Aberdeen	CC1	
Auchinleck	577	Ayrshire	East Ayrshire	Ayr	SC6	Glasgow	CC9	Auchinleck
Auchterarder	329	Perth and Kinross	Perth and Kinross	Perth	SC49	Dunblane	CC6	Auchterarder
Auchterderran	405	Fife	Fife	Cupar	SC20	St Andrews	CC20	Cardenden, Lochgelly
Auchtergaven	330	Perth and Kinross	Perth and Kinross	Perth	SC49	Dunkeld	CC7	Bankfoot, Stanley

Parish	No.	County	Region	Forfar	SC	Dunkeld	CC	Alt. name
Auchterhouse	273	Angus	Angus	Forfar	SC47	Dunkeld	CC7	(Kirkton of) Auchterhouse
Auchterless	173	Aberdeenshire	Aberdeenshire	Aberdeen	SC1	Aberdeen	CC1	
Auchtermuchty	406	Fife	Fife	Cupar	SC20	St Andrews	CC20	Auchtermuchty
Auchtertool	407	Fife	Fife	Cupar	SC20	St Andrews	CC20	Auchtertool, Newbigging
Auldearn	121	Nairnshire	Highland	Nairn	SC31	Moray	CC16	Auldearn
Avoch	59	Ross & Cromarty	Highland	Dingwall	SC25	Ross	CC19	
Avondale	621	Lanarkshire	South Lanarkshire	Hamilton	SC37	Glasgow	CC9	Strathaven
Ayr	578	Ayrshire	South Ayrshire	Ayr	SC6	Glasgow	CC9	Ayr, Citadel of Ayr
Ayton	727	Berwickshire	The Scottish Borders	Duns	SC60	Lauder	CC15	Burnmouth
Baldernock	471	Stirlingshire	East Dunbartonshire	Stirling	SC67	Hamilton & Campsie	CC10	
Balfron	472	Stirlingshire	Stirling	Stirling	SC67	Glasgow	CC9	
Ballachulish & Corran of Ardgour (quoad sacra)	506	Argyll	Highland	Dunoon	SC51	Argyll	CC2	
Ballantrae	579	Ayrshire	South Ayrshire	Ayr	SC6	Glasgow	CC9	Ballantrae
Ballingry	408	Fife	Fife	Cupar	SC20	St Andrews	CC20	Corshill Over Inchgall
Balmaclellan	856	Kirkcudbrightshire	Dumfries and Galloway	Kirkcudbright	SC16	Kirkcudbright	CC13	
Balmaghie	857a	Kirkcudbrightshire	Dumfries and Galloway	Kirkcudbright	SC16	Kirkcudbright	CC13	
Balmerino	409	Fife	Fife	Cupar	SC20	St Andrews	CC20	
Balquhidder	331	Perth and Kinross	Stirling	Perth	SC49	Dunblane	CC6	Lochearnhead, Strathyre
Banchory Devenick	251	Kincardineshire	Aberdeenshire	Stonehaven	SC5	Aberdeen	CC1	

Table A1 (continued)

Parish	No.	County	Local authority	Sheriff court		Commissary court		Burgh/town/village
Banchory Ternan	252	Kincardineshire	Aberdeenshire	Stonehaven	SC5	Aberdeen	CC1	
Banff	147	Banffshire	Aberdeenshire	Banff	SC2	Aberdeen	CC1	Banff
Barony	622	Lanarkshire	City of Glasgow	Glasgow	SC36	Glasgow	CC9	Glasgow
Barr	580	Ayrshire	South Ayrshire	Ayr	SC6	Glasgow	CC9	
Barra	108	Inverness-shire	Western Isles	Inverness	SC29	The Isles	CC12	
Barry	274	Angus	Angus	Forfar	SC47	St Andrews	CC20	
Barvas	86a	Ross & Cromarty	Western Isles	Stornoway	SC33	The Isles	CC12	
Bathgate	662	West Lothian	West Lothian	Linlithgow	SC41	Edinburgh	CC8	Bathgate, Armadale
Beath	410	Fife	Fife	Cupar	SC20	St Andrews	CC20	Cowdenbeath
Bedrule	782	Roxburghshire	The Scottish Borders	Jedburgh	SC62	Peebles	CC18	
Beith	581	Ayrshire	North Ayrshire	Ayr	SC6	Glasgow	CC9	
Belhelvie	174	Aberdeenshire	Aberdeenshire	Aberdeen	SC1	Aberdeen	CC1	
Bellie	126	Morayshire	Moray	Elgin	SC26	Moray	CC16	Fochabers
Bendochy	332	Aberdeenshire	Aberdeenshire	Perth	SC49	St Andrews	CC20	
Benholm	253	Kincardineshire	Aberdeenshire	Stonehaven	SC5	St Andrews	CC20	Johnshaven
Bervie (Inverbervie)	254	Kincardineshire	Aberdeenshire	Stonehaven	SC5	St Andrews	CC20	Inverbervie, Gourdon
Biggar	623	Lanarkshire	South Lanarkshire	Lanark	SC38	Lanark	CC14	
Birnie	127	Morayshire	Moray	Elgin	SC26	Moray	CC16	
Birsay	13	Orkney	Orkney	Kirkwall	SC11	Orkney & Shetland	CC17	
Birse	175	Aberdeenshire	Aberdeenshire	Aberdeen	SC1	Aberdeen	CC1	Marywell
Blackford	333	Perth and Kinross	Perth and Kinross	Perth	SC49	Dunblane	CC6	Blackford
Blair Atholl	334	Perth and Kinross	Perth and Kinross	Perth	SC49	Dunkeld	CC7	

Parish	No.	County	Modern area	Court town	SC	Commissary	CC	Locality
Blairgowrie	335	Perth and Kinross	Perth and Kinross	Perth	SC49	St Andrews	CC20	Blairgowrie
Blantyre	624	Lanarkshire	South Lanarkshire	Hamilton	SC37	Glasgow	CC9	Blantyre
Bo'ness	663	West Lothian	Falkirk	Linlithgow	SC41	Edinburgh	CC8	Bo'ness
Boharm	128a	Morayshire	Moray	Banff	SC2	Moray	CC16	
Boleskine	92	Inverness-shire	Highland	Inverness	SC29	Inverness	CC11	Fort Augustus
Bolton	704	East Lothian	East Lothian	Haddington	SC40	Edinburgh	CC8	
Bonhill	493	Dunbartonshire	West Dunbartonshire	Dumbarton	SC65	Glasgow	CC9	Alexandria, Balloch
Borgue	858	Kirkcudbrightshire	Dumfries and Galloway	Kirkcudbright	SC16	Kirkcudbright	CC13	
Borthwick	674	Midlothian	Midlothian	Edinburgh	SC70	Edinburgh	CC8	Middleton
Bothkennar	473	Stirlingshire	Falkirk	Stirling	SC67	Stirling	CC21	Grangemouth
Bothwell	625	Lanarkshire	North Lanarkshire / South Lanarkshire	Hamilton	SC37	Glasgow	CC9	Bellshill, Holytown, Uddingston
Botriphnie	148	Banffshire	Moray	Banff	SC2	Moray	CC16	
Bourtie	176	Aberdeenshire	Aberdeenshire	Aberdeen	SC1	Aberdeen	CC1	
Bowden	783	Roxburghshire	The Scottish Borders	Jedburgh	SC62	Peebles	CC18	
Bower	34	Caithness	Highland	Wick	SC14	Caithness	CC4	
Bowmore (or Kilarrow)	536	Argyll	Argyll and Bute	Dunoon	SC51	The Isles	CC12	
Boyndie	149	Banffshire	Aberdeenshire	Banff	SC2	Aberdeen	CC1	
Bracadale	109	Inverness-shire	Highland	Inverness	SC29	The Isles	CC12	
Braemar (Crathie & Braemar)	183	Aberdeenshire	Aberdeenshire	Aberdeen	SC1	Aberdeen	CC1	Whitehills
Brechin	275	Angus	Angus	Forfar	SC47	Brechin	CC3	Brechin
Bressay (incl. Burra & Quarff)	1	Zetland	Shetland	Lerwick	SC12	Orkney & Shetland	CC17	
Broughton	758	Peeblesshire	The Scottish Borders	Peebles	SC42	Peebles	CC18	
Brydekirk (Q.S. from Annan)	813b	Dumfriesshire	Dumfries and Galloway	Dumfries	SC15	Dumfries	CC5	

Table A1 (continued)

Parish	No.	County	Local authority	Sheriff court		Commissary court		Burgh/town/village
Buchanan	474	Stirlingshire	Stirling	Stirling	SC67	Glasgow	CC9	
Buittle	859	Kirkcudbrightshire	Dumfries and Galloway	Kirkcudbright	SC16	Kirkcudbright	CC13	
Buncle & Preston	728	Berwickshire	The Scottish Borders	Duns	SC60	Lauder	CC15	Preston
Burntisland	411	Fife	Fife	Cupar	SC20	St Andrews	CC20	Burntisland
Burray (see South Ronaldsay)	29	Orkney	Orkney	Kirkwall	SC11	Orkney & Shetland	CC17	
Cabrach	177	Aberdeenshire (Banffshire)	Moray	Aberdeen	SC1	Aberdeen	CC1	
Cadder	626	Lanarkshire	East Dunbartonshire / North Lanarkshire	Glasgow	SC36	Glasgow	CC9	Bishopbriggs
Caerlaverock	815	Dumfriesshire	Dumfries and Galloway	Dumfries	SC15	Dumfries	CC5	
Cairney	178	Aberdeenshire	Aberdeenshire	Aberdeen	SC1	Aberdeen	CC1	
Callander	336	Perth and Kinross	Stirling	Perth	SC49	Dunblane	CC6	
Cambuslang	627	Lanarkshire	South Lanarkshire	Glasgow	SC36	Glasgow	CC9	
Cambusnethan	628	Lanarkshire	North Lanarkshire	Hamilton	SC37	Glasgow	CC9	Wishaw
Cameron	412	Fife	Fife	Cupar	SC20	St Andrews	CC20	
Campbeltown	507	Argyll	Argyll and Bute	Dunoon	SC51	Argyll	CC2	Campbeltown
Campsie	475	Stirlingshire	East Dunbartonshire	Stirling	SC67	Hamilton & Campsie	CC10	
Canisbay	35	Caithness	Highland	Wick	SC14	Caithness	CC4	
Canonbie	814	Dumfriesshire	Dumfries and Galloway	Dumfries	SC15	Dumfries	CC5	

Parish	No.	Historic county	Council area	Sheriff Court	SC	Commissariot	CC	Other name
Caputh	337	Perth and Kinross	Perth and Kinross	Perth	SC49	Dunkeld	CC7	Meikleour
Cardross	494	Dunbartonshire	Argyll and Bute	Dumbarton	SC65	Hamilton & Campsie	CC10	
Careston	277	Angus	Angus	Forfar	SC47	Brechin	CC3	
Cargill	338	Perth and Kinross	Perth and Kinross	Perth	SC49	Dunkeld	CC7	
Carluke	629	Lanarkshire	South Lanarkshire	Lanark	SC38	Lanark	CC14	Carluke
Carmichael	630	Lanarkshire	South Lanarkshire	Hamilton	SC37	Lanark	CC14	
Carmunnock	631	Lanarkshire	South Lanarkshire	Glasgow	SC36	Glasgow	CC9	
Carmyllie	276	Angus	Angus	Forfar	SC47	Brechin	CC3	
Carnbee	413	Fife	Fife	Cupar	SC20	St Andrews	CC20	
Carnock	414	Fife	Fife	Cupar	SC20	Stirling	CC21	
Carnwath	632	Lanarkshire	South Lanarkshire	Lanark	SC38	Lanark	CC14	Carnwath
Carriden	664	West Lothian	Falkirk	Linlithgow	SC41	Edinburgh	CC8	Bridgeness, Grangepans
Carrington	675	Midlothian	Midlothian	Edinburgh	SC70	Edinburgh	CC8	Carrington
Carsphairn	860	Kirkcudbrightshire	Dumfries and Galloway	Kirkcudbright	SC16	Kirkcudbright	CC13	Kirkton of Carsphairn
Carstairs	633	Lanarkshire	South Lanarkshire	Lanark	SC38	Lanark	CC14	Carstairs
Castleton	784	Roxburghshire	The Scottish Borders	Jedburgh	SC62	Peebles	CC18	
Cathcart	560	Renfrewshire	East Renfrewshire / Glasgow	Paisley	SC58	Glasgow	CC9	
Cavers	785	Roxburghshire	The Scottish Borders	Jedburgh	SC62	Peebles	CC18	
Cawdor	122	Nairnshire	Highland	Nairn	SC31	Moray	CC16	
Ceres	415	Fife	Fife	Cupar	SC20	St Andrews	CC20	Ceres
Channelkirk	729	Berwickshire	The Scottish Borders	Duns	SC60	Lauder	CC15	
Chapel of Garioch	179	Aberdeenshire	Aberdeenshire	Aberdeen	SC1	Aberdeen	CC1	
Chirnside	730	Berwickshire	The Scottish Borders	Duns	SC60	Lauder	CC15	
Clackmannan	466	Clackmannanshire	Clackmannan	Alloa	SC64	Stirling	CC21	Clackmannan

Table A1   (continued)

Parish	No.	County	Local authority	Sheriff court		Commissary court		Burgh/town/village
Clatt	180	Aberdeenshire	Aberdeenshire	Aberdeen	SC1	Aberdeen	CC1	Clatt
Cleish	460	Kinross-shire	Perth and Kinross	Kinross	SC22	St Andrews	CC20	
Closeburn	816	Dumfriesshire	Dumfries and Galloway	Dumfries	SC15	Dumfries	CC5	Dalgarnock
Clunie	339	Perth and Kinross	Perth and Kinross	Perth	SC49	Dunkeld	CC7	
Cluny	181	Aberdeenshire	Aberdeenshire	Aberdeen	SC1	Aberdeen	CC1	
Clyne	45	Sutherland	Highland	Dornoch	SC9	Caithness	CC4	Inverbrora
Cockburnspath	731	Berwickshire	The Scottish Borders	Duns	SC60	Lauder	CC15	Cockburnspath
Cockpen	676	Midlothian	Midlothian	Edinburgh	SC70	Edinburgh	CC8	
Coldingham	732	Berwickshire	The Scottish Borders	Duns	SC60	Lauder	CC15	Coldingham
Coldstream (formerly Lennel)	733	Berwickshire	The Scottish Borders	Duns	SC60	Lauder	CC15	Hyndlawhill
Colinton (or Hailes)	677	Midlothian	City of Edinburgh	Edinburgh	SC70	Edinburgh	CC8	
Coll (see Tiree)	551	Argyll	Argyll and Bute	Dunoon	SC51	The Isles	CC12	
Collace	340	Perth and Kinross	Perth and Kinross	Perth	SC49	St Andrews	CC20	
Collessie	416	Fife	Fife	Cupar	SC20	St Andrews	CC20	Ladybank
Colmonell	582	Ayrshire	South Ayrshire	Ayr	SC6	Glasgow	CC9	
Colonsay (see Jura)	539	Argyll	Argyll and Bute	Dunoon	SC51	The Isles	CC12	
Colvend & Southwick	861	Kirkcudbrightshire	Dumfries and Galloway	Kirkcudbright	SC16	Dumfries	CC5	
Comrie	341	Perth and Kinross	Perth and Kinross	Perth	SC49	Dunblane	CC6	Comrie, St Fillans
Contin	60	Ross & Cromarty	Highland	Dingwall	SC25	Ross	CC19	Strathpeffer
Corstorphine	678	Midlothian	City of Edinburgh	Edinburgh	SC70	Edinburgh	CC8	
Cortachy & Clova	278	Angus	Angus	Forfar	SC47	Brechin	CC3	

Coull	182	Aberdeenshire	Aberdeenshire	Aberdeen	SC1	Aberdeen	CC1	
Coupar-Angus	279	Perth and Kinross / Angus	Perth and Kinross	Forfar	SC47	Dunkeld	CC7	Coupar-Angus
Covington & Thankerton	634	Lanarkshire	South Lanarkshire	Lanark	SC38	Lanark	CC14	
Coylton	583	Ayrshire	East Ayrshire	Ayr	SC6	Glasgow	CC9	
Craig (Inchbrayock)	280	Angus	Angus	Forfar	SC47	St Andrews	CC20	
Craigie	584	Ayrshire	South Ayrshire	Ayr	SC6	Glasgow	CC9	
Craignish	508	Argyll	Argyll and Bute	Dunoon	SC51	Argyll	CC2	
Crail	417	Fife	Fife	Cupar	SC20	St Andrews	CC20	Crail, Fifeness
Crailing	786	Roxburghshire	The Scottish Borders	Jedburgh	SC62	Peebles	CC18	
Cramond	679	Midlothian	City of Edinburgh	Edinburgh	SC70	Edinburgh	CC8	
Cranshaws	734	Berwickshire	The Scottish Borders	Duns	SC60	Lauder	CC15	
Cranston	680	Midlothian	Midlothian	Edinburgh	SC70	Edinburgh	CC8	Cousland, Pathhead
Crathie & Braemar	183	Aberdeenshire	Aberdeenshire	Aberdeen	SC1	Aberdeen	CC1	
Crawford (incl. Leadhills)	635	Lanarkshire	South Lanarkshire	Lanark	SC38	Lanark	CC14	Crawford, Leadhills
Crawfordjohn	636	Lanarkshire	South Lanarkshire	Lanark	SC38	Lanark	CC14	Abington,
Creich	418	Fife	Fife	Cupar	SC20	St Andrews	CC20	
Creich	46	Sutherland	Highland	Dornoch	SC9	Caithness	CC4	Bonar Bridge
Crichton	681	Midlothian	Midlothian	Edinburgh	SC70	Edinburgh	CC8	Crichton
Crieff	342	Perth and Kinross	Perth and Kinross	Perth	SC49	Dunkeld	CC7	Crieff
Crimond	184	Aberdeenshire	Aberdeenshire	Aberdeen	SC1	Aberdeen	CC1	
Cromarty	61	Ross & Cromarty	Highland	Dingwall	SC25	Ross	CC19	Cromarty
Cromdale (incl. Inverallan & Advie)	128b	Morayshire	Highland	Elgin	SC26	Moray	CC16	Cromdale, Grantown on Spey

Table A1 (continued)

Parish	No.	County	Local authority	Sheriff court		Commissary court		Burgh/town/village
Crossmichael	863	Kirkcudbrightshire	Dumfries and Galloway	Kirkcudbright	SC16	Kirkcudbright	CC13	
Croy & Dalcross	94	Inverness-shire	Highland	Inverness	SC29	Inverness	CC11	
Cruden	185	Aberdeenshire	Aberdeenshire	Aberdeen	SC1	Aberdeen	CC1	
Cullen	150	Banffshire	Moray	Banff	SC2	Aberdeen	CC1	Cullen
Culross	343	Perth and Kinross	Fife	Perth	SC49	Dunblane	CC6	Culross, Valleyfield
Culsalmond	186	Aberdeenshire	Aberdeenshire	Aberdeen	SC1	Aberdeen	CC1	
Culter	637	Lanarkshire	South Lanarkshire	Lanark	SC38	Lanark	CC14	
Cults	419	Fife	Fife	Cupar	SC20	St Andrews	CC20	Pitlessie
Cumbernauld	495	Dunbartonshire	North Lanarkshire	Dumbarton	SC65	Glasgow	CC9	Cumbernauld, Condorrat
Cumbraes	552	Buteshire	North Ayrshire	Rothesay	SC8	The Isles	CC12	
Cummertrees	817	Dumfriesshire	Dumfries and Galloway	Dumfries	SC15	Dumfries	CC5	
Cunningsburgh (see Dunrossness)	3	Zetland	Shetland	Lerwick	SC12	Orkney & Shetland	CC17	
Cupar	420	Fife	Fife	Cupar	SC20	St Andrews	CC20	Cupar
Currie	682	Midlothian	City of Edinburgh	Edinburgh	SC70	Edinburgh	CC8	Currie, Balerno
Dailly	585	Ayrshire	South Ayrshire	Ayr	SC6	Glasgow	CC9	
Dairsie	421	Fife	Fife	Cupar	SC20	St Andrews	CC20	
Dalgety	422	Fife	Fife	Cupar	SC20	St Andrews	CC20	
Dalkeith	683	Midlothian	Midlothian	Edinburgh	SC70	Edinburgh	CC8	Dalkeith
Dallas	129	Morayshire	Moray	Elgin	SC26	Moray	CC16	
Dalmellington	586	Ayrshire	East Ayrshire	Ayr	SC6	Glasgow	CC9	Dalmellington

Dalmeny	665	West Lothian	City of Edinburgh	Linlithgow	SC41	Edinburgh	CC8	Dalmeny
Dalry	865	Kirkcudbrightshire	Dumfries and Galloway	Kirkcudbright	SC16	Kirkcudbright	CC13	
Dalry	587	Ayrshire	North Ayrshire	Ayr	SC6	Glasgow	CC9	
Dalrymple	588	Ayrshire	East Ayrshire	Ayr	SC6	Glasgow	CC9	
Dalserf	638	Lanarkshire	South Lanarkshire	Hamilton	SC37	Hamilton & Campsie	CC10	Larkhall
Dalton	818	Dumfriesshire	Dumfries and Galloway	Dumfries	SC15	Dumfries	CC5	
Dalziel	639	Lanarkshire	North Lanarkshire	Hamilton	SC37	Glasgow	CC9	Motherwell
Daviot	187	Aberdeenshire	Aberdeenshire	Aberdeen	SC1	Aberdeen	CC1	
Daviot & Dunlichty	95	Inverness-shire	Highland	Inverness	SC29	Inverness	CC11	
Deerness	14	Orkney	Orkney	Kirkwall	SC11	Orkney & Shetland	CC17	
Delting	2	Zetland	Shetland	Lerwick	SC12	Orkney & Shetland	CC7	
Denny	476	Stirlingshire	Falkirk	Stirling	SC67	Stirling	CC21	
Deskford	151	Banffshire	Moray	Banff	SC2	Aberdeen	CC1	Deskford
Dingwall	62	Ross & Cromarty	Highland	Dingwall	SC25	Ross	CC19	Dingwall
Dirleton	705	East Lothian	East Lothian	Haddington	SC40	Edinburgh	CC8	Dirleton, Gullane
Dollar	467	Clackmannanshire	Clackmannan	Alloa	SC64	Stirling	CC21	Dollar
Dolphinton	640	Lanarkshire	South Lanarkshire	Lanark	SC38	Lanark	CC14	
Dores	96a	Inverness-shire	Highland	Inverness	SC29	Inverness	CC11	
Dornoch	47	Sutherland	Highland	Dornoch	SC9	Caithness	CC4	Dornoch
Dornock	819	Dumfriesshire	Dumfries and Galloway	Dumfries	SC15	Dumfries	CC5	
Douglas	641	Lanarkshire	South Lanarkshire	Lanark	SC38	Lanark	CC14	Douglas
Dowally	344	Perth and Kinross	Perth and Kinross	Perth	SC49	Dunkeld	CC7	

Table A1 (continued)

Parish	No.	County	Local authority	Sheriff court		Commissary court		Burgh/town/village
Drainie	130	Morayshire	Moray	Elgin	SC26	Moray	CC16	Lossiemouth
Dreghorn	589	Ayrshire	North Ayrshire	Ayr	SC6	Glasgow	CC9	
Dron	345	Perth and Kinross	Perth and Kinross	Perth	SC49	Dunblane	CC6	
Drumblade	188	Aberdeenshire	Aberdeenshire	Aberdeen	SC1	Aberdeen	CC1	
Drumelzier	759	Peeblesshire	The Scottish Borders	Peebles	SC42	Peebles	CC18	
Drumoak	189	Aberdeenshire	Aberdeenshire	Aberdeen	SC1	Aberdeen	CC1	
Dryfesdale	820	Dumfriesshire	Dumfries and Galloway	Dumfries	SC15	Dumfries	CC5	Lockerbie
Drymen	477	Stirlingshire	Stirling	Stirling	SC67	Glasgow	CC9	
Duddingston	684	Midlothian	City of Edinburgh	Edinburgh	SC70	Edinburgh	CC8	Duddingston
Duffus	131	Morayshire	Moray	Elgin	SC26	Moray	CC16	Burghead, Hopeman
Duirinish	110	Inverness-shire	Highland	Inverness	SC29	The Isles	CC12	Dunvegan
Dull	346	Perth and Kinross	Perth and Kinross	Perth	SC49	Dunkeld	CC7	Aberfeldy
Dumbarton	496	Dunbartonshire	West Dunbartonshire	Dumbarton	SC65	Glasgow	CC9	Dumbarton
Dumfries	821	Dumfriesshire	Dumfries and Galloway	Dumfries	SC15	Dumfries	CC5	Dumfries
Dun	281	Angus	Angus	Forfar	SC47	St Andrews	CC20	
Dunbar	706	East Lothian	East Lothian	Haddington	SC40	Edinburgh	CC8	Dunbar, Belhaven
Dunbarney	347	Perth and Kinross	Perth and Kinross	Perth	SC49	St Andrews	CC20	
Dunblane	348	Perth and Kinross	Stirling	Perth	SC49	Dunblane	CC6	Dunblane
Dunbog	423	Fife	Fife	Cupar	SC20	St Andrews	CC20	Dunbog
Dundee	282	Angus	Dundee	Forfar	SC47	Brechin	CC3	Dundee
Dundonald	590	Ayrshire	South Ayrshire	Ayr	SC6	Glasgow	CC9	Kirkton of Dundonald

Dundurcas (see Rothes)	141	Morayshire	Moray	Elgin	SC26	Moray	CC16	
Dunfermline	424	Fife	Fife	Cupar	SC20	St Andrews	CC20	Dunfermline, North Queensferry
Dunino	425	Fife	Fife	Cupar	SC20	St Andrews	CC20	
Dunipace	478	Stirlingshire	Falkirk	Stirling	SC67	Stirling	CC21	
Dunkeld	349	Perth and Kinross	Perth and Kinross	Perth	SC49	Dunkeld	CC7	Dunkeld
Dunlop	591	Ayrshire	East Ayrshire	Ayr	SC6	Glasgow	CC9	
Dunnet	36	Caithness	Highland	Wick	SC14	Caithness	CC4	
Dunnichen	283	Angus	Angus	Forfar	SC47	Brechin	CC3	
Dunning	350	Perth and Kinross	Perth and Kinross	Perth	SC49	Dunblane	CC6	Dunning
Dunnottar	255	Kincardineshire	Aberdeenshire	Stonehaven	SC5	St Andrews	CC20	Stonehaven
Dunoon & Kilmun	510	Argyll	Argyll and Bute	Dunoon	SC51	Argyll	CC2	
Dunrossness (incl. Sandwick, Cunningsburgh)	3	Zetland	Shetland	Lerwick	SC12	Orkney & Shetland	CC17	
Duns	735	Berwickshire	The Scottish Borders	Duns	SC60	Lauder	CC15	Duns
Dunscore	822	Dumfriesshire	Dumfries and Galloway	Dumfries	SC15	Dumfries	CC5	
Dunsyre	642	Lanarkshire	South Lanarkshire	Lanark	SC38	Lanark	CC14	
Durness	48	Sutherland	Highland	Dornoch	SC9	Caithness	CC4	
Durris	256	Kincardineshire	Aberdeenshire	Stonehaven	SC5	St Andrews	CC20	Durris
Durrisdeer	823	Dumfriesshire	Dumfries and Galloway	Dumfries	SC15	Dumfries	CC5	
Duthil & Rothiemurchus	96b	Inverness-shire	Highland	Inverness	SC29	Inverness	CC11	
Dyce	190	Aberdeenshire	Aberdeen City	Aberdeen	SC1	Aberdeen	CC1	
Dyke	133	Morayshire	Moray	Elgin	SC26	Moray	CC16	Darnaway
Dysart	426	Fife	Fife	Cupar	SC20	St Andrews	CC20	Dysart
Eaglesham	561	Renfrewshire	East Renfrewshire	Paisley	SC58	Glasgow	CC9	

Table A1 (continued)

Parish	No.	County	Local authority	Sheriff court		Commissary court		Burgh/town/village
Earlston	736	Berwickshire	The Scottish Borders	Duns	SC60	Lauder	CC15	Earlston
Eassie & Nevay	284	Angus	Angus	Forfar	SC47	St Andrews	CC20	
East Calder (see Kirknewton)	690	Midlothian	West Lothian	Edinburgh	SC70	Edinburgh	CC8	
East Kilbride	643	Lanarkshire	South Lanarkshire	Hamilton	SC37	Hamilton & Campsie	CC10	
Eastwood	562	Renfrewshire	East Renfrewshire	Paisley	SC58	Glasgow	CC9	Pollokshaws, Clarkston
Eccles	737	Berwickshire	The Scottish Borders	Duns	SC60	Lauder	CC15	
Ecclesmachan	666	West Lothian	West Lothian	Linlithgow	SC41	Edinburgh	CC8	
Echt	191	Aberdeenshire	Aberdeenshire	Aberdeen	SC1	Aberdeen	CC1	Echt
Eckford	787a	Roxburghshire	The Scottish Borders	Jedburgh	SC62	Peebles	CC18	
Eday & Pharay	15	Orkney	Orkney	Kirkwall	SC11	Orkney & Shetland	CC17	Carrick
Edderton	63	Ross & Cromarty	Highland	Dingwall	SC25	Ross	CC19	
Eddlestone	760	Peeblesshire	The Scottish Borders	Peebles	SC42	Peebles	CC18	Eddleston
Eddrachillis	49	Sutherland	Highland	Dornoch	SC9	Caithness	CC4	Scourie
Edinburgh	685-1	Midlothian	City of Edinburgh	Edinburgh	SC70	Edinburgh	CC8	Edinburgh
Edinburgh: Canongate	685-3	Midlothian	City of Edinburgh	Edinburgh	SC70	Edinburgh	CC8	
Edinburgh: St Cuthbert's	685-2	Midlothian	City of Edinburgh	Edinburgh	SC70	Edinburgh	CC8	
Edinkillie	134	Morayshire	Moray	Elgin	SC26	Moray	CC16	
Ednam	788	Roxburghshire	The Scottish Borders	Jedburgh	SC62	Peebles	CC18	
Edrom	738	Berwickshire	The Scottish Borders	Duns	SC60	Lauder	CC15	

Edzell	285	Angus	Angus	Forfar	SC47	St Andrews	CC20	Edzell
Elgin	135	Morayshire	Moray	Elgin	SC26	Moray	CC16	Elgin
Elie	427	Fife	Fife	Cupar	SC20	St Andrews	CC20	Elie & Earlsferry
Ellon	192	Aberdeenshire	Aberdeenshire	Aberdeen	SC1	Aberdeen	CC1	Ellon
Enzie (*quoad sacra* Bellie & Rathven)	152	Banffshire	Moray	Banff	SC2	Moray	CC16	
Errol	351	Perth and Kinross	Perth and Kinross	Perth	SC49	St Andrews	CC20	Errol
Erskine	563	Renfrewshire	Renfrewshire	Paisley	SC58	Glasgow	CC9	Bishopton
Eskdalemuir	824	Dumfriesshire	Dumfries and Galloway	Dumfries	SC15	Dumfries	CC5	
Ettrick	774b	Selkirkshire	The Scottish Borders	Selkirk	SC63	Peebles	CC18	
Evie & Rendall	16	Orkney	Orkney	Kirkwall	SC11	Orkney & Shetland	CC17	
Ewes	825	Dumfriesshire	Dumfries & Galloway	Dumfries	SC15	Dumfries	CC5	
Eyemouth	739	Berwickshire	The Scottish Borders	Duns	SC60	Lauder	CC15	Eyemouth
Fala & Soutra	686	Midlothian	Midlothian	Edinburgh	SC70	Edinburgh	CC8	
Falkirk	479	Stirlingshire	Falkirk	Stirling	SC67	Stirling	CC21	Falkirk
Falkland	428	Fife	Fife	Cupar	SC20	St Andrews	CC20	Falkland, Freuchie
Farnell	286	Angus	Angus	Forfar	SC47	Brechin	CC3	
Farr	50	Sutherland	Highland	Dornoch	SC9	Caithness	CC4	Bettyhill
Fearn	287	Angus	Angus	Forfar	SC47	Brechin	CC3	
Fearn	64	Ross & Cromarty	Highland	Dingwall	SC25	Ross	CC19	Balintore
Fenwick	592	Ayrshire	East Ayrshire	Ayr	SC6	Glasgow	CC9	
Ferry Port on Craig	429	Fife	Fife	Cupar	SC20	St Andrews	CC20	Tayport
Fetlar (incl. North Yell)	4	Zetland	Shetland	Lerwick	SC12	Orkney & Shetland	CC17	
Fettercairn	257	Kincardineshire	Aberdeenshire	Stonehaven	SC5	St Andrews	CC20	Fettercairn

Table A1 (continued)

Parish	No.	County	Local authority	Sheriff court		Commissary court		Burgh/town/village
Fetteresso	258	Kincardineshire	Aberdeenshire	Stonehaven	SC5	St Andrews	CC20	Stonehaven, Cowie
Findo-Gask	352	Perth and Kinross	Perth and Kinross	Perth	SC49	Dunblane	CC6	
Fintray	193	Aberdeenshire	Aberdeenshire	Aberdeen	SC1	Aberdeen	CC1	Hatton of Fintray
Fintry	480	Stirlingshire	Stirling	Stirling	SC67	Glasgow	CC9	
Firth & Stenness	17	Orkney	Orkney	Kirkwall	SC11	Orkney & Shetland	CC17	
Flisk	430	Fife	Fife	Cupar	SC20	St Andrews	CC20	
Flotta (see Walls)	32	Orkney	Orkney	Kirkwall	SC11	Orkney & Shetland	CC17	
Fodderty	65	Ross & Cromarty	Highland	Dingwall	SC25	Ross	CC19	
Fogo	740	Berwickshire	The Scottish Borders	Duns	SC60	Lauder	CC15	
Fordoun	259	Kincardineshire	Aberdeenshire	Stonehaven	SC5	St Andrews	CC20	Fordoun, Auchenblae
Fordyce	153	Banffshire	Aberdeenshire	Banff	SC2	Aberdeen	CC1	Fordyce, Portsoy
Forfar	288	Angus	Angus	Forfar	SC47	St Andrews	CC20	Forfar
Forgan	431	Fife	Fife	Cupar	SC20	St Andrews	CC20	Newport
Forgandenny	353	Perth and Kinross	Perth and Kinross	Perth	SC49	Dunkeld	CC7	Forgandenny
Forglen	154	Banffshire	Aberdeenshire	Banff	SC2	Aberdeen	CC1	
Forgue	194	Aberdeenshire	Aberdeenshire	Aberdeen	SC1	Aberdeen	CC1	Forgue
Forres	137	Morayshire	Moray	Elgin	SC26	Moray	CC16	Forres
Forteviot	354	Perth and Kinross	Perth and Kinross	Perth	SC49	St Andrews	CC20	
Fortingall	355a	Perth and Kinross	Perth and Kinross	Perth	SC49	Dunkeld	CC7	
Fossoway & Tulliebole	461	Kinross-shire	Perth and Kinross	Kinross	SC22	St Andrews	CC20	Crook of Devon

Foula (see Walls)	12	Zetland	Shetland	Lerwick	SC12	Orkney & Shetland	CC17	
Foulden	741	Berwickshire	The Scottish Borders	Duns	SC60	Lauder	CC15	
Foveran	195	Aberdeenshire	Aberdeenshire	Aberdeen	SC1	Aberdeen	CC1	Newburgh
Fowlis Easter	356	Angus	Angus	Forfar	SC47	St Andrews	CC20	
Fowlis Wester	357	Perth and Kinross	Perth and Kinross	Perth	SC49	Dunblane	CC6	Abercairney
Fraserburgh	196	Aberdeenshire	Aberdeenshire	Aberdeen	SC1	Aberdeen	CC1	Fraserburgh
Fyvie	197	Aberdeenshire	Aberdeenshire	Aberdeen	SC1	Aberdeen	CC1	Fyvie, Woodhead
Gairloch	66	Ross & Cromarty	Highland	Dingwall	SC25	Ross	CC19	Gairloch
Galashiels	775	Selkirkshire	The Scottish Borders	Selkirk	SC63	Peebles	CC18	Galashiels
Galston	593	Ayrshire	East Ayrshire	Ayr	SC6	Glasgow	CC9	
Gamrie (incl. Macduff and Down)	155a	Banffshire	Aberdeenshire	Banff	SC2	Aberdeen	CC1	Macduff, Gardenstown
Gargunnock	481	Stirlingshire	Stirling	Stirling	SC67	Stirling	CC21	Gargunnock
Gartly	198	Aberdeenshire	Aberdeenshire	Aberdeen	SC1	Moray	CC16	
Garvald & Bara	707	East Lothian	East Lothian	Haddington	SC40	Edinburgh	CC8	
Garvock	260	Kincardineshire	Aberdeenshire	Stonehaven	SC5	St Andrews	CC20	
Gigha & Cara	537	Argyll	Argyll and Bute	Dunoon	SC51	The Isles	CC12	
Girthon	866	Kirkcudbrightshire	Dumfries and Galloway	Kirkcudbright	SC16	Kirkcudbright	CC13	Gatehouse of Fleet
Girvan	594	Ayrshire	South Ayrshire	Ayr	SC6	Glasgow	CC9	Girvan
Gladsmuir	708	East Lothian	East Lothian	Haddington	SC40	Edinburgh	CC8	
Glamis	289	Angus	Angus	Forfar	SC47	St Andrews	CC20	Glamis
Glasgow	644-1	Lanarkshire	City of Glasgow	Glasgow	SC36	Glasgow	CC9	Glasgow, Anderston
Glass	199	Aberdeenshire	Aberdeenshire	Aberdeen	SC1	Moray	CC16	
Glassary	511	Argyll	Argyll and Bute	Dunoon	SC51	Argyll	CC2	
Glasserton	885	Wigtownshire	Dumfries and Galloway	Wigtown	SC19	Wigtown	CC22	

Table A1 (continued)

Parish	No.	County	Local authority	Sheriff court	Commissary court	Burgh/town/village
Glassford	645	Lanarkshire	South Lanarkshire	Hamilton SC37	Hamilton & Campsie CC10	
Glenbervie	261	Kincardineshire	Aberdeenshire	Stonehaven SC5	Brechin CC3	Drumlithie
Glenbuchat (Glenbucket)	200	Aberdeenshire	Aberdeenshire	Aberdeen SC1	Aberdeen CC1	
Glencairn	826	Dumfriesshire	Dumfries and Galloway	Dumfries SC15	Dumfries CC5	Moniaive
Glencorse (formerly Woodhouselee)	687	Midlothian	Midlothian	Edinburgh SC70	Edinburgh CC8	
Glendevon	358	Perth and Kinross	Perth and Kinross	Perth SC49	Dunblane CC6	
Glenelg	97	Inverness-shire	Highland	Inverness SC29	Inverness CC11	
Glenholm	761	Peeblesshire	The Scottish Borders	Peebles SC42	Peebles CC18	
Glenisla	290	Angus	Angus	Forfar SC47	Brechin CC3	
Glenmoriston (see Urquhart)	107	Inverness-shire	Highland	Inverness SC29	Inverness CC11	
Glenmuck, Tullich & Glengairn	201	Aberdeenshire	Aberdeenshire	Aberdeen SC1	Aberdeen CC1	
Glenorchy & Inishail	512	Argyll	Argyll and Bute	Dunoon SC51	Argyll CC2	
Glenshiel	67	Ross & Cromarty	Highland	Dingwall SC25	Ross CC19	
Golspie	51	Sutherland	Highland	Dornoch SC9	Caithness CC4	
Gorbals	644-2	Lanarkshire	City of Glasgow	Glasgow SC36	Hamilton & Campsie CC10	Glasgow
Gordon	742	Berwickshire	The Scottish Borders	Duns SC60	Lauder CC15	
Govan	646	Lanarkshire	City of Glasgow	Glasgow SC36	Hamilton & Campsie CC10	

Graemsay (see Hoy)	20	Orkney	Orkney	Kirkwall	SC11	Orkney & Shetland	CC17	
Grange	156	Banffshire	Moray	Banff	SC2	Moray	CC16	
Greenlaw	743	Berwickshire	The Scottish Borders	Duns	SC60	Lauder	CC15	Greenlaw
Greenock (Middle, East & West)	564	Renfrewshire	Inverclyde	Paisley	SC58	Glasgow	CC9	Greenock, Crawfordsdyke
Gretna	827	Dumfriesshire	Dumfries and Galloway	Dumfries	SC15	Dumfries	CC5	
Guthrie	291	Angus	Angus	Forfar	SC47	Brechin	CC3	
Haddington	709	East Lothian	East Lothian	Haddington	SC40	Edinburgh	CC8	Haddington
Halfmorton	828	Dumfriesshire	Dumfries and Galloway	Dumfries	SC15	Dumfries	CC5	
Halkirk	37	Caithness	Highland	Wick	SC14	Caithness	CC4	
Hamilton	647	Lanarkshire	South Lanarkshire	Hamilton	SC37	Hamilton & Campsie	CC10	Hamilton
Harray	18	Orkney	Orkney	Kirkwall	SC11	Orkney & Shetland	CC17	
Harris (incl. St Kilda)	111	Inverness-shire	Western Isles	Inverness	SC29	The Isles	CC12	
Hawick	789	Roxburghshire	The Scottish Borders	Jedburgh	SC62	Peebles	CC18	Hawick
Heriot	688	Midlothian	The Scottish Borders	Edinburgh	SC70	Edinburgh	CC8	
Hobkirk	790	Roxburghshire	The Scottish Borders	Jedburgh	SC62	Peebles	CC18	
Hoddam	829	Dumfriesshire	Dumfries and Galloway	Dumfries	SC15	Dumfries	CC5	Ecclefechan
Holm & Paplay	19	Orkney	Orkney	Kirkwall	SC11	Orkney & Shetland	CC17	
Holywood	830	Dumfriesshire	Dumfries and Galloway	Dumfries	SC15	Dumfries	CC5	
Houston & Killellan	565	Renfrewshire	Renfrewshire	Paisley	SC58	Glasgow	CC9	Houston

Table A1 (continued)

Parish	No.	County	Local authority	Sheriff court	Commissary court	Burgh/town/village
Hownam	791	Roxburghshire	The Scottish Borders	Jedburgh SC62	Peebles CC18	
Hoy & Graemsay	20	Orkney	Orkney	Kirkwall SC11	Orkney & Shetland CC17	
Humbie	710	East Lothian	East Lothian	Haddington SC40	Edinburgh CC8	
Hume (see Stitchell)	808	Berwickshire	The Scottish Borders	Duns SC60	Lauder CC15	
Huntly	202	Aberdeenshire	Aberdeenshire	Aberdeen SC1	Aberdeen CC1	Huntly
Hutton	745	Berwickshire	The Scottish Borders	Duns SC60	Lauder CC15	
Hutton & Corrie	831	Dumfriesshire	Dumfries and Galloway	Dumfries SC15	Dumfries CC5	
Inch	886	Wigtownshire	Dumfries and Galloway	Wigtown SC19	Wigtown CC22	Lochryan
Inchinnan	566	Renfrewshire	Renfrewshire	Paisley SC58	Glasgow CC9	
Inchture	359	Perth and Kinross	Perth and Kinross	Perth SC49	St Andrews CC20	
Innerleithen	762	Peeblesshire	The Scottish Borders	Peebles SC42	Peebles CC18	Walkerburn
Innerwick	711	East Lothian	East Lothian	Haddington SC40	Edinburgh CC8	Innerwick
Insch	203	Aberdeenshire	Aberdeenshire	Aberdeen SC1	Aberdeen CC1	Insch
Insh (see Kingussie)	102	Inverness-shire	Highland	Inverness SC29	Inverness CC11	
Inveraray & Glenaray	513	Argyll	Argyll and Bute	Dunoon SC51	Argyll CC2	Inveraray
Inverarity & Methy	292	Angus	Angus	Forfar SC47	St Andrews CC20	
Inveravon	157	Banffshire	Moray	Banff SC2	Moray CC16	
Inverchaolain	514	Argyll	Argyll and Bute	Dunoon SC51	Argyll CC2	
Inveresk	689	Midlothian	East Lothian	Edinburgh SC70	Edinburgh CC8	Musselburgh, Wallyford
Inverkeillor	293	Angus	Angus	Forfar SC47	St Andrews CC20	

				Cupar		St Andrews		
Inverkeithing	432	Fife	Fife	Cupar	SC20	St Andrews	CC20	Inverkeithing, Rosyth
Inverkeithny	158	Banffshire	Aberdeenshire	Banff	SC2	Moray	CC16	
Inverkip	567	Renfrewshire	Inverclyde	Paisley	SC58	Glasgow	CC9	Gourock, Wemyss Bay
Inverness	98	Inverness-shire	Highland	Inverness	SC29	Inverness	CC11	Inverness
Invernochtie (Strathdon)	240	Aberdeenshire	Aberdeenshire	Aberdeen	SC1	Aberdeen	CC1	
Inverurie	204	Aberdeenshire	Aberdeenshire	Aberdeen	SC1	Aberdeen	CC1	Inverurie
Iona	538	Argyll	Argyll and Bute	Dunoon	SC51	The Isles	CC12	
Irongray (Kirkpatrick-Irongray)	867	Kirkcudbrightshire	Dumfries and Galloway	Kirkcudbright	SC16	Dumfries	CC5	
Irvine	595	Ayrshire	North Ayrshire	Ayr	SC6	Glasgow	CC9	Irvine
Jedburgh	792	Roxburghshire	The Scottish Borders	Jedburgh	SC62	Peebles	CC18	Jedburgh
Johnstone	832	Dumfriesshire	Dumfries and Galloway	Dumfries	SC15	Dumfries	CC5	
Jura & Colonsay	539	Argyll	Argyll and Bute	Dunoon	SC51	The Isles	CC12	
Keig	205	Aberdeenshire	Aberdeenshire	Aberdeen	SC1	Aberdeen	CC1	
Keir	833	Dumfriesshire	Dumfries and Galloway	Dumfries	SC15	Dumfries	CC5	
Keith	159	Banffshire	Moray	Banff	SC2	Moray	CC16	Keith, Newmill
Keithhall & Kinkell	206	Aberdeenshire	Aberdeenshire	Aberdeen	SC1	Aberdeen	CC1	
Kells	868	Kirkcudbrightshire	Dumfries and Galloway	Kirkcudbright	SC16	Kirkcudbright	CC13	New Galloway
Kelso	793	Roxburghshire	The Scottish Borders	Jedburgh	SC62	Peebles	CC18	Kelso
Kelton	869	Kircudbrightshire	Dumfries and Galloway	Kirkcudbright	SC16	Kirkcudbright	CC13	Castle Douglas, Kelton
Kemback	433	Fife	Fife	Cupar	SC20	St Andrews	CC20	
Kemnay	207	Aberdeenshire	Aberdeenshire	Aberdeen	SC1	Aberdeen	CC1	

Table A1 (continued)

Parish	No.	County	Local authority	Sheriff court		Commissary court		Burgh/town/village
Kenmore	360	Perth and Kinross	Perth and Kinross	Perth	SC49	Dunkeld	CC7	Kenmore
Kennethmont	212	Aberdeenshire	Aberdeenshire	Aberdeen	SC1	Aberdeen	CC1	
Kennoway	434	Fife	Fife	Cupar	SC20	St Andrews	CC20	Kennoway
Kettins	294	Angus	Perth and Kinross	Forfar	SC47	St Andrews	CC20	
Kettle	435	Fife	Fife	Cupar	SC20	St Andrews	CC20	
Kilbarchan	568	Renfrewshire	Renfrewshire	Paisley	SC58	Glasgow	CC9	Kilbarchan, Bridge of Weir
Kilberry (see Kilcalmonell)	516	Argyll	Argyll and Bute	Dunoon	SC51	Argyll	CC2	
Kilbirnie	596	Ayrshire	North Ayrshire	Ayr	SC6	Glasgow	CC9	Kilbirnie
Kilbrandon & Kilchattan	515	Argyll	Argyll and Bute	Dunoon	SC51	Argyll	CC2	
Kilbride (Bute)	553	Buteshire	North Ayrshire	Rothesay	SC8	The Isles	CC12	Lamlash
Kilbucho	763	Peeblesshire	The Scottish Borders	Peebles	SC42	Peebles	CC18	Kilbucho
Kilcalmonell & Kilberry	516	Argyll	Argyll and Bute	Dunoon	SC51	Argyll	CC2	Tarbert
Kilchoman	540	Argyll	Argyll and Bute	Dunoon	SC51	The Isles	CC12	Port Ellen
Kilchrenan & Dalavich	517	Argyll	Argyll and Bute	Dunoon	SC51	Argyll	CC2	
Kilconquhar	436	Fife	Fife	Cupar	SC20	St Andrews	CC20	Elie, Earlsferry, Colinsburgh
Kildalton	541	Argyll	Argyll and Bute	Dunoon	SC51	The Isles	CC12	Laggan
Kildonan	52	Sutherland	Highland	Dornoch	SC9	Caithness	CC4	
Kildrummy	208	Aberdeenshire	Aberdeenshire	Aberdeen	SC1	Aberdeen	CC1	Kildrummy
Kilfinan	518	Argyll	Argyll and Bute	Dunoon	SC51	Argyll	CC2	
Kilfinichan & Kilvickeon	542	Argyll	Argyll and Bute	Dunoon	SC51	The Isles	CC12	
Killean & Kilchenzie	519	Argyll	Argyll and Bute	Dunoon	SC51	Argyll	CC2	

Killearn	482	Stirlingshire	Stirling	Stirling	SC67	Glasgow	CC9	
Killearnan	68	Ross and Cromarty	Highland	Dingwall	SC25	Ross	CC19	Redcastle
Killellan (see Houston)	565	Renfrewshire	Renfrewshire	Paisley	SC58	Glasgow	CC9	
Killin	361	Perth and Kinross	Stirling	Perth	SC49	Dunkeld	CC7	Killin, Tyndrum
Kilmacolm	569	Renfrewshire	Renfrewshire	Paisley	SC58	Glasgow	CC9	
Kilmadock	362	Perth and Kinross	Stirling	Perth	SC49	Dunblane	CC6	Doune
Kilmallie	520	Argyll	Argyll and Bute	Dunoon	SC51	Argyll	CC2	Fort William
Kilmany	437	Fife	Fife	Cupar	SC20	St Andrews	CC20	
Kilmarnock	597	Ayrshire	East Ayrshire	Ayr	SC6	Glasgow	CC9	Kilmarnock
Kilmaronock	497	Dunbartonshire	West Dunbartonshire	Dumbarton	SC65	Glasgow	CC9	
Kilmartin	521	Argyll	Argyll and Bute	Dunoon	SC51	Argyll	CC2	
Kilmaurs	598	Ayrshire	East Ayrshire	Ayr	SC6	Glasgow	CC9	Kilmaurs
Kilmeny	543	Argyll	Argyll and Bute	Dunoon	SC51	The Isles	CC12	
Kilmichael Glassary	511	Argyll	Argyll and Bute	Dunoon	SC51	Argyll	CC2	Lochgilphead
Kilmodan	522	Argyll	Argyll and Bute	Dunoon	SC51	Argyll	CC2	
Kilmonivaig	99	Inverness-shire	Highland	Inverness	SC29	Inverness	CC11	Invergarry
Kilmorack	100	Inverness-shire	Highland	Inverness	SC29	Inverness	CC11	Beauly, Kilmorack
Kilmore & Kilbride	523	Argyll	Argyll and Bute	Dunoon	SC51	Argyll	CC2	Oban
Kilmory	554	Buteshire	North Ayrshire	Rothesay	SC8	The Isles	CC12	
Kilmuir	112	Inverness-shire	Highland	Inverness	SC29	The Isles	CC12	
Kilmuir Easter	69	Ross & Cromarty	Highland	Dingwall	SC25	Ross	CC19	
Kilninian & Kilmore	544	Argyll	Argyll and Bute	Dunoon	SC51	The Isles	CC12	
Kilninver & Kilmelfort	524	Argyll	Argyll and Bute	Dunoon	SC51	Argyll	CC2	Melfort
Kilrenny	438	Fife	Fife	Cupar	SC20	St Andrews	CC20	Kilrenny, Innergelly
Kilspindie	363	Perth and Kinross	Perth and Kinross	Perth	SC49	St Andrews	CC20	
Kilsyth (formerly Monyabroch)	483	Stirlingshire	North Lanarkshire	Stirling	SC67	Glasgow	CC9	Kilsyth

Table A1 (continued)

Parish	No.	County	Local authority	Sheriff court		Commissary court		Burgh/town/village
Kiltarlity	101	Inverness-shire	Highland	Inverness	SC29	Inverness	CC11	
Kiltearn	70	Ross & Cromarty	Highland	Dingwall	SC25	Ross	CC19	Foulis
Kilwinning	599	Ayrshire	North Ayrshire	Ayr	SC6	Glasgow	CC9	
Kincardine O'Neil	209	Aberdeenshire	Aberdeenshire	Aberdeen	SC1	Aberdeen	CC1	Kincardine O'Neil
Kincardine (Perth and Kinross)	364	Perth and Kinross	Stirling	Perth	SC49	Dunblane	CC6	
Kincardine (Ross)	71	Ross & Cromarty	Highland	Dingwall	SC25	Ross	CC19	Ardgay
Kinclaven	365	Perth and Kinross	Perth and Kinross	Perth	SC49	Dunkeld	CC7	
Kinfauns	366	Perth and Kinross	Perth and Kinross	Perth	SC49	St Andrews	CC20	
King Edward	210	Aberdeenshire	Aberdeenshire	Aberdeen	SC1	Aberdeen	CC1	
Kingarth	555	Buteshire	Argyll and Bute	Rothesay	SC8	The Isles	CC12	
Kinghorn	439	Fife	Fife	Cupar	SC20	St Andrews	CC20	Kinghorn
Kinglassie	440	Fife	Fife	Cupar	SC20	St Andrews	CC20	
Kingoldrum	295	Angus	Angus	Forfar	SC47	Brechin	CC3	
Kingsbarns	441	Fife	Fife	Cupar	SC20	St Andrews	CC20	
Kingussie & Insh	102	Inverness-shire	Highland	Inverness	SC29	Inverness	CC11	Kingussie, Newtonmore, Dalwhinnie
Kinloch (see Lethendy)	372	Perth and Kinross	Perth and Kinross	Perth	SC49	Dunkeld	CC7	
Kinlochspelvie	545	Argyll	Argyll and Bute	Dunoon	SC51	The Isles	CC12	
Kinloss	138	Morayshire	Moray	Elgin	SC26	Moray	CC16	Findhorn, Kinloss, Muirtown
Kinnaird	368	Perth and Kinross	Perth and Kinross	Perth	SC49	St Andrews	CC20	
Kinneff & Catterline	262	Kincardineshire	Aberdeenshire	Stonehaven	SC5	St Andrews	CC20	

No.	Parish	Old county	New county	Sheriff court	SC	Commissary court	CC	Other
296	Kinnell	Angus	Angus	Forfar	SC47	St Andrews	CC20	
211	Kinnellar	Aberdeenshire	Aberdeenshire	Aberdeen	SC1	Aberdeen	CC1	
297	Kinnettles	Angus	Angus	Forfar	SC47	St Andrews	CC20	
369	Kinnoull	Perth and Kinross	Perth and Kinross	Perth	SC49	St Andrews	CC20	Kinnoull
462	Kinross	Kinrossshire	Perth and Kinross	Kinross	SC22	St Andrews	CC20	Kinross
72	Kintail	Ross & Cromarty	Highland	Dingwall	SC25	Ross	CC19	
213	Kintore	Aberdeenshire	Aberdeenshire	Aberdeen	SC1	Aberdeen	CC1	Kintore
484	Kippen	Stirlingshire	Stirling	Stirling	SC67	Dunblane	CC6	Kippen, Buchlyvie
870	Kirkbean	Kirkcudbrightshire	Dumfries and Galloway	Kirkcudbright	SC16	Dumfries	CC5	Preston
442	Kirkcaldy	Fife	Fife	Cupar	SC20	St Andrews	CC20	Kirkcaldy
887	Kirkcolm	Wigtownshire	Dumfries and Galloway	Wigtown	SC19	Wigtown	CC22	Stewarton
834	Kirkconnel	Dumfriesshire	Dumfries and Galloway	Dumfries	SC15	Dumfries	CC5	
888	Kirkcowan	Wigtownshire	Dumfries and Galloway	Wigtown	SC19	Wigtown	CC22	Knockreavie
871	Kirkcudbright	Kirkcudbrightshire	Dumfries and Galloway	Kirkcudbright	SC16	Kirkcudbright	CC13	Kirkcudbright
298	Kirkden	Angus	Angus	Forfar	SC47	St Andrews	CC20	Friockheim
872	Kirkgunzeon	Kirkcudbrightshire	Dumfries and Galloway	Kirkcudbright	SC16	Kirkcudbright	CC13	
103	Kirkhill	Inverness-shire	Highland	Inverness	SC29	Inverness	CC11	
776	Kirkhope	Selkirkshire	The Scottish Borders	Selkirk	SC63	Peebles	CC18	
889	Kirkinner	Wigtownshire	Dumfries and Galloway	Wigtown	SC19	Wigtown	CC22	
498	Kirkintilloch	Dunbartonshire	East Dunbartonshire	Dumbarton	SC65	Glasgow	CC9	Kirkintilloch, Lenzie

Table A1 (continued)

Parish	No.	County	Local authority	Sheriff court		Commissary court		Burgh/town/village
Kirkliston	667	West Lothian	City of Edinburgh	Linlithgow	SC41	Edinburgh	CC8	Kirkliston, Winchburgh
Kirkmabreck	873	Kirkcudbrightshire	Dumfries and Galloway	Kirkcudbright	SC16	Kirkcudbright	CC13	Creetown
Kirkmahoe	835	Dumfriesshire	Dumfries and Galloway	Dumfries	SC15	Dumfries	CC5	
Kirkmaiden	890	Wigtownshire	Dumfries and Galloway	Wigtown	SC19	Wigtown	CC22	Port Logan
Kirkmichael	370	Perth and Kinross	Perth and Kinross	Perth	SC49	Dunkeld	CC7	Kirkmichael
Kirkmichael (Ayr)	600	Ayrshire	South Ayrshire	Ayr	SC6	Glasgow	CC9	
Kirkmichael (Banffshire)	160	Banffshire	Moray	Banff	SC2	Moray	CC16	
Kirkmichael (Dumfries)	836	Dumfriesshire	Dumfries and Galloway	Dumfries	SC15	Dumfries	CC5	
Kirknewton & East Calder	690	Midlothian	West Lothian	Edinburgh	SC70	Edinburgh	CC8	
Kirkoswald	601	Ayrshire	South Ayrshire	Ayr	SC6	Glasgow	CC9	
Kirkpatrick-Durham	874	Kirkcudbrightshire	Dumfries and Galloway	Kirkcudbright	SC16	Dumfries	CC5	Troquen
Kirkpatrick-Fleming	837	Dumfriesshire	Dumfries and Galloway	Dumfries	SC15	Dumfries	CC5	
Kirkpatrick-Irongray	867	Kirkcudbrightshire	Dumfries and Galloway	Kirkcudbright	SC16	Dumfries	CC5	
Kirkpatrick-Juxta	838	Dumfriesshire	Dumfries and Galloway	Dumfries	SC15	Dumfries	CC5	Beattock

Parish	No.	County	Council area	Registration district	SC	Sheriff court	CC	Commissariot
Kirktown	794	Roxburghshire	The Scottish Borders	Jedburgh	SC62	Peebles	CC18	
Kirkurd	764	Peeblesshire	The Scottish Borders	Peebles	SC42	Peebles	CC18	
Kirkwall & St Ola	21	Orkney	Orkney	Kirkwall	SC11	Orkney & Shetland	CC7	Kirkwall
Kirriemuir	299	Angus	Angus	Forfar	SC47	St Andrews	CC20	Kirriemuir
Kishorn (see Applecross)	58	Ross & Cromarty	Highland	Dingwall	SC25	Ross	CC19	
Knockando	139	Morayshire	Moray	Elgin	SC26	Moray	CC16	
Knockbain (formerly Kilmuir Wester)	73	Ross & Cromarty	Highland	Dingwall	SC25	Ross	CC19	
Ladykirk	746	Berwickshire	The Scottish Borders	Duns	SC60	Lauder	CC15	
Laggan	104	Inverness-shire	Highland	Inverness	SC29	Inverness	CC11	
Lairg	53	Sutherland	Highland	Dornoch	SC9	Caithness	CC4	Lairg
Lamington & Wandell	659	Lanarkshire	South Lanarkshire	Lanark	SC38	Lanark	CC14	
Lanark	648	Lanarkshire	South Lanarkshire	Lanark	SC38	Lanark	CC14	Lanark
Langholm	839	Dumfriesshire	Dumfries and Galloway	Dumfries	SC15	Dumfries	CC5	Langholm
Langton	747	Berwickshire	The Scottish Borders	Duns	SC60	Lauder	CC15	Langton
Larbert	485	Stirlingshire	Falkirk	Stirling	SC67	Stirling	CC21	Larbert
Largo	443	Fife	Fife	Cupar	SC20	St Andrews	CC20	Largo
Largs	602	Ayrshire	North Ayrshire	Ayr	SC6	Glasgow	CC9	Largs, Fairlie
Lasswade	691	Midlothian	Midlothian	Edinburgh	SC70	Edinburgh	CC8	Roslin, Clerkington
Latheron	38	Caithness	Highland	Wick	SC14	Caithness	CC4	Berridale, Dunbeath, Lybster
Lauder	748	Berwickshire	The Scottish Borders	Duns	SC60	Lauder	CC15	Lauder, Thirlestane
Laurencekirk	263	Kincardineshire	Aberdeenshire	Stonehaven	SC5	St Andrews	CC20	Laurencekirk
Lecropt	371	Perth and Kinross	Stirling	Perth	SC49	Dunblane	CC6	
Legerwood	749	Berwickshire	The Scottish Borders	Duns	SC60	Lauder	CC15	

Table A1 (continued)

Parish	No.	County	Local authority	Sheriff court	Commissary court	Burgh/town/village
Leith: North	692-1	Midlothian	City of Edinburgh	Edinburgh SC70	Edinburgh CC8	Leith
Leith: South	692-2	Midlothian	City of Edinburgh	Edinburgh SC70	Edinburgh CC8	Leith, Restalrig
Leochel-Cushnie	214	Aberdeenshire	Aberdeenshire	Aberdeen SC1	Aberdeen CC1	
Lerwick	5	Zetland	Shetland	Lerwick SC12	Orkney & Shetland CC17	Lerwick
Leslie	215	Aberdeenshire	Aberdeenshire	Aberdeen SC1	Aberdeen CC1	Leslie
Leslie	444	Fife	Fife	Cupar SC20	Dunkeld CC7	Leslie
Lesmahagow	649	Lanarkshire	South Lanarkshire	Lanark SC38	Lanark CC14	Lesmahagow
Leswalt	891	Wigtownshire	Dumfries and Galloway	Wigtown SC19	Wigtown CC22	
Lethendy & Kinloch	372	Perth and Kinross	Perth and Kinross	Perth SC49	Dunkeld CC7	
Lethnot & Navar	300	Angus	Angus	Forfar SC47	Brechin CC3	
Leuchars	445	Fife	Fife	Cupar SC20	St Andrews CC20	Leuchars, Balmullo
Lhanbryde (see St Andrews)	142	Morayshire	Moray	Elgin SC26	Moray CC16	Lhanbryde
Libberton	650	Lanarkshire	South Lanarkshire	Lanark SC38	Lanark CC14	
Liberton	693	Midlothian	City of Edinburgh	Edinburgh SC70	Edinburgh CC8	
Liff, Benvie & Invergowrie	301	Angus	Dundee	Forfar SC47	St Andrews CC20	
Lilliesleaf	795	Roxburghshire	The Scottish Borders	Jedburgh SC62	Peebles CC18	
Linlithgow	668	West Lothian	West Lothian	Linlithgow SC41	Edinburgh CC8	Linlithgow
Linton	796	Roxburghshire	The Scottish Borders	Jedburgh SC62	Peebles CC18	Linton
Lintrathen	302	Angus	Angus	Forfar SC47	St Andrews CC20	
Lismore (incl. Appin, Duror)	525	Argyll	Argyll and Bute	Dunoon SC51	Argyll CC2	Ballachulish

Little Dunkeld	373	Perth and Kinross	Perth and Kinross	Perth	SC49	Dunkeld	CC7	Birnam
Livingston	669	West Lothian	West Lothian	Linlithgow	SC41	Edinburgh	CC8	Livingston
Lochalsh	74	Ross & Cromarty	Highland	Dingwall	SC25	Ross	CC19	Plockton
Lochbroom	75	Ross & Cromarty	Highland	Dingwall	SC25	Ross	CC19	Ullapool
Lochcarron	76	Ross & Cromarty	Highland	Dingwall	SC25	Ross	CC19	Lochcarron
Lochgilphead	526	Argyll	Argyll and Bute	Dunoon	SC51	Argyll	CC2	
Lochgoilhead & Kilmorich	527	Argyll	Argyll and Bute	Dunoon	SC51	Argyll	CC2	
Lochlee	303	Angus	Angus	Forfar	SC47	Brechin	CC3	
Lochmaben	840	Dumfriesshire	Dumfries and Galloway	Dumfries	SC15	Dumfries	CC5	Lochmaben
Lochranza (see also Kilmory, 554)	556	Buteshire	North Ayrshire	Rothesay	SC8	The Isles	CC12	
Lochrutton	875	Kirkcudbrightshire	Dumfries and Galloway	Kirkcudbright	SC16	Dumfries	CC5	
Lochs	87	Ross & Cromarty	Western Isles	Stornoway	SC33	The Isles	CC12	
Lochwinnoch	570	Renfrewshire	Renfrewshire	Paisley	SC58	Glasgow	CC9	Howwood
Logie	374	Perth and Kinross	Stirling	Perth	SC49	Dunblane	CC6	Bridge of Allan
Logie Buchan	216	Aberdeenshire	Aberdeenshire	Aberdeen	SC1	Aberdeen	CC1	
Logie Coldstone	217	Aberdeenshire	Aberdeenshire	Aberdeen	SC1	Aberdeen	CC1	
Logie Easter	77	Ross & Cromarty	Highland	Dingwall	SC25	Ross	CC19	
Logie (Fife)	446	Fife	Fife	Cupar	SC20	St Andrews	CC20	
Logie-Pert	304	Angus	Angus	Forfar	SC47	St Andrews	CC20	
Logie Wester (see Urquhart)	84	Ross & Cromarty	Highland	Dingwall	SC25	Ross	CC19	
Logierait	376	Perth and Kinross	Perth and Kinross	Perth	SC49	Dunkeld	CC7	Logierait
Longforgan	377	Perth and Kinross	Perth and Kinross	Perth	SC49	St Andrews	CC20	Longforgan
Longformacus	750	Berwickshire	The Scottish Borders	Duns	SC60	Lauder	CC15	Longformacus

Table A1 (continued)

Parish	No.	County	Local authority	Sheriff court		Commissary court		Burgh/town/village
Longside	218	Aberdeenshire	Aberdeenshire	Aberdeen	SC1	Aberdeen	CC1	
Lonmay	219	Aberdeenshire	Aberdeenshire	Aberdeen	SC1	Aberdeen	CC1	
Loth	54	Sutherland	Highland	Dornoch	SC9	Caithness	CC4	
Loudon	603	Ayrshire	East Ayrshire	Ayr	SC6	Glasgow	CC9	Newmilns
Lumphannan	220	Aberdeenshire	Aberdeenshire	Aberdeen	SC1	Aberdeen	CC1	
Lunan	305	Angus	Angus	Forfar	SC47	St Andrews	CC20	
Lundie & Fowlis	306	Angus	Angus	Forfar	SC47	St Andrews	CC20	
Lunnasting (see Nesting)	7	Zetland	Shetland	Lerwick	SC12	Orkney & Shetland	CC7	
Luss	499	Dunbartonshire	Argyll and Bute	Dumbarton	SC65	Glasgow	CC9	Luss
Lyne & Megget	765	Peeblesshire	The Scottish Borders	Peebles	SC42	Peebles	CC18	
Macduff (see Gamrie)	155a	Banffshire	Aberdeenshire	Banff	SC2	Aberdeen	CC1	
Madderty	378	Perth and Kinross	Perth and Kinross	Perth	SC49	Dunkeld	CC7	Craig
Mains & Strathmartine	307	Angus	Dundee	Forfar	SC47	St Andrews	CC20	Auchry
Makerston	797	Roxburghshire	The Scottish Borders	Jedburgh	SC62	Peebles	CC18	
Manor	766	Peeblesshire	The Scottish Borders	Peebles	SC42	Peebles	CC18	
Markinch	447	Fife	Fife	Cupar	SC20	St Andrews	CC20	Markinch
Marnoch	161	Banffshire	Aberdeenshire	Banff	SC2	Moray	CC16	Aberchirder
Maryculter	264	Kincardineshire	Aberdeenshire	Stonehaven	SC5	Aberdeen	CC1	
Marykirk (formerly Aberluthnot)	265	Kincardineshire	Aberdeenshire	Stonehaven	SC5	St Andrews	CC20	Luthermuir
Maryton	308	Angus	Angus	Forfar	SC47	Brechin	CC3	
Mauchline	604	Ayrshire	East Ayrshire	Ayr	SC6	Glasgow	CC9	Mauchline

Parish								
Maxton	798	Roxburghshire	The Scottish Borders	Jedburgh	SC62	Peebles	CC18	Maxton
Maxwelltown (see Troqueer)	882	Kirkcudbrightshire	Dumfries and Galloway	Kirkcudbright	SC16	Kirkcudbright	CC13	
Maybole	605	Ayrshire	South Ayrshire	Ayr	SC6	Glasgow	CC9	Maybole
Mearns	571	Renfrewshire	East Renfrewshire	Paisley	SC58	Glasgow	CC9	Newton Mearns, Busby
Meigle	379	Perth and Kinross	Perth and Kinross	Perth	SC49	Dunkeld	CC7	Meigle
Melrose	799	Roxburghshire	The Scottish Borders	Jedburgh	SC62	Peebles	CC18	Melrose
Menmuir	309	Angus	Angus	Forfar	SC47	Brechin	CC3	
Mertoun	751	Berwickshire	The Scottish Borders	Duns	SC60	Lauder	CC15	Dryburgh
Methlick	221	Aberdeenshire	Aberdeenshire	Aberdeen	SC1	Aberdeen	CC1	
Methven	380	Perth and Kinross	Perth and Kinross	Perth	SC49	St Andrews	CC20	
Mid-Calder	694	Midlothian	West Lothian	Edinburgh	SC70	Edinburgh	CC8	
Mid & South Yell	6	Zetland	Shetland	Lerwick	SC12	Orkney & Shetland	CC17	
Middlebie	841	Dumfriesshire	Dumfries and Galloway	Dumfries	SC15	Dumfries	CC5	
Midmar	222	Aberdeenshire	Aberdeenshire	Aberdeen	SC1	Aberdeen	CC1	
Minnigaff	876	Kirkcudbrightshire	Dumfries and Galloway	Kirkcudbright	SC16	Wigtown	CC22	Minnigaff
Minto	800	Roxburghshire	The Scottish Borders	Jedburgh	SC62	Peebles	CC18	Minto
Mochrum	892	Wigtownshire	Dumfries and Galloway	Wigtown	SC19	Wigtown	CC22	Port William
Moffat	842	Dumfriesshire	Dumfries and Galloway	Dumfries	SC15	Dumfries	CC5	Moffat
Moneydie	381	Perth and Kinross	Perth and Kinross	Perth	SC49	Dunkeld	CC7	
Monifieth	310	Angus	Angus/Dundee	Forfar	SC47	St Andrews	CC20	Monifieth
Monikie	311	Angus	Angus	Forfar	SC47	Brechin	CC3	

Table A1 (continued)

Parish	No.	County	Local authority	Sheriff court		Commissary court		Burgh/town/village
Monimail	448	Fife	Fife	Cupar	SC20	St Andrews	CC20	
Monkton & Prestwick	606	Ayrshire	South Ayrshire	Ayr	SC6	Glasgow	CC9	
Monquhitter	223	Aberdeenshire	Aberdeenshire	Aberdeen	SC1	Aberdeen	CC1	Cuminestown
Montrose	312	Angus	Angus	Forfar	SC47	Brechin	CC3	Montrose, Hillside
Monymusk	224	Aberdeenshire	Aberdeenshire	Aberdeen	SC1	Aberdeen	CC1	Monymusk
Monzie	382	Perth and Kinross	Perth and Kinross	Perth	SC49	Dunblane	CC6	
Monzievaird & Strowan	383	Perth and Kinross	Perth and Kinross	Perth	SC49	Dunblane	CC6	
Moonzie	449	Fife	Fife	Cupar	SC20	St Andrews	CC20	
Mordington	752	Berwickshire	The Scottish Borders	Duns	SC60	Lauder	CC15	
Morebattle	801	Roxburghshire	The Scottish Borders	Jedburgh	SC62	Peebles	CC18	
Morham	712	East Lothian	East Lothian	Haddington	SC40	Edinburgh	CC8	
Mortlach	162	Banffshire	Moray	Banff	SC2	Aberdeen	CC1	Dufftown
Morton	843	Dumfriesshire	Dumfries and Galloway	Dumfries	SC15	Dumfries	CC5	Thornhill
Morvern	528	Argyll	Highland	Dunoon	SC51	Argyll	CC2	
Moulin	384	Perth and Kinross	Perth and Kinross	Perth	SC49	Dunkeld	CC7	Pitlochry
Mouswald	844	Dumfriesshire	Dumfries and Galloway	Dumfries	SC15	Dumfries	CC5	
Moy & Dalarossie	105	Inverness-shire	Highland	Inverness	SC29	Inverness	CC11	
Muckairn	529	Argyll	Argyll and Bute	Dunoon	SC51	Argyll	CC2	
Muckhart	385	Perth and Kinross	Perth and Kinross	Perth	SC49	St Andrews	CC20	
Muiravonside	486	Stirlingshire	Falkirk	Stirling	SC67	Stirling	CC21	
Muirkirk	607	Ayrshire	East Ayrshire	Ayr	SC6	Glasgow	CC9	
Murroes	313	Angus	Dundee	Forfar	SC47	St Andrews	CC20	

Muthill	386a	Perth and Kinross	Perth and Kinross	Perth	SC49	Dunblane	CC6	
Nairn	123	Nairnshire	Highland	Nairn	SC31	Moray	CC16	Nairn, Geddes
Neilston	572	Renfrewshire	East Renfrewshire	Paisley	SC58	Glasgow	CC9	Neilston, Barrhead
Nenthorn	753	Berwickshire	The Scottish Borders	Duns	SC60	Lauder	CC15	
Nesting	7	Zetland	Shetland	Lerwick	SC12	Orkney & Shetland	CC17	
New Abbey	877	Kirkcudbrightshire	Dumfries and Galloway	Kirkcudbright	SC16	Dumfries	CC5	
New Cumnock	608	Ayrshire	East Ayrshire	Ayr	SC6	Glasgow	CC9	
New Deer	225	Aberdeenshire	Aberdeenshire	Aberdeen	SC1	Aberdeen	CC1	
New Kilpatrick	500	Dunbartonshire	East Dunbartonshire	Dumbarton	SC65	Glasgow	CC9	Bearsden, Milngavie
New Luce	893	Wigtownshire	Dumfries and Galloway	Wigtown	SC19	Wigtown	CC22	
New Machar	227	Aberdeenshire	Aberdeenshire	Aberdeen	SC1	Aberdeen	CC1	
New Monkland	651	Lanarkshire	North Lanarkshire	Hamilton	SC37	Hamilton & Campsie	CC10	Airdrie
New Spynie	136	Morayshire	Moray	Elgin	SC26	Moray	CC16	
Newbattle	695	Midlothian	Midlothian	Edinburgh	SC70	Edinburgh	CC8	Newbattle
Newburgh	450	Fife	Fife	Cupar	SC20	St Andrews	CC20	Newburgh
Newburn	451	Fife	Fife	Cupar	SC20	St Andrews	CC20	
Newhills	226	Aberdeenshire	Aberdeenshire	Aberdeen	SC1	Aberdeen	CC1	
Newlands	767	Peeblesshire	The Scottish Borders	Peebles	SC42	Peebles	CC18	
Newton	696	Midlothian	Midlothian	Edinburgh	SC70	Edinburgh	CC8	
Newton upon Ayr	612	Ayrshire	South Ayrshire	Ayr	SC6	Glasgow	CC9	Newton-upon-Ayr
Newtyle	314	Angus	Angus	Forfar	SC47	St Andrews	CC20	Newtyle
Nigg	266	Kincardineshire	Aberdeen City	Stonehaven	SC5	St Andrews	CC20	Torry
Nigg	78	Ross & Cromarty	Highland	Dingwall	SC23	Ross	CC19	
North Berwick	713	East Lothian	East Lothian	Haddington	SC40	Edinburgh	CC8	North Berwick

Table A1 (continued)

Parish	No.	County	Local authority	Sheriff court	Commissary court		Burgh/town/village
North Bute	557	Buteshire	Argyll and Bute	Rothesay	SC8	The Isles CC12	
North Knapdale	530	Argyll	Argyll and Bute	Dunoon	SC51	Argyll CC2	
North Ronaldsay	22	Orkney	Orkney	Kirkwall	SC11	Orkney & Shetland CC17	
North Uist	113	Inverness-shire	Western Isles	Inverness	SC29	The Isles CC12	
Northmavine	8	Zetland	Shetland	Lerwick	SC12	Orkney & Shetland CC17	
Oa	546	Argyll	Argyll and Bute	Dunoon	SC51	The Isles CC12	
Oathlaw	315	Angus	Angus	Forfar	SC47	Brechin CC3	
Oban (see Kilmore & Kilbride)	523	Argyll	Argyll and Bute	Dunoon	SC51	Argyll CC2	Oban
Ochiltree	609	Ayrshire	East Ayrshire	Ayr	SC6	Glasgow CC9	
Old Cumnock	610	Ayrshire	East Ayrshire	Ayr	SC6	Glasgow CC9	Cumnock
Old Deer	228	Aberdeenshire	Aberdeenshire	Aberdeen	SC1	Aberdeen CC1	
Old Kilpatrick	501	Dunbartonshire	West Dunbartonshire	Dumbarton	SC65	Glasgow CC9	Clydebank, Bowling
Old Luce	894	Wigtownshire	Dumfries and Galloway	Wigtown	SC19	Wigtown CC22	Glenluce, Ballinclach
Old Machar	168b	Aberdeenshire	Aberdeen City	Aberdeen	SC1	Aberdeen CC1	Balgownie
Old Monkland	652	Lanarkshire	North Lanarkshire	Hamilton	SC37	Hamilton & Campsie CC10	Coatbridge
Oldhamstocks	714	East Lothian	East Lothian	Haddington	SC40	Edinburgh CC8	
Oldmeldrum (Meldrum)	229	Aberdeenshire	Aberdeenshire	Aberdeen	SC1	Aberdeen CC1	Oldmeldrum
Olrig	39	Caithness	Highland	Wick	SC14	Caithness CC4	Castletown
Ordiquhill	163	Banffshire	Aberdeenshire	Banff	SC2	Aberdeen CC1	

Parish	No.	County	Council area	Sheriff Court	SC	Commissary Court	CC	
Ormiston	715	East Lothian	East Lothian	Haddington	SC40	Edinburgh	CC8	
Orphir	23	Orkney	Orkney	Kirkwall	SC11	Orkney & Shetland	CC17	
Orwell	463	Kinross	Perth and Kinross	Kinross	SC22	St Andrews	CC20	Milnathort
Oxnam	802	Roxburghshire	The Scottish Borders	Jedburgh	SC62	Peebles	CC18	
Oyne	230	Aberdeenshire	Aberdeenshire	Aberdeen	SC1	Aberdeen	CC1	
Paisley (High, Middle & Low)	573	Renfrewshire	Renfrewshire	Paisley	SC58	Glasgow	CC9	Paisley
Panbride	316	Angus	Angus	Forfar	SC47	Brechin	CC3	East Haven
Papa Westray	33	Orkney	Orkney	Kirkwall	SC11	Orkney & Shetland	CC7	
Parton	878	Kirkcudbrightshire	Dumfries and Galloway	Kirkcudbright	SC16	Kirkcudbright	CC13	
Peebles	768	Peeblesshire	The Scottish Borders	Peebles	SC42	Peebles	CC18	Peebles
Pencaitland	716	East Lothian	East Lothian	Haddington	SC40	Edinburgh	CC8	Pencaitland
Penicuik	697	Midlothian	Midlothian	Edinburgh	SC70	Edinburgh	CC8	
Penninghame	895	Wigtownshire	Dumfries and Galloway	Wigtown	SC19	Wigtown	CC22	Newton Stewart
Penpont	845	Dumfriesshire	Dumfries and Galloway	Dumfries	SC15	Dumfries	CC5	
Perth	387	Perth and Kinross	Perth and Kinross	Perth	SC49	St Andrews	CC20	Perth
Peterculter	231	Aberdeenshire	Aberdeen City	Aberdeen	SC1	Aberdeen	CC1	
Peterhead	232	Aberdeenshire	Aberdeenshire	Aberdeen	SC1	Aberdeen	CC1	Peterhead, Boddam
Pettinain	653	Lanarkshire	South Lanarkshire	Lanark	SC38	Lanark	CC14	
Petty	106	Inverness-shire	Highland	Inverness	SC29	Moray	CC16	Petty
Pitsligo	233	Aberdeenshire	Aberdeenshire	Aberdeen	SC1	Aberdeen	CC1	Rosehearty
Pittenweem	452	Fife	Fife	Cupar	SC20	St Andrews	CC20	Pittenweem
Polmont	487	Stirlingshire	Falkirk	Stirling	SC67	Stirling	CC21	Polmont

Table A1 (continued)

Parish	No.	County	Local authority	Sheriff court	Commissary court	Burgh/town/village
Polwarth	754	Berwickshire	The Scottish Borders	Duns SC60	Lauder CC15	
Poolewe (see Gairloch)	66	Ross & Cromarty	Highland	Dingwall SC25	Ross CC19	
Port Glasgow	574	Renfrewshire	Renfrewshire	Paisley SC58	Glasgow CC9	Port Glasgow
Port of Menteith	388	Perth and Kinross	Stirling	Perth SC49	Dunblane CC6	Port of Menteith
Portmoak	464	Kinrossshire	Perth and Kinross	Kinross SC22	St Andrews CC20	
Portnahaven	547	Argyll	Argyll and Bute	Dunoon SC51	The Isles CC12	
Portpatrick	896	Wigtownshire	Dumfries and Galloway	Wigtown SC19	Wigtown CC22	Portpatrick
Portree	114	Inverness-shire	Highland	Inverness SC29	The Isles CC12	
Premnay	234	Aberdeenshire	Aberdeenshire	Aberdeen SC1	Aberdeen CC1	
Prestonkirk	717	East Lothian	East Lothian	Haddington SC40	Edinburgh CC8	East Linton
Prestonpans	718	East Lothian	East Lothian	Haddington SC40	Edinburgh CC8	Prestonpans
Prestwick (see Monkton)	606	Ayrshire	South Ayrshire	Ayr SC6	Glasgow CC9	Prestwick
Quarff	1	Zetland	Shetland	Lerwick SC12	Orkney & Shetland CC17	
Queensferry	670	West Lothian	City of Edinburgh	Linlithgow SC41	Edinburgh CC8	Queensferry
Rafford	140	Morayshire	Moray	Elgin SC26	Moray CC16	
Rathen	235	Aberdeenshire	Aberdeenshire	Aberdeen SC1	Aberdeen CC1	
Ratho	698a	Midlothian	City of Edinburgh	Edinburgh SC70	Edinburgh CC8	
Rathven	164	Banffshire	Moray	Banff SC2	Aberdeen CC1	Buckie, Portessie, Portgordon, Portknockie
Rattray	389	Perth and Kinross	Perth and Kinross	Perth SC49	Dunkeld CC7	

Rayne	236	Aberdeenshire	Aberdeenshire	Aberdeen	SC1	Aberdeen	CC1	Rayne
Reay	40	Caithness	Highland	Wick	SC14	Caithness	CC4	Reay
Redgorton	390	Perth and Kinross	Perth and Kinross	Perth	SC49	Dunkeld	CC7	
Renfrew	575	Renfrewshire	Renfrewshire	Paisley	SC58	Hamilton & Campsie	CC10	Renfrew
Rerrick	879	Kirkcudbrightshire	Dumfries and Galloway	Kirkcudbright	SC16	Kirkcudbright	CC13	
Rescobie	317	Angus	Angus	Forfar	SC47	St Andrews	CC20	
Resolis (formerly Kirkmichael & Cullicudden)	79	Ross & Cromarty	Highland	Dingwall	SC25	Ross	CC19	
Rhynd	391	Perth and Kinross	Perth and Kinross	Perth	SC49	St Andrews	CC20	
Rhynie (incl. Essie)	237A	Aberdeenshire	Aberdeenshire	Aberdeen	SC1	Moray	CC16	Rhynie
Riccarton	611	Ayrshire	East Ayrshire	Ayr	SC6	Glasgow	CC9	
Roberton	777	Selkirkshire	The Scottish Borders	Selkirk	SC63	Peebles	CC18	
Roberton (Lanarks., see Wiston)	660	Lanarkshire	South Lanarkshire	Lanark	SC38	Lanark	CC14	Roberton
Rogart	55	Sutherland	Highland	Dornoch	SC9	Caithness	CC4	
Rosemarkie	80	Ross & Cromarty	Highland	Dingwall	SC25	Ross	CC19	Fortrose
Roseneath	502	Dunbartonshire	Argyll and Bute	Dumbarton	SC65	Glasgow	CC9	
Rosskeen	81	Ross & Cromarty	Highland	Dingwall	SC25	Ross	CC19	Invergordon
Rothes (incl. Dundurcas)	141	Morayshire	Moray	Elgin	SC26	Moray	CC16	Rothes
Rothesay	558	Buteshire	Argyll and Bute	Rothesay	SC8	The Isles	CC12	Rothesay
Rothiemay	165	Banffshire	Moray	Banff	SC2	Moray	CC16	Rothiemay
Rothiemurchus (see Duthil)	96b	Inverness-shire	Highland	Inverness	SC29	Inverness	CC11	
Rousay & Egilsay	24	Orkney	Orkney	Kirkwall	SC11	Orkney & Shetland	CC17	

Table A1 (continued)

Parish	No.	County	Local authority	Sheriff court		Commissary court		Burgh/town/village
Row (Rhu)	503	Dunbartonshire	Argyll and Bute	Dumbarton	SC65	Glasgow	CC9	Helensburgh, Garelochhead
Roxburgh	803	Roxburghshire	The Scottish Borders	Jedburgh	SC62	Peebles	CC18	Roxburgh
Rutherglen	654	Lanarkshire	South Lanarkshire	Glasgow	SC36	Glasgow	CC9	Rutherglen
Ruthven	318	Angus	Angus	Forfar	SC47	Dunkeld	CC7	
Ruthwell	846	Dumfriesshire	Dumfries and Galloway	Dumfries	SC15	Dumfries	CC5	Ruthwell
Saddell & Skipness	531	Argyll	Argyll and Bute	Dunoon	SC51	Argyll	CC2	
Salen	548	Argyll	Argyll and Bute	Dunoon	SC51	The Isles	CC12	
Saline	455	Fife	Fife	Cupar	SC20	Stirling	CC21	Saline
Saltoun	719	East Lothian	East Lothian	Haddington	SC40	Edinburgh	CC8	
Sanday	26	Orkney	Orkney	Kirkwall	SC11	Orkney & Shetland	CC17	
Sandsting & Aithsting	9	Zetland	Shetland	Lerwick	SC12	Orkney & Shetland	CC17	
Sandwick	27	Orkney	Orkney	Kirkwall	SC11	Orkney & Shetland	CC17	
Sandwick (see Dunrossness)	3	Zetland	Shetland	Lerwick	SC12	Orkney & Shetland	CC17	
Sanquhar	848	Dumfriesshire	Dumfries and Galloway	Dumfries	SC15	Dumfries	CC5	Sanquhar
Savoch	237B	Aberdeenshire	Aberdeenshire	Aberdeen	SC1	Aberdeen	CC1	
Scone	394a	Perth and Kinross	Perth and Kinross	Perth	SC49	St Andrews	CC20	

Parish	No.	Old County	Council Area		SC		CC	
Scoonie	456	Fife	Fife	Cupar	SC20	St Andrews	CC20	Leven
Selkirk	778	Selkirkshire	The Scottish Borders	Selkirk	SC63	Peebles	CC18	Selkirk
Shapinsay	28	Orkney	Orkney	Kirkwall	SC11	Orkney & Shetland	CC17	
Shieldaig (see Applecross)	58	Ross & Cromarty	Highland	Dingwall	SC25	Ross	CC19	
Shisken (see Kilmory)	554	Buteshire	North Ayrshire	Rothesay	SC8	The Isles	CC12	
Shotts	655	Lanarkshire	North Lanarkshire	Hamilton	SC37	Hamilton & Campsie	CC10	
Skene	238	Aberdeenshire	Aberdeenshire	Aberdeen	SC1	Aberdeen	CC1	
Skerries (see Nesting)	7	Zetland	Shetland	Lerwick	SC12	Orkney & Shetland	CC17	
Skirling	769	Peeblesshire	The Scottish Borders	Peebles	SC42	Peebles	CC18	Skirling
Slains	239	Aberdeenshire	Aberdeenshire	Aberdeen	SC1	Aberdeen	CC1	
Slamannan	489	Stirlingshire	Falkirk	Stirling	SC67	Stirling	CC21	
Sleat	115	Inverness-shire	Highland	Inverness	SC29	The Isles	CC12	
Smailholm	805	Roxburghshire	The Scottish Borders	Jedburgh	SC62	Peebles	CC18	Smailholm
Small Isles	116	Inverness-shire (Argyll)	Highland	Inverness	SC29	The Isles	CC12	
Snizort	117	Inverness-shire	Highland	Inverness	SC29	The Isles	CC12	
Sorbie	897	Wigtownshire	Dumfries and Galloway	Wigtown	SC19	Wigtown	CC22	Garliestown
Sorn (formerly Dalgain)	613	Ayrshire	East Ayrshire	Ayr	SC6	Glasgow	CC9	
South Knapdale	533	Argyll	Argyll and Bute	Dunoon	SC51	Argyll	CC2	Ardrishaig
South Ronaldsay & Burray	29	Orkney	Orkney	Kirkwall	SC11	Orkney & Shetland	CC17	St Margaret's Hope
South Uist	118	Inverness-shire	Western Isles	Inverness	SC29	The Isles	CC12	

Table A1 (continued)

Parish	No.	County	Local authority	Sheriff court		Commissary court		Burgh/town/village
Southdean & Abbotrule	806	Roxburghshire	The Scottish Borders	Jedburgh	SC62	Peebles	CC18	
Southend	532	Argyll	Argyll and Bute	Dunoon	SC51	Argyll	CC2	
Speymouth (formerly Essil & Dipple)	143	Morayshire	Moray	Elgin	SC26	Moray	CC16	
Spott	720	East Lothian	East Lothian	Haddington	SC40	Edinburgh	CC8	
Sprouston	807	Roxburghshire	The Scottish Borders	Jedburgh	SC62	Peebles	CC18	
St Andrews (incl. Lhanbryde)	142	Morayshire	Moray	Elgin	SC26	Moray	CC16	
St Andrews (Orkney)	25	Orkney	Orkney	Kirkwall	SC11	Orkney & Shetland	CC7	
St Andrews & St Leonards	453	Fife	Fife	Cupar	SC20	St Andrews	CC20	St Andrews, Boarhills, Strathkinness
St Boswells	804	Roxburghshire	The Scottish Borders	Jedburgh	SC62	Peebles	CC18	St Boswells
St Cyrus	267	Kincardineshire	Aberdeenshire	Stonehaven	SC5	St Andrews	CC20	St Cyrus
St Fergus	166	Aberdeenshire (orig. Banffshire)	Aberdeenshire	Aberdeen	SC1	Aberdeen	CC1	
St Kilda (see Harris)	111	Inverness-shire	Western Isles	Inverness	SC29	The Isles	CC12	
St Madoes	392	Perth and Kinross	Perth and Kinross	Perth	SC49	Dunblane	CC6	
St Martins	393	Perth and Kinross	Perth and Kinross	Perth	SC49	Dunkeld	CC7	
St Monance (or Abercrombie)	454	Fife	Fife	Cupar	SC20	St Andrews	CC20	St Monance

St Mungo	847	Dumfriesshire	Dumfries and Galloway	Dumfries	SC15	Dumfries	CC5	
St Ninians	488	Stirlingshire	Stirling	Stirling	SC67	Stirling	CC21	Stirling, Bannockburn
St Quivox & Newton-upon-Ayr	612	Ayrshire	South Ayrshire	Ayr	SC6	Glasgow	CC9	Newton-upon-Ayr
St Vigeans	319	Angus	Angus	Forfar	SC47	St Andrews	CC20	Auchmithie
Stair	614	Ayrshire	East Ayrshire	Ayr	SC6	Glasgow	CC9	
Stenness (see Firth)	17	Orkney	Orkney	Kirkwall	SC11	Orkney & Shetland	CC17	
Stenton	721	East Lothian	East Lothian	Haddington	SC40	Edinburgh	CC8	
Stevenston	615	Ayrshire	North Ayrshire	Ayr	SC6	Glasgow	CC9	Saltcoats
Stewarton	616	Ayrshire	East Ayrshire	Ayr	SC6	Glasgow	CC9	
Stirling	490	Stirlingshire	Stirling	Stirling	SC67	Stirling	CC21	Stirling
Stitchel & Hume	808	Roxburghshire	The Scottish Borders	Jedburgh	SC62	Peebles	CC18	
Stobo	770	Peeblesshire	The Scottish Borders	Peebles	SC42	Peebles	CC18	
Stonehouse	656	Lanarkshire	South Lanarkshire	Hamilton	SC37	Glasgow	CC9	Stonehouse
Stoneykirk	898	Wigtownshire	Dumfries and Galloway	Wigtown	SC19	Wigtown	CC22	
Stornoway	88	Ross & Cromarty	Western Isles	Stornoway	SC33	The Isles	CC12	Stornoway
Stow	699	Midlothian	The Scottish Borders	Edinburgh	SC70	Edinburgh	CC8	
Stracathro	320	Angus	Angus	Forfar	SC47	Brechin	CC3	
Strachan	268	Kincardineshire	Aberdeenshire	Stonehaven	SC5	Brechin	CC3	
Straiton	617	Ayrshire	South Ayrshire	Ayr	SC6	Glasgow	CC9	
Stralachlan (incl. Strachur)	534	Argyll	Argyll and Bute	Dunoon	SC51	Argyll	CC2	
Stranraer	899	Wigtownshire	Dumfries and Galloway	Wigtown	SC19	Wigtown	CC22	Stranraer

Table A1 (continued)

Parish	No.	County	Local authority	Sheriff court		Commissary court		Burgh/town/village
Strath	119	Inverness-shire	Highland	Inverness	SC29	The Isles	CC12	Broadford, Kyleakin
Strathblane	491	Stirlingshire	Stirlingshire	Stirling	SC67	Glasgow	CC9	Blanefield
Strathdon (incl. Corgarff)	240	Aberdeenshire	Aberdeenshire	Aberdeen	SC1	Aberdeen	CC1	Strathdon
Strathmiglo	457	Fife	Fife	Cupar	SC20	Dunkeld	CC7	Strathmiglo
Strichen	241	Aberdeenshire	Aberdeenshire	Aberdeen	SC1	Aberdeen	CC1	Strichen
Stromness	30	Orkney	Orkney	Kirkwall	SC11	Orkney & Shetland	CC17	Stromness
Stronsay	31	Orkney	Orkney	Kirkwall	SC11	Orkney & Shetland	CC17	
Swinton (incl. Simprim)	755	Berwickshire	The Scottish Borders	Duns	SC60	Lauder	CC15	
Symington	618	Ayrshire	South Ayrshire	Ayr	SC6	Glasgow	CC9	
Symington (Lanarks.)	657	Lanarkshire	South Lanarkshire	Lanark	SC38	Lanark	CC14	
Tain	82	Ross & Cromarty	Highland	Dingwall	SC25	Ross	CC19	Tain
Tannadice	321	Angus	Angus	Forfar	SC47	St Andrews	CC20	
Tarbat	83	Ross & Cromarty	Highland	Dingwall	SC25	Ross	CC19	Portmahomack, Tarbat
Tarbolton	619	Ayrshire	South Ayrshire	Ayr	SC6	Glasgow	CC9	Tarbolton
Tarland & Migvie	242	Aberdeenshire	Aberdeenshire	Aberdeen	SC1	Aberdeen	CC1	Tarland
Tarves	243	Aberdeenshire	Aberdeenshire	Aberdeen	SC1	Aberdeen	CC1	Tarves
Tealing	322	Angus	Angus	Forfar	SC47	Dunkeld	CC7	
Temple	700	Midlothian	Midlothian	Edinburgh	SC70	Edinburgh	CC8	Gorebridge
Terregles	880	Kirkcudbrightshire	Dumfries and Galloway	Kirkcudbright	SC16	Dumfries	CC5	Terregles

Teviothead	809	Roxburghshire	The Scottish Borders	Jedburgh	SC62	Peebles	CC18	
Thurso	41	Caithness	Highland	Wick	SC14	Caithness	CC4	Thurso, Scrabster
Tibbermore	395	Perth and Kinross	Perth and Kinross	Perth	SC49	Dunkeld	CC7	
Tillicoultry	468	Clackmannanshire	Clackmannan	Alloa	SC64	Dunblane	CC6	Tillicoultry
Tingwall	10	Zetland	Shetland	Lerwick	SC12	Orkney & Shetland	CC17	
Tinwald	849	Dumfriesshire	Dumfries and Galloway	Dumfries	SC15	Dumfries	CC5	Amisfield
Tiree (incl. Coll)	551	Argyll	Argyll and Bute	Dunoon	SC51	The Isles	CC12	
Tobermory (see also Kilninian)	544	Argyll	Argyll and Bute	Dunoon	SC51	The Isles	CC12	
Tongland	881	Kirkcudbrightshire	Dumfries and Galloway	Kirkcudbright	SC16	Kirkcudbright	CC13	
Tongue	56	Sutherland	Highland	Dornoch	SC9	Caithness	CC4	
Torosay	550	Argyll	Argyll and Bute	Dunoon	SC51	The Isles	CC12	
Torphichen	671	West Lothian	West Lothian	Linlithgow	SC41	Edinburgh	CC8	
Torryburn	458	Fife	Fife	Cupar	SC20	Stirling	CC21	
Torthorwald	850	Dumfriesshire	Dumfries and Galloway	Dumfries	SC15	Dumfries	CC5	Torthorwald
Tough	244	Aberdeenshire	Aberdeenshire	Aberdeen	SC1	Aberdeen	CC1	
Towie	245	Aberdeenshire	Aberdeenshire	Aberdeen	SC1	Aberdeen	CC1	
Tranent	722	East Lothian	East Lothian	Haddington	SC40	Edinburgh	CC8	Tranent, Cockenzie, Port Seton
Traquair	771	Peeblesshire	The Scottish Borders	Peebles	SC42	Peebles	CC18	
Trinity Gask	396	Perth and Kinross	Perth and Kinross	Perth	SC49	Dunblane	CC6	
Troqueer	882	Kirkcudbrightshire	Dumfries and Galloway	Kirkcudbright	SC16	Dumfries	CC5	Maxwelltown

Table A1 (continued)

Parish	No.	County	Local authority	Sheriff court		Commissary court		Burgh/town/village
Tulliallan	397	Perth and Kinross (later Fife)	Fife	Perth	SC49	Dunblane	CC6	Kincardine-on-Forth
Tullynessle & Forbes	246	Aberdeenshire	Aberdeenshire	Aberdeen	SC1	Aberdeen	CC1	
Tundergarth	851	Dumfriesshire	Dumfries and Galloway	Dumfries	SC15	Dumfries	CC5	
Turriff	247	Aberdeenshire	Aberdeenshire	Aberdeen	SC1	Aberdeen	CC1	Turriff
Tweedsmuir	772	Peeblesshire	The Scottish Borders	Peebles	SC42	Peebles	CC18	
Twynholm	883	Kirkcudbrightshire	Dumfries and Galloway	Kirkcudbright	SC16	Kirkcudbright	CC13	
Tyninghame (see Whitekirk)	723	East Lothian	East Lothian	Haddington	SC40	Edinburgh	CC8	Tyninghame
Tynron	852	Dumfriesshire	Dumfries and Galloway	Dumfries	SC15	Dumfries	CC5	
Tyrie	248	Aberdeenshire	Aberdeenshire	Aberdeen	SC1	Aberdeen	CC1	
Udny	249	Aberdeenshire	Aberdeenshire	Aberdeen	SC1	Aberdeen	CC1	
Uig	89	Ross & Cromarty	Western Isles	Stornoway	SC33	The Isles	CC12	
Unst	11	Zetland	Shetland	Lerwick	SC12	Orkney & Shetland	CC7	
Uphall	672	West Lothian	West Lothian	Linlithgow	SC41	Edinburgh	CC8	Broxburn
Urquhart	144	Morayshire	Moray	Elgin	SC26	Moray	CC16	Garmouth
Urquhart & Glenmoriston	107	Inverness-shire	Highland	Inverness	SC29	Inverness	CC11	
Urquhart & Logie Wester	84	Ross & Cromarty	Highland	Dingwall	SC25	Ross	CC19	

Urr	884	Kirkcudbrightshire	Dumfries and Galloway	Kirkcudbright	SC16	Kirkcudbright	CC13	Dalbeattie
Urray	85	Ross & Cromarty	Highland	Dingwall	SC25	Ross	CC19	
Walls	12	Zetland	Shetland	Lerwick	SC12	Orkney & Shetland	CC7	
Walls (incl. Flotta)	32	Orkney	Orkney	Kirkwall	SC11	Orkney & Shetland	CC17	Evie, Rendall
Walston	658	Lanarkshire	South Lanarkshire	Lanark	SC38	Lanark	CC14	
Wamphray	853a	Dumfriesshire	Dumfries and Galloway	Dumfries	SC15	Dumfries	CC5	
Wandell & Lamington	659	Lanarkshire	South Lanarkshire	Lanark	SC38	Lanark	CC14	
Watten	42	Caithness	Highland	Wick	SC14	Caithness	CC4	
Weem	398	Perth and Kinross	Perth and Kinross	Perth	SC49	Dunkeld	CC7	
Weisdale (see Tingwall)	10	Zetland	Shetland	Lerwick	SC12	Orkney & Shetland	CC17	
Wemyss	459	Fife	Fife	Cupar	SC20	St Andrews	CC20	Buckhaven, Methil, Wemysss
West Calder	701	Midlothian	West Lothian	Edinburgh	SC70	Edinburgh	CC8	
West Kilbride	620	Ayrshire	North Ayrshire	Ayr	SC6	Glasgow	CC9	
West Linton	773	Peeblesshire	The Scottish Borders	Peebles	SC42	Peebles	CC18	
Westerkirk	854	Dumfriesshire	Dumfries and Galloway	Dumfries	SC15	Dumfries	CC5	
Westray (incl. Papa Westray)	33	Orkney	Orkney	Kirkwall	SC11	Orkney & Shetland	CC17	
Westruther	756	Berwickshire	The Scottish Borders	Duns	SC60	Lauder	CC15	
Whalsay (see Nesting)	7	Zetland	Shetland	Lerwick	SC12	Orkney & Shetland	CC17	

Table A1 (continued)

Parish	No.	County	Local authority	Sheriff court		Commissary court		Burgh/town/village
Whitburn	673	West Lothian	West Lothian	Linlithgow	SC41	Edinburgh	CC8	
Whitekirk & Tyninghame	723	East Lothian	East Lothian	Haddington	SC40	Edinburgh	CC8	Tyninghame
Whiteness (see Tingwall)	10	Zetland	Shetland	Lerwick	SC12	Orkney & Shetland	CC17	
Whithorn	900	Wigtownshire	Dumfries and Galloway	Wigtown	SC19	Wigtown	CC22	Whithorn
Whitsome & Hilton	757	Berwickshire	The Scottish Borders	Duns	SC60	Lauder	CC15	
Whittinghame	724	East Lothian	East Lothian	Haddington	SC40	Edinburgh	CC8	
Wick	43	Caithness	Highland	Wick	SC14	Caithness	CC4	Wick, Keiss
Wigtown	901	Wigtownshire	Dumfries and Galloway	Wigtown	SC19	Wigtown	CC22	Wigtown
Wilton	810	Roxburghshire	The Scottish Borders	Jedburgh	SC62	Peebles	CC18	
Wiston & Roberton	660	Lanarkshire	South Lanarkshire	Lanark	SC38	Lanark	CC14	
Yarrow	779	Selkirkshire	The Scottish Borders	Selkirk	SC63	Peebles	CC18	
Yester	725	East Lothian	East Lothian	Haddington	SC40	Edinburgh	CC8	Gifford
Yetholm	811	Roxburghshire	The Scottish Borders	Jedburgh	SC62	Peebles	CC18	Town Yetholm

2 Scottish archives

Website links to archives holding Scottish material

ARCHON	www.archon.nationalarchives.gov.uk
	Art galleries, museums, district archives and universities
FAMILIA	www.familia.org.uk
	Family history resources in public libraries
HUB	www.archiveshub.ac.uk
	Holdings of British universities, colleges, libraries and special collections
SCAN	www.scan.org.uk
	Online catalogues of Scottish archives
SCOTLANDS PEOPLE	www.scotlandspeople.gov.uk
	Access to statutory registers, census returns, OPRs and testaments

Addresses of Scottish archives

Note: Scottish local authority archives are in bold. Other main archives within each authority are also given.

It is wise to check the addresses of archives before visiting as some archives may have moved to new buildings.

There are a great many other libraries, museums and bodies which hold records. Search through one of the above websites or consult *Exploring Scottish history* (Cox, 1999).

Aberdeen City Archives, Town House, Broad Street, Aberdeen AB10 1AQ
University of Aberdeen, Special libraries and archives, King's College, Aberdeen AB24 3SW
Aberdeenshire Council Archives, Old Aberdeen House, Dunbar Street, Aberdeen AB24 3UJ
Angus Archives, Hunter Library, Restenneth, by Forfar DD8 2SZ
Argyll and Bute Council Archives, Kilmory, Manse Brae, Lochgilphead, Argyll PA31 8QU
Bute Archives, Mount Stuart House and Gardens, Rothesay, Isle of Bute PA20 9LR
Ayrshire Archives Centre, Ayrshire Archives Centre, Craigie Estate, Ayr KA8 0SS
Clackmannanshire Council Archives, 26–28 Drysdale Street, Alloa FK10 1JL
Comhairle nan Eilean Siar (Western Isles), Sandwick Road, Stornoway, Isle of Lewis HS1 2BW
Dumfries and Galloway Archives, Archive Centre, 33 Burns Street, Dumfries DG1 1PS
Dumfries and Galloway Libraries – Ewart Library, Catherine Street, Dumfries DG1 1JB

Dundee City Archives, Archive and Record Centre, 21 City Square, Dundee
DD1 3BY

Dundee University Archives, Tower Building, University of Dundee DD1 4HN

East Dunbartonshire Council Information and Archives, William Patrick
Library, 20–24 West High Street, Kirkintilloch G66 1AD

East Lothian Council Local History Centre, Haddington Library, Newton
Port, Haddington EH41 3HA

Edinburgh City Archives, City Chambers, High Street, Edinburgh EH1 1YJ

Edinburgh University Library, Special Collections, George Square, Edinburgh
EH8 9LJ

Edinburgh University School of Scottish Studies, 27 George Square,
Edinburgh EH8 9LD

Edinburgh City Library, Central Library, George IV Bridge, Edinburgh EH1
1EG (Edinburgh Room and Scottish Room)

General Register Office for Scotland, New Register House, Princes Street,
Edinburgh EH1 3YT

National Archives of Scotland, HM General Register House, 2 Princes Street,
Edinburgh EG1 3YY

National Library of Scotland, George IV Bridge, Edinburgh EH1 1EW
(maps, printed books and manuscripts)

Falkirk Council Archives, History Research Centre, Callendar House,
Callendar Park, Falkirk FK1 1YR

Fife Council Archive Centre, Carleton House, Haig Business Park, Balgonie
Road, Markinch KY7 6AQ

(Fife Council Family History is opening centres at St Andrews, Dunfermline
and Kirkcaldy)

St Andrews University Library, Department of Special Collections, North
Street, St Andrews KY16 9TR

Glasgow City Council Archives and special collections, Level 2, The Mitchell
Library, North Street, Glasgow G3 7DN

Glasgow University Archive Services (business records), 13 Thurso Street,
Glasgow G11 6PE

Glasgow University Library (special collections and local history), Hillhead
Street, Glasgow G12 8QE

Highland Council Archive, Inverness Library, Farraline Park, Inverness IV1
1NH

North Highland Archive, Wick Library, Sinclair Terrace, Wick, Caithness
KW1 5AB

Clan Donald Centre Library (Skye), Armadale, Sleat, Isle of Skye IV45 8RS

Midlothian Council Archives, Local Studies Centre, Midlothian Library
Headquarters, 2 Clerk Street, Loanhead, Midlothian EH20 9DR

Moray Council Archives, East End Primary School, Institution Road, Elgin
IV30 1RP

North Lanarkshire Archive, Lenziemill Centre, 10 Kelvin Road, Cumbernauld
G67 2BA

Orkney Library and Archives, 44 Junction Road, Kirkwall KW15 1AG

Perth and Kinross Council Archives, A. K. Bell Library, 2–8 York Place, Perth PH2 8EP
Renfrewshire Council Museum Service, Room 24, North Building, Cotton Street, Paisley, PA1 1TR
Scottish Borders Archive and Local History Centre, St Mary's Mill, Selkirk TD7 5EU
Shetland Museum and Archives, Hay's Dock, Lerwick (opening 2006)
South Lanarkshire Council Archives, 30 Hawbank Road, College Milton, East Kilbride G74 5EX
Stirling Council Archives Services, 5 Borrowmeadow Road, Springkerse Industrial Estate, Stirling FK7 7UW
Stirling University Library special collections, University of Stirling, Stirling FK9 4LA
West Lothian Council Archives, 9 Dunlop Square, Deans Industrial Estate, Livingston, West Lothian EH54 85B
Western Isles (see Comhairle nan Eilean Siar)

3 Scottish family history societies

All the following are members of the Scottish Association of Family History Societies (SAFHS). Up-to-date details of addresses, e-mail addresses and websites can be found on the SAFHS website at www.safhs.org.uk. A number of other national and regional associations with Scottish interests round the world are also members or associate members of the Association and are listed on their site.

Aberdeen and North East of Scotland Family History Society
Alloway and Southern Ayrshire Family History Society
Anglo-Scottish Family History Society
Borders Family History Society
Caithness Family History Society
Central Scotland Family History Society
Dumfries and Galloway Family History Society
East Ayrshire Family History Society
Fife Family History Society
Glasgow and West of Scotland Family History Society
Highland Family History Society
Lanarkshire Family History Society
Largs and North Ayrshire Family History Society
Lothian Family History Society
Orkney Family History Society
Renfrewshire Family History Society
Scottish Genealogy Society
Shetland Family History Society
Tay Valley Family History Society
Troon and Ayrshire Family History Society
West Lothian Family History Society

4 Sources for Scottish family history

The reference in the left-hand column is the class reference for such records in the National Archives of Scotland. 'A' in the right-hand column indicates that further records relating to the subject may be found in local archives and libraries.

Church records

CH2	Kirk session	Minutes; accounts; disciplinary cases; testimonials; lair lists; communion rolls; parish listings; some baptisms; marriages (irregular and others); burials; poor relief; parish listings	A
CH2	Presbytery	Cases referred from kirk session; matters concerning schools, churches, and ministers	
CH2	Synod	Some disciplinary cases; church administration	
CH1	General Assembly	Admission of new ministers, disputed calls; discipline cases; early eighteenth-century lists of Catholics	
HR	Heritors' minutes	Upkeep of kirk, manse and school; care of poor; raising cess	A
CH3	Dissenting churches (Free Church, UP and others)	Session, presbytery and synod – remit as for Established Church; some baptismal, marriage and burial records	A
CH10	Quaker records	Births, marriages, deaths and other material	
CH12	Episcopal records		A
CH13	United Free Church		A
RH21	Roman Catholic Church	Baptisms, marriages and burials	A

Court and legal records

CS	Court of Session	Processes, hearings and judgments in civil cases; bankruptcy; court of appeal
RD	Register of deeds	Books of Council and Session (contracts, bonds, leases, testamentary material etc.)
AD	Lord Advocate's or Crown Office	Precognitions, indictments in criminal cases
JC	High Court of Justiciary	Reports on criminal trials including courts on circuit: books of adjournal; trials of those later transported
PC	Privy Council	Judicial and administrative functions up to 1707

PS	Register of Privy Seal	Legitimation, Crown grants of land, remissions
E	Court of Exchequer (up to 1856)	Revenue cases, seizure of smuggled goods, illicit brewing
AC	Admiralty court	Maritime and seafaring jurisdiction; piracy; mutiny; salvage A
CC	Commissary courts	Testaments and inventories (till *c.*1823); court cases for slander, divorce, small debt
SC	Sheriff courts	Court records; commissary business (after 1823); deeds; retours; diligence; licences; militia; miscellaneous
B	Royal burghs	Court records; council minutes; retours; deeds; sasines; admission of burgesses; apprenticeships; protocol books; guildry records; miscellaneous A
JP	Justices of the Peace	Court records; licensing; militia A
RH11	Regality, stewartry and bailiery (franchise courts abolished 1747)	Accounts, rentals, deeds, hornings, court books A
RH11	Baron courts (franchise courts)	Court books (local); rentals A
NP	Notaries public	Protocol books (deeds, sasines) A
DI	Diligence records	Actions for debt – inhibitions and adjudications (also in sheriff, burgh and regality courts)

Government records

AF	Agriculture and fisheries	Crofting, emigration, agricultural censuses A
BR	British Rail records	Records of Scottish railways A
CB	National Coal Board	Records of Scottish coalmines – see also GD A
CO	County councils	Poor relief; miscellaneous A
ED	Education department	School inspections; endowment schemes; universities A
FS	Friendly societies	Minutes, members A
HD	Highland destitution	Famine relief and emigration A
HH	Scottish Home Office	Prisons, poor relief, police, health
PO	Post office	
PC	Privy council	Administrative and judicial business

Trade, revenue and tax records

E	Exchequer rolls	Payments to Crown of casualties and duties
E	Hearth and poll tax	Tax on hearths – all Scotland 1691–95; poll tax 1693–99 A

E	Eighteenth-century taxes	Farm horse tax, income tax, windows, servants and others
CE	Customs and Excise	Trade, customs letter books; import/export records; fishing and whaling returns A

Land records

RS	Registers of sasines	General and particular (see also burghs)
NP	Protocol books	Early registers of sasines A
C	Chancery	Register of the Great Seal (charters); retours (services of heirs)
RT	Tailzies	Entails
SIG	Signatures	First drafts of Crown charters
E	Forfeited estate papers	Administration of estates forfeited after the 1745 rebellion
GD	Family papers	Land titles, correspondence, rentals, accounts etc. A
NRAS	National Register of Archives in Scotland	Catalogues of records still in private hands
OS	Ordnance Survey	Name books
RHP	Register House plans	Estate and other plans A
VR	Valuation rolls	Annual valuations of lands 1855–1974

5 Scottish money, numbers and dates

Scottish money

Scots money was abolished by the terms of the Act of Union in 1707, at which time one penny Scots equalled one twelfth of a penny sterling. In fact, references to Scots money continue through the first half of the eighteenth century.

Money was often expressed in merks – a merk being worth 13s. 4d. Scots. 'li' or 'lib' is used for a pound; 's' or 'sh' for a shilling and 'd' for a penny.

Scottish numbers

Numbers were usually expressed in Roman numerals:

'i' (one) standing alone or as the last in a group of numerals is written as 'j'. Thus 'viij' = 8; 'iij' = 3.
Four may be written as 'iiij' – not as 'iv'.
'xx' is used for a score or 20; it is usually written as raised letters. Thus vj^{xx} = six score or 120.
Raised 'c' represents 100. Thus ij^c = 200.
'm' is used for 1,000. 'jaj' is often written for 1,000, being a corruption of 'jm' or 'im' – 1,000. This often occurs in dates.

Term days

There were four term days on which certain payments might be due, leases start or finish and contracts of employment begin or end.
Old Scottish term days:

Candlemas – 2 February
Whitsunday – the legal term day was fixed at 15 May
Lammas – 1 August
Martinmas (known as 'St Martin in winter') – 11 November

From 1886 onwards, term days for removals and hirings were fixed at:

Candlemas – 28 February
Whitsunday – 28 May
Lammas – 28 August
Martinmas – 28 November

Dating

Before 1600, the new year began in March. From 1600 onwards the official start of the new year was 1 January but there was a period of overlap in adopting the new dating.

Bibliography

Note: if the book has been published by a society, this is given instead of the place of publication.

Periodicals

Ancestors
Family Tree Magazine
Innes Review
Scottish Archives
Scottish Local History
Scottish Genealogist

Histories of Scotland (political and social)

Devine, T. M. (1999), The Scottish Nation 1700–2000, London
Dickinson, W. C. and Pryde, George S. (1961–62), A new history of Scotland, Edinburgh
Donaldson, Gordon, ed. (1965–74), The Edinburgh history of Scotland, Edinburgh
Fry, Michael (2001), *The Scottish empire*, Phantassie
Lynch, Michael (1991), *Scotland: a new history*, London
Smout, T. C. (1969), *A history of the Scottish people 1560–1830*, London
Smout, T. C. (1986), *A history of the Scottish people 1830–1950*, London

The law

Brunton, George and Haig, David (1832), *An historical account of the Senators of the College of Justice*, Edinburgh
Gibb, A. D., ed. (1971), *Students' glossary of Scottish legal terms*, Edinburgh
Gouldesbrough, Peter (1985), *Formulary of old Scots legal documents*, Stair Society
Grant, Sir Francis J. (1944), *Faculty of Advocates 1532–1943*, Scottish Record Society
Henderson, John, ed. (1912), *History of the Society of Advocates in Aberdeen*, New Spalding Club
McKechnie, Hector, ed. (1936), *Society of Writers to H.M. Signet*, Edinburgh
Signet Library (1983), *Register of the Society of Writers to Her Majesty's Signet*, Edinburgh
Various authors (1936), *An introductory survey of the sources and literature of Scots law*, Stair Society

Walker, David M. (1988–2001), *A legal history of Scotland*, 6 vols, Edinburgh
Watson, George (1882), *Bell's dictionary and digest of the law of Scotland*, Edinburgh

The Church

Baptie, Diane (2000), *Records of baptisms, marriages and deaths in the Scottish secession churches*, Edinburgh
Baptie, Diane (2001), *Parish registers in the kirk session records of the Church of Scotland*, Aberdeen
Bertie, David M. (2000), *Scottish episcopal clergy 1689–2000*, Edinburgh
Cameron, N. M., ed. (1993), *Dictionary of Scottish church history and theology*, Edinburgh
Drummond, Andrew and Bulloch, James (1973), *The Scottish church 1688–1843*, Edinburgh
Drummond, Andrew and Bulloch, James (1975), *The church in Victorian Scotland 1843–74*, Edinburgh
Ewing, W. (1914), *Annals of the Free Church of Scotland 1843–1900*, Edinburgh
Gandy, Michael (1993a), *Catholic missions and registers 1700–1880*, published by the author
Gandy, Michael (1993b), *Catholic parishes in England, Wales and Scotland: an atlas*, published by the author
Lamb, John, ed. (1956), *Fasti of the United Free Church of Scotland 1900–1929*, Edinburgh
McNaughton, William D. (1993), *The Scottish congregational ministry 1794–1993*, Glasgow
Scott, D. (1886), *Annals of the Original Secession Church to 1852*, Edinburgh
Scott, Hew ed. (1961 reprinted), *Fasti ecclesiae Scoticanae*, Edinburgh
Small, Robert (1904), *History of the congregations of the United Presbyterian Church 1733–1900*, Edinburgh
Watt, D. E. R. (1969), *Fasti ecclesiae Scoticanae medii aevi ad annum 1638*, SRS

The army and the navy

Fowler, Simon (1992), *Army records for family historians*, PRO
Fowler, Simon, Spencer, William and Tamblin, Stuart (1997), *Army service records of the First World War*, PRO
Hamilton-Edwards, Gerald (1977), *In search of army ancestry*, London
Kitzmiller, J. M. (1987–88), *British regiments and their records 1640-WW1*, Salt Lake City
Livingstone, A., Aikman, C. and Hart, Betty, eds (1984), *Muster roll of Prince Charles Edward Stuart's army 1845–46*, Aberdeen
Morrison, Arnold (1996), *Some Scottish sources on militias, fencibles and volunteers*, published by the author
Rodger, N. A. M. (1988), *Naval records for genealogists*, PRO

Scottish Record Office (1996), *A military source list*, 2 vols, Edinburgh

Watts, Michael J. and Christopher T. (1991), *My ancestor was a merchant seaman*, London

Watts, Michael J. and Christopher T. (1992), *My ancestor was in the British army*, London

Wise, Terence and Shirley (2001), *A guide to military museums and other places of military interest*, Knighton

Emigration

Filby, P. W. (1981), *Passenger and immigration lists index: a guide to published arrival records of about 500,000 passengers in the United States and Canada*, Detroit

Whyte, Donald, ed. (1972 Part I, 1995 Part II) *A dictionary of Scottish emigrants to the USA*, Baltimore

Whyte, Donald, ed. (1986 Part I, 2002 Part II) *A dictionary of Scottish emigrants to Canada before Confederation*, Ontario Genealogical Society

General

Adam, R. J., ed. (1960), *John Home's survey of Assynt*, SHS

Adams, Ian H. (1966–88), *Descriptive list of plans in the Scottish Record Office*, Edinburgh

Adamson, Duncan, ed. (1981), *West Lothian hearth tax, 1691*, SRS

Addison, William, I. (1913) *Matriculation albums of the University of Glasgow 1728–1858*, Glasgow

Arnot, Hugo (1998 reprinted), *History of Edinburgh*, Edinburgh

Baird, W. W. and Whittles, K. H. (1998), *Directory of Scotland's organisations*, Latheronwheel

Barron, D. G., ed. (1892), *The court book of the barony of Urie*, SHS

Begg, Allan (2002), *Deserted settlements of Glassary parish*, Dunoon

Bigwood, A. R. (1987), 'Dissenting congregations in pre-Disruption Ayrshire and their importance to the genealogist', *The Scottish Genealogist*, 34:2, 328–9.

Bigwood, Frank (2001a), *Argyll commissary court*, published by the author

Bigwood, Frank (2001b), *The burgh court of Campbeltown*, published by the author

Bigwood, Frank (2001c), *The burgh court of Inveraray*, published by the author

Bigwood, Frank (2001d), *Justices of the peace in Argyll, processes 1723–1825*, published by the author

Bigwood, Frank (2001e), *The vice-admiral court of Argyll*, published by the author

Black, George F. (1946 and reprints), *The surnames of Scotland*, New York

Blatchford, Robert, ed. (annually), *The family and local history handbook*, York

Bloxham, V. Ben, ed. (1970), *Key to the parochial registers of Scotland*, Salt Lake City

Brander, Michael (1996), *The world directory of Scottish associations*, Glasgow
Cowper, A. S., ed. (1997), *SSPCK schoolmasters, 1709–1872*, SRS
Cox, Michael, ed. (1999), *Exploring Scottish history*, Scottish Library Association, Scottish Local History Forum and Scottish Records Association
Cramond, William (1893), *Annals of Banff*, New Spalding Club
Cregeen, Eric (1963), *Inhabitants of the Argyll estate 1779*, SRS
Drake, Michael and Finnegan, Ruth, eds (1994), *Studying family and community history: sources and methods*, Cambridge
Ferguson, Joan P., ed. (1984), *Directory of Scottish newspapers*, Edinburgh
Ferguson, P. S., ed. (1986), *Scottish family histories*, Edinburgh
Flinn, Michael (1977), *Scottish population history*, Cambridge
Ford, P. and G. (1953), *Select list of British parliamentary papers 1833–1899*, Oxford.
Ford, P. and G. (1968), *Hansard's catalogue and breviate of parliamentary papers 1696–1834*, Dublin
Forbes, Kirsty M. and H. J. Urquhart (2002), 'Records in the National Archives of Scotland relating to Poor Relief, 1845–1930', *Scottish Archives* 8, 9–32.
Foster, Joseph (1882), *Members of Parliament, Scotland 1357–1882*, privately printed
Gilchrist, George (1975), *Annan parish censuses 1801–1821*, SRS
Ginsburg, Madeleine (1982), *Victorian dress in photographs*, London
Grant, Francis J., ed. (1908), *Index to genealogies, birthbriefs and funeral escutcheons recorded in the Lyon Office*, SRS
Gray, Iain (1994), *A guide to dean of guild court records*, Glasgow
Groome, Francis H. (1882), *Ordnance gazetteer of Scotland*, Edinburgh
Hamilton-Edwards, Gerald (1972), *In search of Scottish ancestry*, Chichester
Hamilton-Edwards, Gerald (1978), *Perthshire marriage contracts*, privately printed
Hancock, P. D. (1960), *Bibliography of works relating to Scotland 1916–50*, Edinburgh
Haythornthwaite, J. A. (1993), *Scotland in the nineteenth century: analytical bibliography of material relating to Scotland in parliamentary papers 1800–1900*, Aldershot
Irvine, James M. (2004), *Trace your Orkney ancestors*, privately published
Irvine, Sherry (2003), *Scottish ancestry*, Utah
Johnson, K. A. and Sainty, Malcolm R., eds (annually), *Genealogical research directory*, Melbourne
Kilmorack Heritage Association (2001), *The glens and straths, parish of Kilmorack*, privately printed
Kyd, James Gray, ed. (1952), *Scottish population statistics including Webster's analysis of population 1755*, SHS
Leneman, Leah (2003), *Promises, promises*, Edinburgh
Levitt, Ian, ed. (1988), *Government and social conditions in Scotland 1845–1919*, SHS
Livingstone, M. (1905), *Guide to the public records of Scotland*, Edinburgh

Local Studies Group, Scottish Branch (2002) *Photographic collections in Scotland's local studies libraries*, Glasgow

MacDougall, Ian (1978), *Labour records in Scotland*, Edinburgh

Mackenzie, Osgood (1921), *A hundred years in the Highlands*, London

Maclean-Bristol, Nicholas, ed. (1998), *Inhabitants of the Inner Isles, Morvern and Arnamurchan 1716*, SRS

Macleod, John, ed. (1934) *Roxburghshire services of heirs 1636–1847*, SRS

McNab, P. B., ed. (1903), *The history of the Incorporation of Gardeners of Glasgow 1626–1903*, Glasgow

Malcolm, Charles A. (1931), *Minutes of the Justices of the Peace for Lanarkshire 1707–23*, SHS

Marshall, J. S., ed. (1968), *Calendar of irregular marriages in the South Leith kirk session records 1697–1818*, SRS

Matheson, C. (1928), *A catalogue of the publications of Scottish historical and kindred clubs and societies 1908–1927*, Aberdeen

Mitchell, Sir A. and Cash, C. G. (1917), *A contribution to the bibliography of Scottish topography*, SHS

Mitchison, Rosalind and Leneman, Leah (1989), *Sexuality and social control, Scotland 1660–1780*, Oxford

Moir, D. G., ed. (1973 and 1983), *The early maps of Scotland*, Edinburgh

Monteith, Robert (1704 and 1713), *Ane theater of mortality*, Edinburgh

Moody, David (1986), *Scottish local history*, London

Moody, David (1988), *Scottish family history*, London

Moody, David (1992), *Scottish towns*, London

Musgrave, Sir William (1899–1901), *Obituary prior to 1800*, Harleian Society

National Archives of Scotland (2003), *Tracing your Scottish ancestors*, Edinburgh

New (or Second) Statistical Account of Scotland (1834–45), Edinburgh

Oliver, George (1989), *Photographs and local history*, London

Paul, Sir James Balfour (1904–14), *The Scots peerage*, Edinburgh

Payne, Peter (1967), *Studies in Scottish business history*, London

Pols, Robert (1992), *Dating old photographs*, Federation of Family History Societies

Pryde, George Smith (1965), *The burghs of Scotland*, Glasgow

Raymond, Stuart A. (2002), *Scottish family history on the web*, Federation of Family History Societies

Registrar General (1872), *Detailed list of the old parochial registers of Scotland*, Edinburgh

Richards, Tom (1989), *Was your grandfather a railwayman?*, Birmingham

Robinson, Mairi, ed. (1985), *The concise Scots dictionary*, Aberdeen

Rosie, Alison, ed. (1994), *Scottish handwriting 1500–1700*, SRO

Scotland, James (1969), *History of Scottish education*, London

Scottish Record Office (1966–88, 4 vols), *Descriptive list of plans in the SRO*, SRO

Scottish Record Office (1973), *Statistics of the annexed estates 1755–1756*, HMSO

Scottish Record Office (1996), *Guide to the National Archives of Scotland*, HMSO and Stair Society

Seton, Bruce and Arnot, J. eds (1928–29), *Prisoners of the '45*, SHS

Seton, George (1854), *Sketch of the history and imperfect condition of the parochial records in Scotland*, Edinburgh

Shaw, Gareth and Tipper, Allison (1988), *British directories*, Leicester

Shennan, John Hay (1892), *The boundaries of the counties and parishes in Scotland*, Edinburgh

Simpson, Grant G. (1973), *Scottish handwriting 1150–1650*, Edinburgh

Sinclair, Cecil (1994), *Tracing Scottish local history in the Scottish Record Office*, HMSO

Sinclair, Cecil (2000), *Jock Tamson's bairns*, Edinburgh

Sinclair, Sir John (1791–99), *Old (or First) Statistical Account of Scotland*, Edinburgh

Sinclair, Sir John (1825), *Analysis of the Statistical Account of Scotland*, Edinburgh

Smith, Annette (1982), *Jacobite estates of the Forty-Five*, Edinburgh

Steel, D. J. (1970), *Sources for Scottish genealogy and family history*, London

Stenton, M. and Lees, S. (1976–81), *Who's who of British Members of Parliament 1832–1979*, 4 vols, Sussex

Stevenson, David and Wendy (1987), *Scottish texts and calendars*, SHS

Stewart, Alan (2004), *Gathering the clans*, Chichester

Stewart, I. (1991), *List of inhabitants upon the Duke of Argyle's property in Kintyre in 1792*, SRS

Stuart, John, ed. (1844), *List of pollable persons within the shire of Aberdeen 1696*, Spalding Club

Stuart, Margaret (1978), *Scottish Family history*, Baltimore

Symon, J. A. (1959), *Scottish farming past and present*, Edinburgh

Terry, C. S. (1909), *A catalogue of the publications of Scottish historical and kindred clubs and societies 1780–1908*, Glasgow

Thomson, J. M. (1922), *The public records of Scotland*, Glasgow

Thomson, John Maitland, ed. (1984 reprinted), *The register of the Great Seal of Scotland*, Edinburgh

Timperley, Loretta R. (1976), *A directory of landownership in Scotland c.1770*, SRS

Torrance, D. R. (1998), *Scottish trades, professions, vital records and directories*, Scottish Association of Family History Societies

Warrack, Alexander, ed. (1965), *Chambers's Scots Dictionary*, Edinburgh

Wilkins, Frances (1993), *Family histories in Scottish customs records*, Kidderminster

Wills, Virginia, ed. (1973), *Reports on the annexed estates 1755–1769*, Edinburgh

Willsher, Betty (1985), *Understanding Scottish graveyards*, Edinburgh

Young, Margaret D. (1992–93), *The parliaments of Scotland*, Edinburgh

Index

East India Company 93
economic trends 149
Edinburgh Central Library 20
education 187–90
electors 190
emigrant links 9–11
emigrants 198–9
emigration 148
employment records 159–60
entail *see* tailzies
Episcopal Church 192
Episcopalians 71–2
  marriage registers of 84
Established Church of Scotland
    191
Exchequer 143–4, 146
Excise
  see Customs and Excise; licensing
    courts

factory 207
family letters 7
family muniments 113–14, 173
fatal accidents 89
fencibles 194
feudal system 208
finding sources 119–23
First Statistical Account 26, 126,
    164
forfeited estate papers 144,
    167–8
franchise courts 140
  registers of deeds 205
friendly societies 160

gazetteers 126
General Assembly 72, 131–2
General Register Office for Scotland
    17
Glasgow University Archives 160
graveyard records 95–9
guilds *see* crafts

health boards 187
hearth tax 144–5, 169
heritors 132–3

High Court of Justiciary 143, 176,
    221–3
  procedure 221–2
  records of 222–3

immigration records 10
indexes 12
information sites 13
inheritance 114–18
International Genealogical Index
    15–16, 37, 77
internet 11–13, 119

judges *see* Senators
Justices of the Peace 139

kirk session records 67–8
  irregular marriages in 82–3
  lists of population in 45
    see also church records

labourers 155–6, 159
  in the towns 159
lair registers 98–9
landowners 171–6
landownership 208–21
lawyers 186–7
LDS *see* Church of Jesus Christ of
    the Latter-Day Saints
libraries 20
licensing courts 184
Lieutenancy 139
living relatives 30
local authorities 21
local government records 128
local histories 127

maps 19, 123–4, 173
marriage 72–87 *passim*
  border 84
  by consent 74
  by declaration 73
  by promise 73
  cohabitation 73
  consular returns of 75
  contracts of 84–6